Interpreting the Ambiguous

Archaeology and interpretation in early 21st century Britain

Proceedings of a session from the 2001
Institute of Field Archaeologists annual conference,
held at the University of Newcastle upon Tyne

Edited by

Paul Frodsham

Northumberland
NATIONAL PARK

Conference session and proceedings supported by
Northumberland National Park Authority

BAR British Series 362
2004

Published in 2016 by
BAR Publishing, Oxford

BAR British Series 362

Interpreting the Ambiguous

ISBN 978 1 84171 583 4

BAR Publishing is the trading name of British Archaeological Reports (Oxford) Ltd.
British Archaeological Reports was first incorporated in 1974 to publish the BAR
Series, International and British. In 1992 Hadrian Books Ltd became part of the BAR
group. This volume was originally published by Archaeopress in conjunction with
British Archaeological Reports (Oxford) Ltd / Hadrian Books Ltd, the Series principal
publisher, in 2004. This present volume is published by BAR Publishing, 2016.

Printed in England

BAR
PUBLISHING

BAR titles are available from:

BAR Publishing
122 Banbury Rd, Oxford, OX2 7BP, UK
EMAIL   info@barpublishing.com
PHONE   +44 (0)1865 310431
FAX   +44 (0)1865 316916
www.barpublishing.com

Contents

List of contributors ii

Foreword and acknowledgements iii

1. 'So much history in this landscape. So much confusion, so much doubt.' 1
   Paul Frodsham

2. Sowing the seeds of doubt. The presentation of the past to the public. 27
   Emma Carver

3. Virtually the Ice Age. Interpreting the Palaeolithic archaeology of Creswell Crags. 42
   Ian Wall

4. Telling stories. Archaeology, interpretation and the National Trust at Avebury. 43
   Ruth Taylor

5. The Maelmin Heritage Trail. Archaeological research and the public. 49
   Clive Waddington

6. Drama on Gardom's Edge. The use of theatre groups in public interpretation of prehistory. 59
   Bill Bevan

7. Changing interpretations. Public access and interpretation on a developer-funded excavation
   at Braehead, Glasgow. 67
   Ronan Toolis and Clare Ellis

8. 'Valley of the First Iron Masters'. A case study in inclusion and interpretation. 75
   Peter Halkon

9. Roundhouses in the Landscape. Interpreting the Iron Age at Castell Henllys. 83
   Phil Bennett

10. High Street, Londinium. Reconstructing Roman London. 89
    Hedley Swain

11. Access to the evidence. Interpretation of an excavation at a Scottish castle. 95
    Adrian Cox

12. 'But didn't the horses drown?' Interpreting historic narrowboats in the Working Boats Project 105
    Jo Bell

13. Endpiece. Whither interpretation? 113
    Peter Stone

List of contributors

Jo Bell
National Trust Regional Office for the East Midlands, Clumber Park Stableyard, Worksop, Nottinghamshire, England, S80 3BE. (Previously the Working Boats Project Officer, British Waterways).

Phil Bennett
Castell Henllys Iron Age Fort, (Pembrokeshire Coast National Park Authority), Meline, nr Crymych, Pembrokeshire, Wales, SA41 3UT.

Bill Bevan
Archaeology Service, Peak District National Park Authority, Aldern House, Bakewell, Derbyshire, England, DE45 1AE.

Emma Carver
Historic Scotland, Longmore House, Salisbury Place, Edinburgh, Scotland, EH9 1SH.

Adrian Cox
Scottish Urban Archaeological Trust Ltd., 55 South Methven Street, Perth, Scotland, PH1 5NX.

Clare Ellis
AOC Archaeology Group, Edgefield Industrial Estate, Edgefield Road, Loanhead, Scotland, EH20 9SY.

Paul Frodsham
Northumberland National Park Authority, Eastburn, South Park, Hexham, Northumberland, England, NE46 1BS.

Peter Halkon
The Department of History, University of Hull, Cottingham Road, Hull, East Yorkshire, England, HU6 7RX.

Peter Stone
International Centre for Cultural and Heritage Studies, Bruce Building, University of Newcastle upon Tyne, Newcastle upon Tyne, England, NE1 7RU.

Hedley Swain
Museum of London, London Wall, London, England, EC2Y 5HN.

Ruth Taylor
The National Trust, Rowan, Kembrey Park, Swindon, Wiltshire, England, SN2 8YL.

Ronan Toolis
AOC Archaeology Group, Edgefield Industrial Estate, Edgefield Road, Loanhead, Scotland, EH20 9SY.

Clive Waddington
Archaeological Research Services, 6 Laverdene Drive, Totley, Sheffield, England, S17 4HH.

Ian Wall
Creswell Heritage Trust, Creswell Crags Visitor Centre, Crags Road, Welbeck, Worksop, Nottinghamshire, England, S80 3LH.

Foreword and acknowledgements

This volume is based on a session entitled 'Interpreting the Ambiguous' at the 2001 Institute of Field Archaeologists (IFA) annual conference at the University of Newcastle upon Tyne. It is hoped that the papers included here (all but two of which were presented at the conference) will be of some value to anyone planning archaeological interpretation work in the near future.

The volume's relative lack of contributions from southern England is unusual for an archaeological book that seeks to be relevant throughout Britain (and perhaps further afield). This lack of southern English material presumably relates to the location of the original conference session. However, as Newcastle upon Tyne is the closest city to the centre of Britain, this shouldn't really have precluded contributions from anywhere. Regardless of a possible regional bias in content, the papers collected here range over large expanses of both space and time. While they vary considerably in terms of subject matter, they are all united by one basic aim: the desire to encourage people to think for themselves about the past.

Readers will note that the vast majority of contributions are rooted in prehistory. This was not the original intention, but reflects the response to the initial call for papers when the session was first suggested. Does this mean that prehistorians tend to think more about the presentation of their subject than archaeologists specialising in later periods? Perhaps the very nature of prehistory means that this is naturally the case?

The conference session was initially planned as a joint exercise between archaeologists and environmental interpreters. Its purpose was to enable presentations and discussion aimed at strengthening the links between the two professions, thus reducing the potential for misunderstanding and frustration which can occur when archaeologists and interpreters are brought together within a particular project. It was thought that such an approach would be of great benefit to the planning of future projects. In the event, for reasons over which I had no control, the session had to be amended so that it consisted essentially of archaeologists talking about the interpretation of their work for the general public. The session, therefore, had a rather different slant than was originally intended, but I hope the results will still be of interest to archaeologists and interpreters alike, as well as to those who like to describe themselves as 'archaeological interpreters'.

The 'Interpreting the Ambiguous' session outline, as presented in the 2001 IFA conference programme, reads as follows:

'This session is all about getting the message across to the public. We now have a bewildering array of interpretive options at our disposal: leaflets, books, on-site panels, guided walks, conferences, television and radio, theatre, the web, visitor centres etc etc. In some cases the use of high-tech options is justified, but in others the good old leaflet and self-guided trail are still the best option. This session seeks to examine case studies of recent archaeological projects where interpretation and research have been developed hand-in-hand from the start. Very often in the past interpretation for the public was a bolt-on extra, considered when research or conservation work at a particular site had been completed, but this should no longer be the case as the actual 'doing' of archaeology is often of as much interest to the public as the end result of investigations, and this 'doing' can in itself offer vast scope for exciting and innovative interpretation. Nevertheless, it does appear that research and interpretation are increasingly being undertaken by different individuals, and in many cases different organisations, and this can pose problems with regard to the nature of the message being provided to the public. Is it the archaeologists or the interpreters who should be setting the agenda?

Presentations will also consider the extent to which interpretation should dwell on 'facts', and how much should be left to the public's imagination. What, after all, is the real meaning of the word 'interpretation'?

The session includes presentations on a variety of recent projects which have attempted to integrate research and interpretation, including small-scale initiatives and larger scale projects, covering all periods from prehistory through until recent times. The aim is to publish the proceedings as a record of good practice to aid those involved in future projects.'

Readers will judge for themselves how effectively the various contributors have addressed the agenda set out in this session outline. Feedback from the conference was very positive and the volume reflects the conference session quite closely, so I hope that the publication will prove to be worthwhile.

I am very grateful to everyone who attended the conference session, especially those who took part in the discussion. Special thanks go to all the contributors to this volume. I must apologise (especially to those who sent me their papers soon after the event) for the length of time that has elapsed between the conference and the eventual appearance of this publication (although I should state that am not solely responsible for the delay!). I would also like to record my gratitude to Rachel Boning at the IFA office, whose help was instrumental in organising the conference session, and to Jonathan Mullard (Director of Park Management, Northumberland National Park Authority) for enthusiastically backing the session and allowing me some 'work time' in which to edit the volume. Thanks also to David Davison at BAR for accepting the original publication proposal, for cheerfully putting up with numerous delays and excuses while the manuscript underwent several phases of editing, and for seeing the project successfully through to publication.

PF
Hexham
June 2003

'So much history in this landscape, so much confusion, so much doubt'

Paul Frodsham

Introduction

The above title is taken from the lyrics of the Elton John song 'American Triangle' (copyright Elton John/Bernie Taupin, 2001). On first hearing this song, on New Year's Day 2002, I realised immediately that I would struggle to find a more appropriate title for this paper. A couple of months later, in the cold, sober light of a February afternoon in the office, the same words seem no less relevant. Although taken somewhat out of context, they sum up beautifully what this volume is all about. How can we, as archaeologists, effectively interpret the history in our landscape, about which we readily acknowledge so much confusion and so much doubt, for the benefit of the general public?

I opened the conference session on which this volume is based with the words:

"*Every archaeological job in Britain is dependent at the end of the day on public support for archaeology and the historic environment. The effective provision of information to the general public about our archaeological heritage must, therefore, be a major priority, if not the major priority, underlying everything we do as archaeologists.*"

All archaeologists know this to be the case, but many of us would do well to remind ourselves of it on a more regular basis. The purpose of the conference session was to consider how public understanding can best be integrated with academic research, for the benefit of all. The session proved very popular, and was well attended despite the presence of a parallel session organised by English Heritage on the future of British archaeology in the adjacent lecture theatre! It generated much discussion, and the decision to publish the proceedings was taken in the hope that future projects could benefit from the experiences of those considered at the conference.

This paper is based on the notes I used when opening the session, and is intended to raise a number of issues that should be considered when planning interpretive work. I will start with the same little (absolutely true) story with which I began my presentation at the conference. When attempting to engage someone from English Heritage to address the session with regard to the interpretation of the Hadrian's Wall World Heritage Site, I phoned Fortress House and explained to the very pleasant receptionist that

I would like to speak to someone in the English Heritage Interpretation Team. 'Oh' she said, 'I don't think we do interpretation.' I assured her that they did. 'What, you mean like foreign languages?' was the response. 'No,' I explained, 'site panels and leaflets – that sort of thing'. 'Oh,' she said, 'just a minute'. I was then put through to someone who didn't seem to have a clue what I was talking about, but who helpfully suggested that my regional office might be able to help. (It couldn't). A colleague who overheard my end of the conversation said 'you should have asked for *marketing*', which perhaps tells us something. Actually, I happen to know that EH does have an interpretation team that has done some very effective work, but I thought the story was worth telling – read into it what you will. At the very least, it tells us something about the very ambiguity of the word 'interpretation'.

We will consider some definitions of 'interpretation' shortly. Of course, it could legitimately be argued that all archaeology is interpretation, but what we are particularly concerned with here is interpretation for the general public. The initial call for papers for the conference session requested case studies demonstrating an effective relationship between public interpretation and academic research. In all cases contributors were asked to focus on WHY they did what they did, rather than simply how they did it. Of course, the best possible way of encouraging people to engage with their past is to enable direct public participation in archaeological fieldwork. Although this is not always possible (and is not specifically considered within this paper) it must always be given careful consideration when planning new research projects. Quite apart from any moral duty to encourage public participation, funding is increasingly easier to find when genuine public involvement is built into new projects.

It is important, I think, for all archaeologists engaged in public interpretation to ask themselves some basic questions.

Why do we, as archaeologists, do interpretation? There are two basic reasons, relating to my initial statement set out above. We have moral duty to inform the public of our work, and (more selfishly) we wish to develop public interest in our profession in order to maintain and expand the available resources for archaeology. I would also add a third reason – doing archaeological interpretation is fun, or at least it should be!

Another key question is **who** should be setting the agenda regarding **what** we seek to interpret? Are we really doing this for the public? If we are interpreting archaeology for the public, who decides what the public wants to know? Are interpreters there to provide a mechanism for getting an archaeological researcher's ideas across to the public? Or is the interpreter's role also to ask the public what they want to know and therefore actually inform our research strategies? Is research done for the good of the discipline, or the public, as the two don't necessarily have the same priorities, especially in the short term? Also, we must not forget that there are many branches of 'the public', and many different audiences whose needs and expectations must be addressed in the planning of any interpretive project. Good interpretation will appeal to a variety of ages, from primary schoolchildren (fig. 1.1) to pensioners, and to people from all types of background. This point is not treated as fully as it perhaps should be here, but it should be borne in mind throughout the reading of this volume.

The issue of **how** to interpret archaeology is fundamental to all the contributions in this volume. All I would say at this stage is that we must not be drawn into using inappropriate techniques simply because they are available. Modern technology offers unlimited opportunities to the interpreter, but methods of interpretation must be appropriate to the setting. Inappropriate techniques can actually damage or destroy the potential for people to experience atmospheric sites or landscapes for themselves. The relationship between person and place can be heightened by effective interpretation, or destroyed by inappropriate interpretative provision. Either way, that relationship will not be the same as if no interpretation had been provided. There is, therefore, a great responsibility on the shoulders of those who seek to interpret our historic landscape for the benefit of the general public. Such work is not easy, and it is important to recognise that being good at public interpretation is not necessarily any less difficult than being good at archaeological research. As few archaeologists have genuine expertise in both fields, the key to success must, in most cases, lie in effective partnership.

Fig. 1.1. Eight and nine year-old children from Whittingham School, Northumberland, learning about prehistory in the Breamish Valley. The children take part in a variety of interpretive events linked to the Park Authority's archaeological research project in the valley. All children of this age are intrigued by the distant past, and very keen to learn about it. Many pupils leave such events convinced that they want to be archaeologists when they grow up!

Effective archaeological interpretation, like a good novel or film, will generate an emotional response rather than simply tell a story. If we are really seeking to generate a meaningful relationship between the public and the heritage, then we must seek to encourage the development of emotional bonds between modern people and ancient places. This will not be achieved by the simple presentation of facts, but requires the stimulation of minds. When taking visitors to a recently excavated Bronze Age cairn in the Cheviot Hills, I explain the form of the site, the nature of the finds, the radiocarbon dates obtained for the site and various other results of the excavation (Frodsham, in press). Most people are interested in these facts, but not half as interested as they are in the poignant story of the little two year old child who apparently suffered form meningitis and whose cremated remains were interred in an intricately decorated pot within the cairn. This story generates an emotional response, intimately linked to the tragic life of an infant who lived, briefly, in this beautiful valley some 4,000 years ago. People wonder about the form the funeral ceremony may have taken, or how the little tot's parents would have coped. Of course, we will never know such details, but through thinking about them people develop mental links with the distant past that are of value to them personally as well as helping to generate wider support for archaeology. Similarly, though perhaps not quite as intimately, public interpretation of Hadrian's Wall could go much further in considering the effect of the Roman military on the everyday lives of people in central and northern Britain. People today should perhaps be encouraged to consider the anger and resentment which must have existed amongst communities whose ancestral homelands were threatened by the Roman war machine. The key to effective interpretation, in my view, lies in generating emotional ties between people now and people in the past: what would it have felt like? How would I have reacted. Would I have been sad, angry or happy?

These are not new ideas. Back in 1957, in his often quoted book 'Interpreting Our Heritage' Freeman Tilden advocated a number of principles for good interpretive practice. Uzzell (1994), in a useful overview of the principles and practice of heritage interpretation, summarises some of these as follows:

1. *Interpretation should relate to something within the personality or the experience of the visitor.*
2. *Information, as such, is not interpretation. Interpretation is revelation based upon information. These are entirely different things. However, all interpretation includes information.*
3. *The chief aim of interpretation is not instruction, but provocation.*
4. *Interpretation presented to children should not be a dilution of the presentation to adults, but should follow a fundamentally different approach.*

These basic principles remain as relevant today as they were in 1957, and should underlie all archaeological interpretation projects.

A final point which I would like to consider in this introduction is the effective use of humour in archaeological interpretation. While not always appropriate, humour can on occasions be a very effective interpretive or educational tool. During an introductory address (Frodsham 2000) to a major conference some years ago, while considering Neolithic burial practice, I made the casual observation that 'Speaking as someone brought up in Lancashire, it has never surprised me that Yorkshiremen, even as long ago as the Neolithic, chose to be buried with their valuables rather than let them fall into someone else's hands'. To this day, people present at that conference, most of whom will have long forgotten everything else I said, still occasionally make reference to this. They may know nothing else about prehistoric burial practice, but they will always remember that there was something unusual about Neolithic burials in Yorkshire. It is, in my view, a shame that the editors of the proceedings of that conference saw fit to remove the above statement, on the grounds that 'it might cause offence to Yorkshiremen'. How ridiculous! Yorkshire folk are made of sterner stuff than that, and the superiority complex of the true Yorkshireman will never be dented by such feeble jibes. We must, of course, be careful not to cause unnecessary offence to anyone when seeking to interpret the past, but perhaps we should also be prepared to take an occasional risk if we really want our interpretation to be effective.

The following notes represent three papers rolled into one. The first relates to prehistoric rock art (spmething that most people, including most archaeologists, find very difficult to interpret). The second is about Hadrian's Wall (the interpretation of which appears quite straightforward to most people). The third is based loosely on the Anglian place of *Gefrin*, but also considers Hobbits and Winnie the Pooh (who may never previously have been considered in relation to archaeological interpretation but who may, nevertheless, not be wholly irrelevant to the subject). These discussions differ from most subsequent contributions in that they are not about specific projects, but aim to introduce some general issues that should be of relevance throughout the rest of the volume.

Interpreting the Ambiguous: Prehistoric Rock Art in Northern England and the American South-West.

(This volume's main title was originally applied to the following paper, given at a 1996 international conference at York University entitled *Images, Myths and Identity: Interpreting Historic Places in Britain and the United States*. The views expressed within it are now several years old, but are no less relevant to a discussion of archaeological interpretation than they were when originally presented.)

Introduction

'Interpretation' is a word which I often think is misused in the context of the historic landscape. The archaeologist Christopher Tilley has recently described 'interpret' as '*one of those incorrigible and annoying little verbs whose meaning is apparently simple and yet simultaneously remains almost impossible to define*' (Tilley 1993,1). He then asks '*what precisely do we do when we interpret? When does interpretation begin or end, and how do we know when we are interpreting?*' (*ibid*). My copy of the Concise Oxford Dictionary provides some help, defining as it does the verb 'interpret' as '*Expound the meaning of (abstruse words, writings, dreams, etc); make out the meaning of; bring out the meaning of, render, by artistic representation or performance; explain, understand, in specified manner, as this we interpret as a threat; act as interpreter.*' There are, of course a number of alternative definitions of the word interpretation, such as that provided by the Society for the Interpretation of Britain's Heritage: '*Interpretation is the process of communicating to people the significance of a place or object, so that they can enjoy it more, understand their heritage and environment better, and develop a positive attitude to conservation*'. Personally, I like the definition provided by Hodder *et al* (1995, 238) in the glossary of a volume entitled 'Interpreting Archaeology: Finding Meaning in the Past': '*with a particular archaeological aim of understanding the past and a wider interest of providing edifying learning experiences, interpretation is a never-ending process of making sense...Interpretation is essentially open and never final: more can always be said or learned...*'. We could argue for hours about the meaning of the word 'interpretation', but it is probably safe to state that 'archaeological interpretation is a never ending process of trying to make sense of a past about which we can never know everything'.

Professional interpreters may translate a speech made in a foreign language in a number of different ways, none of which need necessarily be considered 'wrong'. This act of interpreting a foreign tongue may be likened in certain respects to the archaeologist attempting to interpret prehistoric rock art and subsequently seeking to pass on this interpretation to the public through a variety of media. However, there are also crucial differences, and I wonder whether the word 'interpretation' is adequate to cover such a wide range of activities. I contend that a lot of what we conventionally call interpretation (for example the provision of information panels at archaeological sites) is not actually interpretation at all, but is better defined as explanation or presentation. As an archaeologist it is certainly not for me to lecture to interpreters about the meaning of interpretation, but in this account I will offer a personal view on the process of interpretation, linked to my own research into prehistoric rock art.

I will deal with the interpretation of prehistoric rock art on two different levels. First, I will examine how, as an archaeologist, I have sought to interpret a particular element of British rock art for myself. Secondly, I will examine how we should attempt to 'interpret' or 'present' rock art for the benefit of the general public: a process which I consider to be in many ways a separate issue from my personal interpretation of the phenomenon.

Prehistoric rock art in Britain and the United States

The prehistoric rock art of northern England and parts of Scotland remains one of the great enigmas of British prehistory (Beckensall 1999). This is due partly to the nature of the subject, but also owes much to the lack of relevant academic research throughout most of the last century.

The rock art which concerns us here dates from the Neolithic and possibly also the early Bronze Age (most of it probably dates from the period 4000 - 2000BC). It is entirely abstract in nature, making its interpretation particularly challenging. Notable concentrations occur on natural rock outcrops, often in locations with spectacular views, in Northumberland (fig. 1.2a), Durham, North Yorkshire and West Yorkshire in England, and in Argyll (fig. 1.2b), Strath Tay and Galloway in Scotland. In addition to the natural outcrops some motifs occur on monuments, such as stone circles and burial cairns, but much of this 'monumental art' appears to consist of reused fragments of previously decorated outcrop rock (fig. 1.3). The principal motif is the simple cup mark, a cup-shaped depression in the rock surface which can be several centimetres in diameter. These cupmarks can occur in isolation, or in combination with concentric rings and wavy lines. Spirals and other motifs are occasionally incorporated into the designs.

North American rock art is considerably more varied than that of Britain, and includes much painted decoration in addition to petroglyphs (a fact which serves to remind us that such painted decoration may also have existed in Neolithic Britain, though no traces survive today). Native rock art has been recorded at thousands of sites

Fig. 1.2 a & b. Rock art in northern Britain. a = Poltalloch, Argyll, Scotland. b = Roughting Linn, Northumberland, England.

Fig. 1.3 a & b. Long Meg stone circle, Cumbria. There is reason to believe that Long Meg was quarried from an already decorated red sandstone river cliff (Frodsham 1996), but what the carvings may have 'meant' to the artists who first produced them, or to the builders of the stone circle, are matters for endless speculation. Many visitors to this splendid monument leave without even noticing the carvings, which is a shame given the potential interpretive challenge that they offer to all visitors who care to think about them for a moment. Detailed interpretive panels may be inappropriate here, but a little on site information to help visitors appreciate the site would be no bad thing.

Fig. 1.4. Cup and ring marked boulder from a site by the Etowah River, Canton, Georgia, USA, now located at Rheinhardt College, Waleska, Georgia. Might the motifs on this stone have a similar 'meaning' to those on the hundreds of similarly decorated panels from Neolithic Britain?

throughout the USA (Grant 1967, 1983), with particularly interesting concentrations in the South-West and the Great Basin area. Much work has been done over the years on the study and classification of this art, which includes many recognisable figures (people, animals deer, sheep, fish etc), along with apparently mythical figures and, crucially to the discussion which follows, a large number of abstract motifs which would not be at all out of place in northern England (fig. 1.4).

Interpreting rock art in Northern England

Having established what we mean by rock art, let us now briefly consider what it all 'means', or, put another way, let us attempt to interpret it for ourselves. We should begin by reminding ourselves that '*rock art interpretation involves making associations between rock art and past cultures and attempting to explain how the rock art functioned and what meaning it might have had to past societies. Explanations of function and meaning are tentative because the rock art now exists out of its living cultural context*' (Cole 1990, 36). Evidently, the interpretation of rock art is more complex than that of many other types of archaeological site, and back in 1864, J. Y. Simpson wrote that '*it is surely better frankly to own that we know not what these markings mean (and possibly may never know it), rather than wander off into that vague mystification and conjecture which in former*

days often brought discredit on the whole study of archaeology' (Simpson 1864, 261). Since then there have been a variety of more or less bizarre, and occasionally rather amusing, explanations. The late Ronald Morris, doyen of Scottish rock art students for over a quarter of a century, listed 104 possible interpretations of the motifs employed in British art that he had heard over the years (Morris 1979, 16-28). These included more or less plausible, but vague, ideas such as that the symbols represented religious or magical symbols, a mother goddess, the sun, eyes, an undecipherable code, maps of the stars, messages from outer space, doodles, or (my personal favourite) marks of sexual prowess, whereby the chief made a cup-and-ring to celebrate each female sexual conquest (Morris omits to tell us why one particular sexual conquest should warrant a cup with seven rings a metre in diameter, while so many others were celebrated by no more than a humble cup mark!). Clearly, these carvings have meant a lot of different things to a lot of different people over the years.

More recent suggestions, based partly on ethnographic analogy, have included the idea that many of the symbols employed in the rock art are related to entoptic phenomena, possibly linked to Shamanic activity. This in my view seems quite probable, and Cambell Grant (1983, 12-14) highlights the importance of Shamanism in American rock art, citing also hunting magic, clan symbols, astronomy, fertility rites, visions and doodles as worthy of consideration when seeking to interpret various motifs. Jean McCann, in one of the most enthralling accounts of European rock carvings to have appeared in recent decades, notes that *'as symbols, the stone age designs contain meanings which could not be precisely translated into our language, even if we had a neolithic symbols rosetta stone'* (McCann 1980, 152). It is important to bear this in mind when discussing the interpretation of rock art. *'Symbols are esoteric, wheras words are exoteric. That is, symbols imply without specifying exactly. They refer to an innate or intuitive knowledge without formulating (and thus limiting) a concept......The symbol, by its powers of evocation, can serve as a synthesiser. It can exist outside time, representing an abstract reality which can be comprehended intuitively, but never objectively expressed'* (*ibid* 148).

In a recent paper I analysed a particular element of British rock art: the spiral (Frodsham 1996). As part of this work I attempted to provide an explanation of the meaning of the spiral to the prehistoric people who used it. This may be regarded by some as a trifle rash, especially in the light of work by scholars such as Nancy Munn, who has demonstrated through her studies of Aboriginal Australian art that such symbols can have several different meanings of varying abstraction and complexity, and that these meanings can fluctuate over time (Munn 1973). However, undaunted by such potential problems, I proceeded to read a few books about native American rock art, and was intrigued by the extent to which some of this art is still regarded as sacred by native communities. This is in complete contrast to the British art, which is generally regarded as fascinating but of no direct relevance to people today. The source that I found most intriguing was a book called 'Signs from the Ancestors: Zuni Cultural Symbolism and Perceptions of Rock Art' by Jane Young (1988). This discusses personal interpretations of rock art by present day Zuni individuals. While it would be foolish to claim that symbols common to both Zuni and British rock art must have had similar original 'meanings', it was nevertheless fascinating to realise that the Zuni explanations of the spiral motif corresponded very closely with certain views of later Neolithic society in Britain which had been drawn up on the basis of the study of monuments and with absolutely no consideration of rock art. In particular, Young records that contemporary Zunis refer to the carvings as 'messages from the ancestors' and the spiral was most frequently interpreted as 'journey in search of the Centre', represented by the inturning arms of the spiral. This makes a lot of sense as we know that the concept of the Centre, or central place, is fundamental to many aspects of Zuni cosmology. Is it reasonable, then, to seek to apply a similar interpretation to the British spirals (and possibly also the much more numerous cup and ring marks, as the Zuni also interpret concentric circles in a similar way)? Obviously, I do not expect there to be direct parallels between Zuni cosmology and that of

Neolithic Britain, but some possible similarities may be worth investigating. For example, it is interesting to note that the archaeologist John Barratt has recently suggested that life in later Neolithic Britain may have been considered as a 'process of becoming', perhaps regarded as 'a movement towards a future state which was described by reference to ancestors or gods and where life itself might be spoken of as ephemeral, as a series of movements through or as a journey through the world' (Barrett 1994, 136). It may not, therefore, be unreasonable to suggest that some common ground may underlie the use of spiral and concentric circle motifs by both the Zuni and the inhabitants of Neolithic Britain. At the very least, an awareness of Zuni symbolism suggests a plausible interpretation of the British spirals that I would otherwise have been most unlikely to think of.

Managing rock art: the art of informing the public.

I am very grateful to Sarah Stuart-Nash of Southampton University for making available to me her discussion of the Native American rock art of the Lava Beds National Park in northern California prior to its publication, as this provides a particularly good example of some the problems associated with interpreting American rock art (Stuart-Nash 1996). Here, at Petroglyph Point, is one of North America's largest concentrations of prehistoric rock engravings. The land traditionally belonged to the Modoc tribe, and was unknown to westerners until the goldrush of 1849. The Modoc were eventually forced out of the area onto a reservation, leading to the Modoc wars of 1872-73 when the tribe attempted to return to its traditional homeland which had by then been settled by white ranchers. Eventually, after holding out in the Lava Beds with only thirty-seven warriors against a thousand government soldiers, Captain Jack (as the Modoc chief was affectionately known when westerners first settled the area) was betrayed by former colleagues and captured. He was 'tried' (the scaffold was constructed while the 'trial' was in progress), found guilty of murder, and hanged. His body was then taken on a tour of the east as a carnival attraction, admission 10 cents (Brown 1991, 220-240). Subsequently the land around the lava beds was agriculturally 'improved', causing much environmental damage and destroying various sacred elements of the Modoc cultural landscape. During World War II the area was used for a Japanese-American internee camp, and much new rock art was added to that of the Modoc. After the war, Petroglyph Point was incorporated within the newly created Lava Beds National Monument, bringing it under the jurisdiction of a distant federal agency subject to the demands of modern tourists. Sarah Stuart-Nash observes that: *'The area where the warriors put up such fierce resistance to losing their homeland is now called 'Captain Jack's Stronghold Picnic Centre', the costliest war undertaken by the government, with so many warriors killed, so that predominantly Euro-American tourists can now eat their sandwiches in true colonial fashion'.* For some reason it seems difficult for modern westerners to appreciate the depths of disgust felt even today by some native Americans at such insensitive and unnecessary interpretation. This paper was originally presented on the day of the funeral of Diana, Princess of Wales, one of the most popular and respected individuals in the western world. Perhaps the average westerner would begin to have some sympathy for our native American colleagues if faced by the prospect of some self-centered, exploitative entrepreneur seeking to open 'Di's Diner' adjacent to the spot where she met her tragic end. I would imagine, however, that even this would not extend to the strength of feeling generated by a community forcibly removed from its ancestral, sacred territory and subsequently made to endure the post-humus humiliation of its leader by an ignorant and largely disinterested population. Perhaps part of the answer to these problems is to involve more native Americans in rock art studies in such a way as to enable serious research while not damaging or destroying the symbolic significance of sacred sites.

It should be stated at this point that the above paragraph was originally written several years ago, and that I have never visited the Lava Beds National Monument and consequently cannot offer any personal views on the place or the interpretive material provided there for visitors. However, in fairness to the US National Parks Service, the Lava Beds website (June 2003) suggests that serious efforts are now being made to provide effective interpretation. For example, the website states that '*A walk through Captain Jacks Stronghold is a unique experience just waiting to happen. The spirit of the Modoc People can still be found there. Think of the courage it took for them to endure the winter of 1872-73 after their village and winter food supplies had been burned by the army. Please walk the trail with respect and with an open heart. Enter the medicine circle reverently, as you would enter your own church. Let the spirits of the winds, the rocks, and the animals speak to you of past events, as they have always spoken to the indigenous peoples. Listen for their silent voices. The traditional culture of an entire people was lost here, yet a modern culture of their descendants still survives. Don't be surprised if you find prayer ribbons or sage offerings hanging on the prayer tree near the junction of the two trails. Feel free to offer your own. The spirituality of the Modoc Stronghold permeates the whole region and captures the hearts of many visitors, calling them back year after year. Will you be among them? (You can borrow a trail guide from the dispenser, but please remember to return it when you're finished. You can buy it for 25 cents.)*'

With specific regard to rock art, the same website tells us that '*there are several possible interpretations. Rock art was most likely an integral part of the ceremonies and rituals performed by the Native American people. Pictographs may have been done in conjunction with a girl's puberty ceremony or the people's fertility rites............Petroglyphs in many areas of the western United States appear to be related to hunting magic and this may be the case with rock art of the Lava Beds, although there is at present time, no evidence for this theory.............rock art may have also been used to describe an event in the tribe's history, or perhaps to record an individual's animal spirit 'helper'. We do know that the symbols left on the rock faces of this area are not writing, as was originally thought, but art, because the Modoc and their predecessors had no written alphabet. We may never truly know what was in the mind of the artist as he or she sat down many ages ago to leave a mark on this fire-broken land.*'

In Britain, we have no surviving communities of 'native Britons' claiming association with the rock art, nor any historic records of any such communities. However, it is important to bear in mind examples such as the Modoc at the Lava Beds when seeking to interpret our British sites, many of which may also have witnessed episodes of disputed 'ownership' back in prehistory.

While the level of interest in rock art at some places in the world is such that National Parks can be created largely to ensure their sympathetic management, and information about such sites can be found on numerous websites, the number of rock art sites officially accessible to the general public throughout Northern England is negligible, and those with any form of on-site (or near-site) interpretation/presentation can be counted on the fingers of one hand. Indeed, until the 1990s the level of professional indifference towards rock art had been extraordinary, and were it not for the meticulous work of Stan Beckensall and a few other enlightened 'amateurs' we would still be unaware of a large proportion of the known examples. Recently, however, we have witnessed a resurgence of academic interest in the subject, largely thanks to the lead provided by Professor Richard Bradley at Reading University (eg Bradley 1997), and public interest in the subject is certainly rising. Archaeologists have a duty to present a sample of rock art sites to the public through negotiations with landowners, and a sample of these sites should receive some form of 'interpretation'.

In Scotland, several examples of rock art are now cut off from the surrounding landscape by green metal fences. These help to protect the art, but do rather detract from the atmosphere of sites by providing a barrier between them and their often magnificent landscape settings. However, these fences can always be removed in the future, and we must at the very least credit the Scottish authorities with having done something positive about their rock art. In my personal defence I should state the only area of the Northumberland National Park which contains a major concentration of rock art is now the focus of a management agreement between the Park Authority and the landowner, The Duke of Northumberland (Frodsham *et al* 1995). This ensures that all elements of the archaeological landscape are conserved for the future, and also enables the interpretation of these sites (including Bronze Age burial cairns, an Iron Age hillfort, a Romano-British settlement and several examples of rock art) for the general public. Such agreements are important, enabling rock art to be interpreted for the public within the context of the wider archaeological landscape rather than considered in splendid isolation. Sadly, there are far too few such agreements elsewhere throughout northern England, although one particular project is worthy of special mention. The Peak District National Park has very few rock art sites, but one of the most spectacular, at Gardom's Edge, was recently buried to ensure its conservation and a replica, flown in by helicopter, was placed on top of it (see Bevan this volume). This was part of a project to research and conserve the important archaeological landscape in the vicinity of the rock art. The project attracted sponsorship, and generated much public interested on a local level. But what should be done in Northumberland, where hundreds of sites, no less interesting or vulnerable than that at Gardom's Edge, exist scattered across the hills?

A final observation with regard to the management and presentation of rock art sites is that this must be done sympathetically. The atmosphere of many prehistoric sites, both locally and internationally, has been dramatically altered by the demand for popular interpretation. Visiting some such sites (such as Stonehenge, Carnac or New Grange) is now only possible under the gaze of uniformed attendants, whereas previously it was a truly inspirational, and much more intimate, experience. Visitors in the not very distant past interacted directly with the mysterious archaeological remains, but today the visitor experience is to an extent sanitised through the medium of the ticket office and the souvenir shop. Unfortunately, many interpreters seem unable to recognise this fact. I have regrettably arrived at the conclusion that some of these people actually have more interest in information panels, coffee shops and visitor numbers than in the archaeological sites themselves. It is, I think, legitimate to question the extent to which some sites should be advertised and interpreted for the public, or left as 'rewards' for people prepared to put some effort into discovering them for themselves.

I firmly believe that the rock art of Northern England is of international importance and deserves a level of management that can only be achieved through adequate funding on a professional basis. British rock art is no less important than that of the American South-West, or indeed of our own better funded archaeological remains such as Hadrian's Wall or any number of medieval abbeys or castles, and it is essential that we accept this now and start to do something about it before it is too late (Frodsham 1995). Recent attempts to address such issues (English Heritage 2000) have yet to make any substantial progress despite considerable expense, and careful thought is needed as to how best to allocate resources to rock art management. An international project covering European rock art, and incorporating new research into the origins and development of rock art (essential to inform fresh interpretations and thus stimulate further public interest) could perhaps be set up to tackle the conservation of rock art sites, a selection of which must be 'interpreted' in some way for the benefit of visitors.

Summary: some final thoughts on the interpretation of prehistoric rock art.

In this paper I have presented a brief overview of my own attempts to interpret a particular element of prehistoric rock art for myself, and have also discussed the ways in which information about this rock art should be presented to the general public. I still have some difficulty deciding exactly what we mean by 'interpretation'. Does this cover the whole process described in the previous sentence, or technically just the first half of it? Perhaps we should now accept interpretation as a kind of umbrella term, encompassing a lot of different activities such as perception, meaning, experience, translation, presentation, dissemination and information. My personal inclination, however, is to view interpretation as a specialised activity which must be accepted as an essential aspect of all archaeological research, but which varies in nature from one project to another. For example, the act of interpreting rock art is, in my view, considerably more complex than the question of how to present information about an old country house or a historic garden: the latter should perhaps be re-labelled 'presentation' rather than interpretation. I feel that the act of interpretation is a very personal thing, and I believe that it would be arrogant of me to assume that I could interpret a site for, or on behalf of, someone else. The interpretation of the spiral in British prehistoric rock art as 'a journey to a central place', based as it is largely on my limited knowledge of American rock art, is a personal view which I choose to present to others as a possibility in order to help them to experience sites on the ground. The actual act of interpretation occurs inside my head, as it does inside the heads of each individual visitor. I am not interpreting the site for others, who, after considering the available evidence, may well prefer an alternative explanation which is entirely their prerogative. I contend that visiting a prehistoric rock art site should be an emotional experience, and no two people will react in exactly the same way to such a site. Indeed, individual visitors should be *encouraged* to develop their own *personal interpretations* based on their experiences of such places.

One final observation, also touched on above, is that we must be honest with the public when seeking to help them interpret rock art sites. There is simply no need to invent fabulous stories or perpetuate silly explanations. Accurate facts, if effectively presented, are ultimately of more interest to 99% of the public than irrelevant, if occasionally entertaining, nonsense. When a complete story cannot be told (which is invariably the case when dealing with ancient sites) then let's present the public with genuine alternatives which they can evaluate for themselves and upon which they can build their own interpretations. Campbell Grant, writing about American rock art in 1967, notes that *'only the original artist or shaman.....would know the precise meaning of the pictures, and it is doubtful if many of us would understand him if he were here to explain. The world of the aboriginal Indian, where the supernatural was as real as the natural, is a world we cannot enter but nothing prevents us from enjoying the intriguing pictures that still exist by the thousands in caves and on cliffs'* (Grant 1967, 152). In the States, where rock art sites are still regarded as sacred 'signs from the ancestors' by some native communities, it is absolutely essential that all the relevant facts are presented to visitors, allowing them to form an unbiased interpretation rather than to be indoctrinated with a carefully edited version of the truth designed to appeal to the 'average Euro-American' of the early 21st century.

Much of the pleasure of rock art (whether in Britain, the USA, or anywhere else in the world) exists in its very ambiguity, the interpretation of which has to be down to individual experience much as it may have been when the art was first produced. We will never know exactly what it all 'means', but we can certainly have a lot of fun thinking about it.

Hadrian's Wall: mighty monument to glory or failure?

Introduction

As the conference on which this volume is based was held in Newcastle upon Tyne, it would have been appropriate for someone from English Heritage's interpretation team to address it with regard to the region's world famous ancient monument, Hadrian's Wall. Close to the event, it was confirmed that no speaker from EH would be available, leaving two options. The first was to ignore the old Wall completely, which wasn't really on. The second was to incorporate my own somewhat unconventional views on the Wall's interpretation into the opening address to the conference: they are thus presented here.

Hadrian's Wall (fig. 1.5) is regarded by most people as a magnificent monument to the glory of the Roman Empire. However, this public perception is based largely on interpretations by classical scholars extending back over three centuries. In fact, a perfectly reasonable case can be made, through the reinterpretation of the very same evidence, for the Wall to be considered largely as a monument to failure (Divine 1995, 23). In reality, the arguments are complex, and will keep academics busy for centuries to come, but it is my firm belief that alternative

Fig. 1.5. Hadrian's Wall. One of the world's most famous and instantly recognisable ancient monuments. But what was it for? How did it work? And was it a failure? If more visitors are to be encouraged to visit this world famous monument and seek to interpret it for themselves, with all the consequent benefits for the tourism-based local economy, how much erosion, such as that visible in this view, should be deemed acceptable to the fabric of the World Heritage Site?

interpretations for this most famous of ancient monuments should be provided, in an accessible form, for the benefit of the general public.

Many people agree with my observation that Roman military sites appear 'alien', somehow isolated from the landscape in which they were built, whereas most 'native' prehistoric sites, and even later sites such as Norman castles, seem to fit 'naturally' into those same landscapes. However, this is no reason why the interpretation of Roman sites should also be done in isolation. I make no attempt to belittle the achievements of Rome, in Britain or elsewhere, but we must now seek to develop a recognition of native society before and during the occupation if we are truly to attempt an interpretation of 'Roman' Britain. I believe that the interpretation of the Wall has suffered from being the preserve of Romanists for too long, and that an approach which seeks to integrate the study and interpretation of the Wall with wider historic and landscape studies is now essential. This argument is as relevant to issues of public interpretation as it is to academic research.

These notes are based on a public lecture in which I questioned much of the popular interpretation of Hadrian's Wall. My intention is to present some alternative interpretations, and invite people to enhance their own appreciation of one of the most famous archaeological monuments in the world by reaching their own conclusions as to its purpose and effectiveness. In the lecture, I examined the historical background to the study of the Wall, and the character of Hadrian, both of which are crucial to an understanding of why the Wall was built. Clearly, space precludes a detailed consideration of such issues here, so what I propose to do is to set out some general thoughts about the Wall and to consider whether or not it could legitimately be considered as a monument to failure. The relevance of this discussion to the current volume lies in the question of whether or not it should be presented to the visiting public, and if so, how?

Who was Hadrian?

If you were to undertake a poll of the general public in Britain, or possibly throughout the world, to ask people to name three Roman Emperors, I suspect that most of those who could name any would name Hadrian. Why should this be the case? Quite simply, it is because of the hype surrounding Hadrian's Wall, the subject of much learned debate amongst academics and a popular tourist destination throughout the 20th century. Given his fame, however, relatively few hard facts are known about Hadrian (Birley 1997; Speller 2002). We know that he was the fourteenth Roman Emperor, that he travelled more extensively about his Empire than any previous or subsequent Emperor, that he set about the consolidation of the Empire's boundaries rather than seek further

expansion, that he reorganised the structure of the army and tightened discipline within it, and that he was a very keen architect. He also appears to have been something of a perfectionist, was highly educated and intelligent, and loved everything to do with ancient Greece. He was the first emperor to wear a beard, which some say was to cover a facial blemish but which was probably inspired by Greek fashion: this trend was continued by his successors. He was married, although never produced an heir. His private life appears to have been extravagant and varied, including intimate relationships with a variety of young men and married women. Relationships between older men and young boys were apparently commonplace in ancient Greece, but whether or not Hadrian's interest in young men was influenced by this remains a matter for conjecture. He could be ruthless, almost certainly being responsible for the murder of possible competitors at the beginning and towards the end of his reign, yet in comparison with many other Emperors he continues to enjoy a very favourable reputation.

What is Hadrian's Wall?

The ancient monument (or rather the collection of ancient monuments) that we refer to today as Hadrian's Wall began life in, or shortly before, AD122, and was not finally abandoned by Rome until AD407. The Wall may therefore be regarded as having been in active service for about three centuries during which it underwent considerable changes, only the briefest sketch of which can be recounted here.

In AD83, Roman troops achieved a significant victory over the Caledonians at the Battle of Mons Graupius (the exact location of which is unknown, but must have been somewhere on the fringes of the Scottish Highlands). Mons Graupius must have been a major battle: literary sources suggest that the Caledonian army consisted of some 30,000 men, and the Roman force probably numbered some 20,000. It should have been the pivotal moment in the Roman conquest of the whole of Britain. But it was not. Instead, troops were withdrawn and Scotland was effectively abandoned (Breeze 1996). Some four decades later, Hadrian visited Britannia and it is generally assumed that he personally ordered the construction of the Wall, from coast to coast across the Tyne-Solway isthmus, that now bears his name. As part of his plans to consolidate the Empire, Hadrian gave up some of Trajan's recently conquered territories in the East, and he must surely have considered giving up Britain and formalising the boundary of the Empire along the Channel coast. However, on balance he must have decided that the division of the island into a Roman south and a barbarian north was the optimum solution. Most of England had effectively been 'Roman' for the best part of a century by this time, so to simply 'hand it back to the natives' was probably never a realistic option. Given Hadrian's love of architecture, however, the fact that the decision to permanently partition Britain enabled him to order the construction of 'his' Wall may not have been entirely irrelevant to this decision. Although rarely commented upon, his love of all things Greek may also be relevant here. Hadrian would have been familiar with Greek walls, such as the 5km long double barrier with internal towers and fortified gateways that joined Athens with its harbour, Piraeus. He would also have been aware of the ancient Greek tradition of building defensive works 'to wall out barbarians' (Birley 1997, 133). Could it be that his desire was to place a magnificent monument to the glory of ancient Greece (and himself) at the northern edge of his empire? It may come as a surprise to many tourists visiting Hadrian's Wall that there are no contemporary sources relating to its original construction. Could it be that the Wall was never actually as critical to the defence of the Empire as most people today assume it to have been?

Although it is normally depicted with battlements and a parapet walkway, the exact form of the Wall is not known. Its original height is unknown but was probably about six metres. It may have been whitewashed, perhaps only on its north face. A substantial ditch, with an outer mound, lay to the north of the Wall along most of its length. A defended gateway, known to us a milecastle, was built each Roman mile along the entire length of the Wall. Two turrets were built at regular intervals between adjacent milecastles. The western sector of the Wall was originally built of turf and timber, but was later rebuilt in stone.

The Wall as originally planned was never completed, which would suggest that the initial plans were recognised as fundamentally flawed at an early stage. It is just possible that the original plans were the work of the British Governor rather than the Emperor, and that it was Hadrian who drew up the revised plan. A more likely scenario, however, has Hadrian drawing up the original blueprint and ordering work to start in advance of his visit to the province in AD 122, subsequently agreeing revisions to the original plan following consultation with various advisors *during* his presumed personal inspection of the frontier. Whatever the explanation for the change, the revised plan saw work on the Wall itself postponed while several large forts were built astride its line. These include today's popular tourist sites of Chesters, Housesteads and Birdoswald. This meant that troops would now be garrisoned on the line of the Wall, rather than in forts to the south. Access to the north was now possible directly from these forts, rather than just through the milecastle gateways. Indeed, access through the milecastles was impeded through the building of the *vallum*, a massive ditch running to the south of the Wall the purpose of which appears to have been to define the southern edge of a military zone. The *vallum* is often regarded as some kind of 'optional extra' within the Wall complex, but it was in itself an enormous undertaking. Given its architectural symmetry and uncertain purpose, it is tempting to see the *vallum* as part of the architect

inspired 'grand design' of an original blueprint, running parallel to the Wall (with its regular, uninterrupted sequence of turrets and milecastles) from coast to coast. However, it appears not to have been constructed until the revised plan had been adopted (Breeze & Dobson 2000, 56-58). The chronology and purpose of the *vallum* remain unresolved and continue to demand further investigation in the attempt to offer a plausible interpretation of the entire Wall complex.

When work recommenced on the Wall, following the construction of the Wall forts, its width was reduced from the original 10 feet to 8 feet or less. The conventional explanation of this is that the reduced width speeded up the construction process, but in practice the time saved would have been minimal. The same quantity of worked stone for the wall faces was required and the only time actually saved related to the reduced need for rubble infill, a matter of little consequence given the effort involved in other aspects of the immense construction project. It is possible that the narrow Wall was somewhat lower, and it may be that the revised plan no longer required a parapet walkway, but no generally accepted explanation for the reduction in width has yet been forthcoming from any source.

Hadrian died in the summer of AD138. He was presumably kept informed of progress with the construction and modification of his wall, at the northern edge of his Empire, right up to his death, though whether or not he paid it much attention during his final years is not recorded. What we do know, however, is that no sooner had he died than the Wall was abandoned. Hadrian's successor, Antoninus Pius, decided to move the frontier north to the Forth-Clyde isthmus, where the Antonine Wall was built, thus bringing southern Scotland firmly back into the clutches of the Empire. This proved to be a short term arrangement. The Antonine Wall was abandoned by the late 160s and the frontier was back on Hadrian's Wall where it remained, despite further military campaigns in the north, until it was finally abandoned by Rome in the early fifth century.

So, all things considered, why should this mighty monument to the glory of Rome be considered as a monument to failure? There are a number of reasons for suggesting that it could be considered thus, and some of these will now be outlined.

A monument to failure? Some thoughts on the purpose and effectiveness of Hadrian's Wall

Why was Hadrian's Wall built?
Hadrian's Wall was built as a response to a number of factors, some Empire wide and some peculiar to Britain. It was one part of a grand scheme which sought to locate the bulk of the army around the fringes of the Empire. This scheme was abandoned a few decades later, following Germanic invasions across the Danube, when it

was realised that an effective defence policy demanded that troops should be located throughout the Empire as well as at its frontiers. I believe that Hadrian's Wall owed much of its grandeur to the architectural interests of its founder, but the fact that it was never entirely abandoned by Rome for as long as the province of Britannia was retained suggests that it must have had a perceived usefulness in the eyes of succeeding Emperors. Indeed, the Wall could be regarded as representative of an extremely radical and praiseworthy attempt by Hadrian to consolidate the edges of his empire along sensible and sustainable boundaries. Some authorities explain this about return in Roman frontier policy by suggesting that all the land that was worth conquering had been conquered by Hadrian's time, but this argument is not really valid. It is probably fair to credit Hadrian with the move from an aggressive 'foreign policy' to one of consolidation, and he may well have done this for what we would regard as highly commendable reasons. Having deprived himself of the chance to seek glory through the traditional route of military conquest, he had to seek personal glory elsewhere, and his impressive architectural achievements probably represent part of this quest.

Few would argue that Hadrian's Wall justifies World Heritage Site status, and most tourists who visit the area are suitably impressed by the quantity and the scale of the ruins that are set out for their perusal. Available interpretation stresses the efficiency and the power of the Roman army, power that we can still feel today embedded in the very fabric of the Wall. But despite what all the Romanists tell us about the might of the Empire and the wonders of Rome, what was the real reason for the building of the Wall? Quite simply it was built because Rome and her mighty army failed, for whatever reason, to conquer Scotland. Had Scotland fallen to the legions (which it very nearly did and surely would have done had successive Emperors not been engaged in other priorities) then nobody would ever have contemplated the bizarre idea of building a massive wall for 80 miles from coast to coast across the centre of Britain. This failure to conquer Scotland is perhaps the main justification for considering the Wall itself as a monument to failure, although, as we will see, there are also others.

Was Hadrian's Wall built in the wrong place?

Hadrian's Wall was the focal point of a military zone that was necessary to defend the province of Britannia. Economically, the expense involved in the maintenance of this military zone, coupled with the need to keep the northern tribes quiet through a combination of threat and bribery, was immense. This expense could have been avoided through either a concerted effort to conquer the whole island, or the abandonment of Britannia which was never really an essential element of the Empire. Roman frontier policy in Britain could be deemed successful in that it enabled southern England to become 'Romanised', but the need to constantly maintain a substantial military

presence in northern England and southern Scotland meant that the conventional public view of a civilised and peaceful Roman society extending up to the Wall, with the 'barbarians' held at bay to the north, was never the case. If Hadrian's Wall was intended to enable the building of such a peaceful Roman society as far as the edge of the Empire, then it failed.

It could legitimately be questioned whether the Wall was ever actually considered as the edge of the Empire. Clearly, Roman influence extended to the north, and some areas to north and south existed at certain times as client kingdoms with their own leaders, albeit ultimately subservient to Rome. It may be that the generally pro-Roman tribal kingdoms to the immediate north of the Wall were considered as some kind of 'buffer zone' between the province and the anti-Roman northern tribes. Perhaps the people of southern Scotland actually welcomed the building of the Wall, seeing it as ensuring their independence from the Empire but with a guarantee of Roman military assistance should they be threatened from the north.

It is generally thought that the Wall was built where it is simply because that is where most of the frontier troops were stationed at the time of Hadrian's visit, but maybe the location was a calculated attempt to separate tribes to the south from those in the north and thus prevent the movement of those opposed to Rome in either direction, thus reducing the likelihood of a major anti-Roman confederation developing on the edge of the Empire. Alternatively, it could be argued that the Wall was simply built in the wrong place and should have been on the Forth-Clyde isthmus (the site of the later Antonine Wall) from where troops could be more easily despatched to deal with any smouldering unrest amongst the northern tribes.

Clearly, the Wall met with some success in controlling the passage of people, but how different things might have been if Hadrian had decided to build it on the Clyde-Forth isthmus rather than from Tyne to Solway. Not only can a case be made for regarding the whole of Roman Britannia as a failure, and Hadrian's Wall as the major symbol of that failure, but perhaps Hadrian's Wall itself actually contributed to the eventual failure of the province by virtue of having been built in the wrong place!

Was Hadrian's Wall successful in helping to control the natives?

Leaving aside the Wall's origins (rooted in the failure to conquer Scotland) and final abandonment (representing the eventual failure of the province), and the few occasions on which it was temporarily abandoned in between, we must conclude that it formed part of a system of frontier defence which enjoyed considerable success over three centuries. However, it is important to stress that this was not the Wall as originally envisaged (presumably by Hadrian), with its architect-inspired symmetry and lack of forts and other military paraphernalia, but a comprehensively redesigned and strongly garrisoned military frontier that functioned as part of a 50 mile deep frontier zone. The original plan must have been deemed a failure well before it was completed.

During the 300 years that Hadrian's Wall was in commission, many changes occurred in the relationships between the army and the local population. At the onset of Roman rule in northern England, nearly half a century before the commencement of work on the Wall, local attitudes to Rome are not recorded but would presumably have been mixed. The initial effect of the Wall on the local population must have been dramatic. Recent air photographic surveys by Tim Gates (1999) for the Northumberland National Park Authority have suggested that the Wall was built in a busy landscape, with much evidence for contemporary settlement and agriculture. This evidence (though currently lacking any accurate dating due to the lack of recent excavations) suggests that the Wall may never have existed, as traditionally assumed, in an unpopulated 'military zone'. As noted above, we do not know the extent to which local people may have supported or opposed the construction of the Wall, but by the 'end' of the Wall, some fifteen generations later, distinctions between 'Roman' and 'native' would inevitably have become blurred. Some 'British' families would no doubt be able to point to generations of military service in the 'Roman' army, and it is interesting to speculate as to the extent that Brigantian or Votadinian individuals may have considered themselves Roman. Perhaps the situation was not dissimilar to that of many people in the same region today, who may consider themselves primarily Northumbrian, English, British or European. These fascinating issues should certainly be considered by those responsible for the presentation of the Wall to the general public.

Although the two are very different, comparisons are sometimes drawn between Hadrian's Wall and the Berlin Wall; the latter being something that only lasted half a century but which people from both sides could not tear down fast enough once the opportunity arose. Both walls were imposed on the landscape and on the population by military dictatorships in an attempt to control the movements of people and the development of ideologies, but they were also very different. The Berlin Wall was constructed primarily to keep people in and western or capitalist ideas out, in order to enable the promotion of 'socialist' ideology. Hadrian's Wall is normally thought to have been built primarily to keep potential enemies out, while enabling the encouragement of Romanisation 'within'. Another difference lies in the grandeur of the architectural styles of the two walls: the Berlin Wall, although it became hugely symbolic, was built rapidly and cheaply as a functional barrier, whereas it has been

argued above that Hadrian's Wall, with its awe-inspiring architecture, was from its inception as much a symbolic as a practical structure. The Berlin Wall was hated by people on both sides of it, and the same may have been true of Hadrian's Wall for much of its effective life. While it was in commission, though, the Berlin Wall was undeniably effective: quite probably much more effective than Hadrian's Wall ever was at controlling the passage of people. Today, regardless of the operational effectiveness of either Wall, Hadrian enjoys an enviable reputation throughout the world, while the same cannot be said of those who supervised the construction of the Berlin Wall. It is not beyond the bounds of possibility that Hadrian had this long term view in mind when ordering the construction of his Wall. Certainly, such matters would have concerned him more than the relative irrelevance of a few people sneaking across the barrier from time to time. It could be argued that while it was properly manned Hadrian's Wall exercised its control through its sheer *demonstration* of power: there was simply no need for Rome to concern herself about occasional individuals seeking to cross it in a fashion akin to the desperate and horrific attempts to cross the Berlin Wall that were occasionally caught so dramatically on camera. It is also important to realise that the Berlin Wall existed in isolation, whereas Hadrian's Wall was only one element of a frontier zone, with troops garrisoned to north and south. The extent to which the actual fabric of Hadrian's Wall made any difference to the defence of the province must be open to much doubt.

Regardless of the views of the immediate local population (and these were probably never uniform, and must have fluctuated over time), it would seem that communities much further to the north remained resolutely opposed to Rome. These people must have regarded the Wall as a hated symbol of imperialist aggression, to be pierced at every available opportunity. As such, the Wall may have actively promoted anti-Roman sentiment, and on the occasions that the province was sacked by marauding northern tribes the actual passage through the Wall, both on the way south and subsequently on the way back home, must have been moments of great symbolic significance. On each such occasion, however, the Wall was subsequently re-garrisoned by the Roman army: in addition to its practical value, the Wall presumably retained considerable symbolic significance for Rome, despite it having occasionally failed the province it was supposed to have defended.

We may conclude that the Wall appears to have met with some success in controlling the activities of the native people in what is now northern England and southern Scotland. However, it had little effect on those further north, for whom it must have acted as a magnet drawing them south to plunder the province whenever the opportunity arose. Such people were not interested in capturing Roman territory, but simply in sacking and looting the province before returning home with as much booty as they could carry. Perhaps the Romans would have fared better had they sought to 'control' the northern natives by direct military force or political negotiation, rather than by constructing an outwardly aggressive looking monument for primarily defensive purposes. In Roman eyes the Wall may have stood as a powerful symbol of the mighty Empire, but in the eyes of successive northern tribal leaders it may well have represented an open invitation, and a challenge, to sack the hated imperial province to the south.

Revolting Romans: Hadrian's Wall and military rebellions against Rome.

As we have seen, the concept of a Roman province based on the occupation of only the southern half of Britain led to the construction of a defensive Wall across the middle of the island. This necessitated the maintenance of a very large garrison in the frontier region, backed up by the permanent presence of three entire legions at York, Chester and Caerleon. Hadrian's Wall differed from all other frontiers in the Empire (with the brief exception of the Antonine Wall) in two particular respects: its comparatively very short length, and the very great concentration of troops necessary to man it. It has been estimated that the Rhine-Danube provinces, with a frontier more than 2000km in length, beyond which lay numerous powerful potential enemies, were garrisoned by some 170,000 soldiers in the Hadrianic period (Maxfield 1990, 5). This contrasts with Britain, where as many as 50,000 men were entrusted with the defence of a frontier only 120km long, and beyond which lay nothing other than the tribes defeated by Agricola a generation or so before Hadrian's accession. This concentration of military personnel in so small a province led to a number of known cases of military rebellions against Rome involving the commanders and men of the 'British' army, and many more smaller scale episodes may have escaped the attention of contemporary writers. It could reasonably be argued that all these problems were a direct result of the decision to base the defence of the province on the static frontier of Hadrian's Wall. A well trained army, designed to undertake offensive field campaigns every year aimed at the acquisition of new territories from which wealth would filter indirectly back to Rome, was transformed into a static army of frontier defence. We should note that such problems were far from unique to Britain. Military commanders and their armies from other far flung regions of the Empire occasionally rebelled against Rome, but none of these regions were as small or as potentially insignificant as Britain. How much easier life would have been for Rome if she had simply exercised her option to conquer the whole of the island in the first place, or perhaps better still, if she had never bothered to set foot in Britain at all!

Hadrian's Wall in the present day landscape – what does it mean to us today?

There are some fine attempts at interpretation at various points along Hadrian's Wall, and many interesting publications aimed at the general visitor are available for purchase. However, it would not be unreasonable to suggest that conventional interpretations of the Wall, as enshrined in much of the currently available interpretive material, are now outdated. These conventional interpretations are rooted in the days of British Imperialism, when both the British (or should that be English?) and Roman Empires were regarded as forces for good, spreading civilisation and Christianity amongst uneducated 'native' populations (Hingley 2000). Today, we must seek to develop new interpretations of the evidence which consider the position of people living their 'ordinary lives' to either side of the Wall, and the relationships between these people and the Roman military over the three centuries that the Wall was manned.

If we are not careful, Hadrian's Wall will reflect not only the failures of the Romans in Britain, but also our own failure to adequately interpret the archaeological evidence available to us. When seeking to tell the fascinating story of the Romans at the edge of their Empire, we must also consider the 'non-Romans' who existed in the same landscape at the same time. In undertaking such work, archaeologists must present the results of their research in a publicly accessible form, and where relevant should provide alternative interpretations of these results. In addition, there must be meaningful interaction with the wider public. Everyone should be invited to develop their own interpretations of what it might have been like to have been alive in the Hadrian's Wall corridor in Roman times, whether one was a 'simple' farmer born and bred in the Northumbrian rain, a Roman commander from some exotic part of the Empire, or any one of the many thousands of individuals who would have experienced the Wall in operation.

Archaeologists are in general agreement that one of the original aims of Hadrian's Wall was to help exercise control over the natives. I cannot help but wonder what the Romans would have thought if they could see the extent to which the ruins of their old wall still control the activities of the natives today! Hadrian, I have no doubt, would be most amused. These ruins, through local, national and international regulations and guidelines, exercise control over everything to do with the landscape, including agricultural production, woodland management, the siting and form of new buildings, and the location of industrial activity. These controls extend far beyond the stones and mortar of the wall itself, so much so that a decision relating to a new quarry or a wind farm several miles away might be determined by its potential impact on the views to be enjoyed from the line of the Wall. This is because Hadrian's Wall is now a World Heritage Site, demanding strict conservation policies which necessitate much control over the activities of the people who live and work in the area.

In addition to conserving this landscape, archaeologists

have a duty to explain to people (locally, regionally and internationally) what the Wall is and why it is important. We could do this much better than we do at present. In doing so, however, we shouldn't forget that some people come to Wall Country for reasons other than archaeology: perhaps to seek the solitude, peace and quiet depicted in the tourist brochures but increasingly hard to find on the ground; to experience the beautiful scenery; or to get themselves photographed beneath 'Kevin Costner's tree' at Sycamore Gap, which has bizarrely become a major attraction in its own right following its role in the 1991 film *Robin Hood: Prince of Thieves*. Such people may not wish to know anything about Romans, and there is nothing wrong with that. However, the provision of alternative interpretations, carefully presented to encourage visitors to formulate their own opinions, certainly has more potential to encourage new levels of interest than the traditional 'boring' discussions of Roman soldiers.

Given that the Wall was, and still is, so much about controlling people, some may think it appropriate that Tynedale District Council (the Local Planning Authority for a large proportion of the Wall corridor) has adopted a coin of Hadrian as its official logo. One wonders whether the individuals responsible for adopting this logo cared about, or were even interested in, the fact that Hadrian was 'universally loathed when he died' (Birley 1997). Although some may consider a loathsome figure an appropriate public face for a planning authority, the

intention was presumably to link the council with Hadrian on more positive economic and marketing grounds. Our public attitude towards Hadrian as a great man, seen in the naming of dozens of local businesses (including hotels, travel agents, dentists, butchers, sandwich makers and even a chop suey house) really is rather strange. It might legitimately be compared to the unlikely future scenarios of the Tibetans glorifying the Chinese, the Poles celebrating Nazi occupation, or the Palestinians praising the creation of Israel. This strange worshipping of all things Roman owes much, albeit subconsciously, to the nature of British Imperialism. Today, just as attitudes to native Americans are generally somewhat different to those expressed in so many good old mid 20th century westerns (consider also the discussion of the Petroglyph Point rock art presented earlier in this paper), so we must now reconsider our attitudes to the 'refined' Romans and the 'nasty' natives of 2000 years ago.

As a final observation on the current interpretation of Hadrian's Wall, I would like to briefly consider the rectangular structure (fig. 1.6) which, from a distance, bears a remarkable resemblance to the mysterious monoliths from Stanley Kubrick's masterful *2001 A Space Odyssey*. Kubrick's monoliths represent a mysterious form of intelligence, beyond the understanding and even the imagination of all those who saw them. This, I fear, does not apply to our Hadrian's Wall monolith. Far from representing any form of

Fig. 1.6. Possibly the worst archaeological 'interpretive' panel in the world (at Sewingshields) set obtrusively within the magnificent landscape of the Hadrian's Wall World Heritage Site (see text for further details).

intelligence, this is the most inappropriate piece of archaeological interpretation that I have ever encountered anywhere in the world, and I have vowed to show it at every relevant opportunity until it is removed. It is an English Heritage panel, thrusting out of the earth in the midst of a beautiful open landscape in which all potentially intrusive developments of whatever scale are strictly controlled. It isn't really interpretation at all, being essentially an advertisement for English Heritage, containing minimal information about the Wall. It is also immediately adjacent to the remains of a Roman turret, which are being destroyed by cattle and sheep that use the panel as a convenient rubbing post. The decision to erect these panels was not taken locally: it was presumably taken in a London office by people who have no understanding of the landscape they are seeking to interpret. Panels like this may be satisfactory in certain contexts, but are wholly inappropriate out here in the vast open landscape of the Northumberland National Park. People come from around the world to visit Hadrian's Wall, but perhaps the interpretation of the heritage (even when the subject under discussion is a World Heritage Site) would be best left to local initiatives rather than imposed on local people by a distant central authority just as the Wall itself was some nineteen centuries ago.

Summary

Any attempt to assess the extent to which Hadrian's Wall may be considered a failure must consider its original purposes, and the extent to which it succeeded with regard to those purposes. As we have seen, experts remain divided as to the Wall's original function, and information about many aspects of its history is, at best, sketchy. Was it primarily a military frontier, a customs barrier, or a monument to the glory of the Emperor? Perhaps it sought to fulfil all three of these objectives in equal measure. Attempts to assess the effectiveness of the Wall must rely to a large extent on the interpretation of flimsy strands of evidence on which other archaeologists may develop very different conclusions. This is, of course, normal practice in prehistory, and had there been no documentary references to Roman Britain it would have been fascinating to see what prehistorians would have made of the Wall in its contemporary landscape. The historic framework is essential to our understanding of Roman military activity in Britain, but we must remember that at the time the Wall was built most local people were still living in 'prehistoric' times. Effective interpretation of Hadrian's Wall will only become possible once 'later prehistoric Britain' and 'the Roman Conquest' are no longer regarded as separate subjects.

Hadrian's Wall was not built as a World Heritage Site for the amusement of 21st century tourists. It was built by a brutally efficient military force as part of the attempt to consolidate a troublesome corner of a vast Empire. Once constructed, an enormous static garrison was required to hold it, which in itself led to serious political problems on several occasions. It was apparently breached several times by 'barbarians'. Today, its atmospheric ruins say as much about the failure of the Roman Empire as they do about its temporary triumphs. It could be considered a failure on a number of grounds, and these should be reflected in its modern day interpretation. However, we must not lose sight of the fact that if Hadrian's main aim in building the wall was self-glorification then it must be considered an unqualified success; a success which is reflected in the fact that you are currently reading about him nearly two millennia after he breathed his last breath!

While not wishing to detract from the extraordinary architectural achievement that the Wall undoubtedly was, I believe that we must be wary of falling into the trap set for us by Hadrian. That trap is to regard the Roman Empire with awe – to look up to the Roman way of life as somehow superior in every way to that of the sorry 'barbarian'. The Roman way of life was certainly different to that of the native Iron Age, but whether or not it was really so much 'better' is certainly open to question. Many regions that were never conquered by Rome have coped quite satisfactorily over the past 2,000 years, and many people today regard the heritage of the Celtic fringe or Scandinavian nations, with their lack of Roman influence, as spiritually much richer than that of England.

To some extent the remains of all Roman military sites in Britain can be regarded as monuments to failure, as the influence of Roman life soon disappeared from Britain after the army was finally withdrawn in the early fifth century and the Britons were left to fight new enemies and forge new kingdoms in *their* land. Neither Roman people nor Roman culture (with the single exception of the Church) were to play much of a role in the subsequent development of Britain. Seen in this context, Hadrian's Wall, as the mightiest and grandest of all the military structures left behind by the Romans, can justly be regarded as *the* monument to the failure of Roman Britain.

Hadrian's Wall represents the failure of the Roman Empire to conquer northern Britain, the failure of Roman Britannia to ever feel entirely secure in the face of the 'Barbarians' to the north, and, eventually, the Roman failure to hold onto what it had, as even the 'Romanised' south of England was lost. Let us hope that in future this Wall will not stand as a reflection of *our* inability to interpret *our* history with both imagination and integrity. To the Romans, it probably represented power and permanence, but in reality it was a brutal monument, imposed on local communities by military force, that only remained in commission for a dozen or so generations. In my view, it should be largely remembered, and interpreted to visitors, as such.

Of Hobbits, Royal Palaces and Winnie the Pooh.

As a child I loved J. R. R. Tolkein's *The Hobbit* (originally published in 1937) and The *Lord the Rings* (originally published as three separate volumes, 1954-55) and read them many times. Given the current hysteria about the *Lord of the Rings* films, I recently retrieved my tatty old copy of the book from my library and was struck immediately by the complete lack of illustrations (other than the front covers and a couple of maps) within it. This is in stark contrast to the very visual nature of the films, and the associated publicity material which, at the time of writing, seems to be everywhere. Although some early versions of *The Hobbit* and *The Lord of the Rings* included illustrations (including a few of Tolkein's own), and some splendid illustrated versions have been published over the years, my copies had no pictures and the magical place that is Middle Earth was created in my mind through a combination of Tolkein's text and my imagination. Today, children either read an illustrated version, including a particular artist's interpretation of selected scenes, or they watch a film, which shows them exactly what all the characters looked like and how they spoke. I suppose this is unavoidable, and that it happens every time a film is made of a story, but it is nevertheless something of a shame as it leaves little to the reader's imagination. Similar concerns relate to the interpretation of archaeological sites – how much should be described in detail, and how much should be left to the imagination of the visitor?

Of course, my love of the experience that I gained from these books developed long before I became aware of the fact that Tolkein was a scholar of Anglo Saxon literature. As a child I also read a version of *Beowulf*, surely one of the greatest stories ever told, and was transfixed by the images that this created in my head. (Incidentally, very few people reading this paper will understand Old English, and thus be able to appreciate the full power of *Beowulf* presented in its original form. The vast majority will only be able to read a translation, which is in effect an individual scholars' personal interpretation of the original Old English. This is why Seamus Heaney (1999) was able, slightly contentiously but in my view entirely justifiably, to win the Booker prize for his recent translation.) More recently, I became familiar with a relatively little known place that is now without question one of my favourite archaeological sites: a magical place if ever there was one drawing its power from a combination of sublime landscape and historical/mythological sources such as Bede and Beowulf. That place is Yeavering, or to give its original name, *Gefrin* – the site of the largest prehistoric hillfort in the Cheviots and of a magnificent 'palace' of the seventh century kings of Northumbria (Frodsham 1999).

I have come to realise that there are similarities between my love of the fictional worlds of Bilbo Baggins, Gollum, Grendel and Beowulf, and the real place that we call *Gefrin*. Although I can't fully explain this to myself, never mind to the public, I know from peoples' reactions to Yeavering that many feel something similar. I am reminded of Jean McCord's comments on rock art (quoted earlier in this paper) and the inadequacy of words to describe certain things. I am reminded also of my first trip to Yeavering with a newly appointed National Park interpretation officer. He asked me to clarify exactly why I thought Yeavering was special, and I remember replying that I didn't really want to think about it too much in case I spoiled my personal relationship with the place by thinking about it too much. Nevertherless, the Park Authority has a duty to interpret the place for visitors, and has attempted to do so in a low key way that encourages visitors to think for themselves and which I hope doesn't detract from the sense of place.

Yeavering is a place where interpretation has to be done with extreme care, or we risk damaging that which we seek, with the best of intentions, to interpret for the benefit of others (fig. 1.7). Often we simply *can't* know the facts, and this is what gives our subject much of its intrigue. We must be aware that as soon as we publicise a reconstruction of the Yeavering hillfort, or the *Gefrin* palace, we influence people's perceptions of these places which can never be the same again. That isn't to say that we shouldn't do it, just that we must think about it very carefully and, in some cases, we might actually be better leaving things to the visitor's imagination rather than trying to impose our own, albeit well intentioned, interpretations.

So how is it that an archaeological site like *Gefrin* can generate an emotional response in me akin to that experienced when reading *Beowulf*, *The Hobbit*, or *The Lord of the Rings*? Well, superficially, there are similarities between them: Beorn's Hall in The Hobbit, the golden hall of Meduseld in the Lord of the Rings, Beowulf's Heorot, and Gefrin. Three fictional places, and one real. All were very similar, and all resounded to the sounds of feasting, fuelled by copious quantities of mead. Beowulf is an ancient story which had its origins in Anglo-Saxon times, so its links with *Gefrin* are clear. But it is also important to note that Tolkien's *The Lord of The Rings* is '*the result of an ancient story-telling tradition that dates back to the dawn of Western culture*' (Day 2001, 11) and that '*In his Lord of the Rings, J. R. R. Tolkein awoke something deep in human consciousness through the universal language of mythic images drawn from the early history of mankind. His epic tale made him the heir of an ancient story-telling tradition that used the common symbolic language of myth to create the largest body of invented mythology in the history of literature*' (*ibid*, 12). Perhaps, as archaeological interpreters, we could learn from Tolkien's skilful combination of a masterful story-telling ability with a great understanding of ancient, and especially Anglo-Saxon, mythology. I am not saying that we should make up stories, but we could learn something from Tolkien about the things that

Fig. 1.7. Sometimes the old tried and tested methods are the best. This guided walk at Yeavering relied on no props or gimmicks: just a fabulous place, a beautiful midwinter day, a leader who new something of what he was talking about, and a particularly attentive and inquisitive audience.

interest the public and attempt to use these to fire public enthusiasm about a 'real' place like *Gefrin*. Other popular works of fiction set in the distant past, such as Jean Auel's Palaeolithic *Earth's Children*, Ellis Peters' medieval *Brother Cadfael*, or Raymond Williams' haunting *People of the Black Mountains* are no less relevant here. Millions of people are enthralled by such novels. Surely these same people would be equally enthralled by real archaeological sites if given the opportunity to experience them through effective interpretation. Interpreters should perhaps consider such the spirit of such novels when seeking to recreate the atmosphere of ancient times at 'real' archaeological sites.

Tolkein was wary of the interpretation of his books by others, and seems to have had a particular dislike of Walt Disney. In a letter written in 1937, he writes '*Let the Americans do what seems good to them by means of illustrating* The Hobbit *in America, as long as it is possible to veto anything from, or influenced by, the Disney studios, for all whose work I have a heartfelt loathing*' (Fowler 2001). This brings me neatly to the final example of interpretive work that I wish to discuss in this paper: Disney's *Winnie the Pooh*.

Winnie the Pooh was introduced to the world by A.A. Milne in 1925, and from the beginning Pooh stories were embellished with the instantly recognisable illustrations of E.H. Shepard. Most of the characters were based on stuffed toys belonging to Milne's son, Christopher Robin Milne, who himself provided the inspiration for the fictional Christopher Robin. However, Shepard's illustrations were not deemed suitable by the Disney Corporation, whose artists reinterpreted the much loved Pooh, Tigger, Piglet, Eeyore, Owl, Rabbit, Kanga, Roo and Christopher Robin, and introduced Gopher (who doesn't figure in any of Milne's stories), to look good on the screen in the 1960s. Walt Disney himself apparently wanted the Disney characters to appear similar to Shepard's 'classic' illustrations, but in the event many changes were made to allow the characters to move, become expressive and be viewed from all angles. In addition, the Disney characters were presumably considered more marketable than Shepard's. Whatever Walt's intentions, the 'new' Pooh and friends are clearly very different from the 'originals'. The new images now form the basis of a multi-million pound Pooh industry, and while they are the same characters as those in Shepard's original illustrations, a young child brought up today on Disney (as many are) might be hard pressed to recognise the originals. Personally, I think the Disney characters are delightful, but what, I wonder, would E.H. Shepard have made of them? My point here is that the characters and their world have been completely reinterpreted, but neither interpretation is right or wrong, and one interpretation is not necessarily any better than the other (toys and ornaments of the 'old style' Pooh still sell by the million, alongside those of the Disney version: fig. 1.8). If such a universally recognised symbol as Winnie the Pooh can be so completely reinvented, then perhaps nothing is immune to reinterpretation. (Incidentally, it would be an interesting exercise to attempt an 'interpretative archaeology of Winnie the Pooh'. The original landscapes that provided the inspiration for the Hundred Acre Wood, the Poohsticks Bridge, Roo's Sandpit and the North Pole can still be visited at Ashdown Forest in East Sussex. Artefacts available for study include many of the original stuffed toys on which the characters were based (now in New York Public Library), as well as an astonishing array of toys, games, books and other merchandise around the world. There is now even a body of theory about the 'Bear with Very Little Brain': John Tyerman Williams' (1995) *Pooh and the Philosophers* and Benjamin Hoff's (1982) *The Tao of Pooh* are now international best sellers!)

Fig. 1.8. Winnie the Pooh and Eeyore. The ornament on the left is based on EH Shepard's original characters from the 1920s, while that on the right depicts Disney's reinterpretation of the characters for a mass market in the latter half of the 20th century. Disney's Pooh is probably the most widely recognised cartoon character in the modern world, and regularly brings pleasure to millions of people. Are there lessons to be learned here regarding the possible reinterpretation of ancient monuments and traditional archaeological 'stories' for a mass market?

This brief consideration of Winnie the Pooh demonstrates the importance of *presentation*, an important element of interpretation. Effective presentation (or packaging) of a message can be the key to success: even if a basic message about the past remains the same, presentations of this message can be updated from time to time with the aim of attracting and maintaining growing levels of public interest in, and support for, archaeology. New discoveries are not necessarily required in order to develop new interpretations. Things will always move with the times, and perhaps the best we should aim for in archaeology is to provide effective interpretations for the present, with the full expectation that these will be superseded by something different (and possibly very different) in due course.

Tolkein's concerns over Disney presumably relate to the reinterpretation of his characters that would undoubtedly have occurred had either The Hobbit or Lord of the Rings been 'Disneyfied'. The process of 'Disneyfication' is clearly demonstrated by the story of Winnie the Pooh, and I can certainly understand Tolkein's concerns as to what might happen to Gollum or Bilbo should Disney ever get hold of them. But need a Disney Middle Earth necessarily be something on which to pour scorn? Indeed, would a Disney story of Hadrian's Wall, with a plot and myriad of bizarre characters loosely based on historical 'fact', necessarily be a bad thing, especially if it provided entertainment for children while presenting a storyline loosely rooted in historical events? Perhaps not. There is no real harm in children gaining an impression of Iron Age life through reading *Asterix the Gaul*, or even of earlier times through *The Flintstones*, and as archaeological interpreters we could try to learn what it is about such characters which children find so addictive, and then use similar techniques to interpret 'real' ancient worlds.

Stories told in olden times, whether round a stone age camp fire or in an Anglo-Saxon great hall, relied on the imagination of the listener for effect. An unillustrated version of the *Lord of the Rings*, or *Beowulf*, likewise stimulates the imagination of the reader. A film cannot hope to do the same as it leaves very little to the imagination, and consequently risks losing some of the magic of the story on which it is based. However, the film can still be enjoyable and, especially in this age of sound-bites and quick thrills, may appeal to a much wider audience than a book. In seeking to interpret archaeology, perhaps the answer is to produce both the 'book' (in the form of quality and challenging interpretation, perhaps incorporating art or verse which fires the imagination) and the 'film' (which gives a more visual and more readily accessible impression) and to let individuals choose for themselves the medium which they prefer. The problem, of course, is that all those who see the 'film' will never truly be able to forget the visual images and thus interpret a site from scratch for themselves, but this is simply a fact of life about which we can do little.

In the introduction to this paper it was noted that interpreters must seek to appeal to people of all ages. With this in mind, the Northumberland National Park Authority (2000) recently produced an education pack telling the 5000-year story of Yeavering in cartoon form. I was initially far from sure that this was the right medium for so atmospheric a site as Yeavering. However, my doubts were misplaced: the education pack is in use at schools throughout northern England and thousands of schoolchildren, who would otherwise have never heard of the place, have enjoyed discovering the story of Yeavering and have benefited from associated literacy lessons based on *Beowulf* and Bede. If cartoon versions of *The Hobbit*, and even of the Bible, are deemed acceptable, then the appropriate use of this technique in archaeological interpretation should perhaps be encouraged, even at special places like Yeavering. It is an inescapable fact that the popularisation and marketing of special places for economic gain is now the norm. Many great churches and cathedrals, originally constructed as places of worship, now find themselves visited primarily by fee-paying tourists rather than worshippers. The popular interpretation of such sites may be considered as somehow inappropriate, or even vulgar, but any archaeological interpreter offering such views is likely to be dismissed as elitist. The challenge lies in finding a delicate balance between maintaining the 'specialness' of such places and somehow encouraging more people to experience them in meaningful ways. This is not easy, and the archaeological interpreter must have many different tools at his or her disposal. Some such tools, either in isolation or in combination, can be effective in certain contexts but entirely inappropriate in others. Only a full knowledge of the available tools, together with an in depth understanding of the subject to be interpreted and of the proposed audience, will enable the development of effective interpretive provision at sensitive locations.

In this technological age, a bewildering array of options is available to the archaeological interpreter, and there is a considerable risk of inappropriate techniques being adopted simply because they are available. This problem has recently been brought into sharp focus within the Northumberland National Park Authority's *Discovering our Hillfort Heritage* project. This £1 million project is focused upon the many Iron Age hillforts of the Northumberland Cheviots, but also has wider aims relating to research, conservation and interpretation throughout the prehistoric landscapes of the northern half of the national park (Hedley 2001). The interpretive element of the project is based upon a specially commissioned interpretive plan. This plan includes a variety of recommended initiatives, some conventional and others rather less so. One proposal is for the introduction of 'wand tours' around some of the hillforts. The proposal is that visitors hire a 'wand', and take it with them up into the hills. At specific points this wand becomes active and presents information about the archaeology of a particular area, along with atmospheric music and other background sounds. It was suggested that the wand 'could play natural sounds like the sound of the wind'. A nice idea, but unfortunately the sound of the real wind would probably render the noise emanating from the wand completed inaudible on many days of an average year! In some environments, such 'wand tours' work very well, and are popular with the visiting public. But even if the technology could be made to work, is this really a suitable medium for the magnificently tranquil environment of the Cheviot hills, where people can walk for miles, exploring the remnants of ancient civilisations, while feeling genuinely removed from the technological world of the 21st century? I fear that this proposal may well be one that takes 'rummaging in the interpretive toy cupboard' (Uzzell 1994, 294) a stage too far. I mention it

here only because it polarised views like no other interpretive project that I have ever been involved with. Some people, familiar with the special qualities of the Cheviots, found it wholly inappropriate, while others demanded that it be introduced to help attract new audiences and bring the interpretation of the national park 'up to date'.

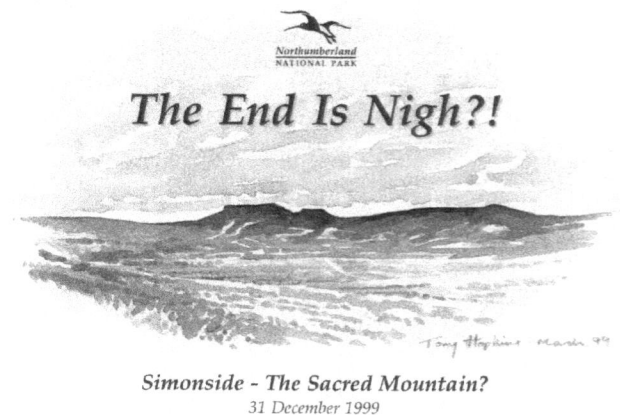

Simonside - The Sacred Mountain?
31 December 1999

Fig. 1.9. The limited edition card, featuring artwork by local artist and environmental interpreter Tony Hopkins, presented to all participants in the National Park Authority's 'The End is Nigh?!' millennium event. Archaeological interpreters should encourage the development of links between present day artists and the distant past.

I should stress that my personal concerns about 'wand tours' in the Cheviots are certainly not illustrative of a general distrust of interpretive techniques employing modern technology. At the time of writing, the *Discovering our Hillfort Heritage* project officer is putting together proposals for a new visitor centre exhibition that it is hoped will use a considerable amount of modern technology to enhance visitor appreciation of the Cheviots. But these will be contained *within* the Visitor Centre, and out in the hills people will be left with nothing more than an informative leaflet and their own imaginations. On some occasions Park staff, and others, will offer guided walks. These events offer the best way of presenting archaeological information to the public, and of establishing what people want to learn more about, but the number of participants in them is necessarily limited. While most such walks are quite conventional, there is always scope for occasional 'special events'. On 31st December 1999, to celebrate the end of the old millennium and the start of the new, I led an event around the 'sacred mountain' of Simonside (fig. 1.9). The event was fully booked up well in advance, and about 80 people took part. We walked through an ancient landscape and visited many archaeological sites, at some of which a professional storyteller appeared to tell tales relating to the sites. At a rock shelter that may have been used during the Mesolithic, the storyteller, sitting at a camp fire, told Australian aboriginal creation myths, and we discussed possible similarities between Mesolithic life in Northumberland and aboriginal society in Australia. At another site, we were all entertained by a Northumberland piper. After watching the final sunset of the millennium from the top of the 'sacred mountain', the participants were treated to a surprise firework display that had been set up earlier in the day (and which was triggered using the now not-so-modern technology of mobile phones). After the fireworks it poured with rain and getting 80 bedraggled people safely down the mountain was not without incident. I doubt whether such an event would now get past the health and safety police, but for those that participated in it, it provided an unforgettable experience. (What did you do on the last day of the second millennium AD?). The availability of many different interpretive techniques offers enormous potential for such events, which I have termed 'landscape theatre'. The bottom line is that people have fun while also learning about their heritage.

To sum up, there are perhaps two main messages from this rather wide ranging discussion. First, anything, including even something as sacred as Winnie the Pooh, can be interpreted or reinterpreted in any number of ways, and society will always reinterpret things of interest to it in different ways to reflect changing times. Archaeological interpreters must always be on the outlook for new and stimulating ways to get their messages across: fresh research invariably adds to the overall picture, but it is not always necessary to have new 'evidence' to tell old stories more effectively. Second, archaeological interpreters who are genuinely serious about engaging with the public could learn potentially valuable lessons from authors such as Tolkein. There is nothing at all wrong with seeking to invoke the spirit of *The Lord of the Rings*, or *Beowulf*, when seeking to interpret a real site such as *Gefrin*. While we must always distinguish between fiction and fact, the firing of peoples' imaginations about the past is no less important than the provision of relevant facts, and the archaeological interpreter must be entitled to a degree of 'artistic licence' when seeking to encourage people to think about what life in the distant past might really have been like.

Summary

I will bring this account to a close by stressing three main themes that I consider crucial to planning of effective archaeological interpretation. These issues are relevant to all three of the above discussions, the subject matter of which could hardly have been more varied.

First, we must stress that if archaeology is about anything it is about *people*: past people (the people we study, and earlier archaeologists or antiquarians); present people (those privileged to be doing archaeological research on behalf of the wider community, and those members of the wider community interested in the results of our studies); and future people (who will undertake further

archaeological research and develop new interpretations, and who provide the justification for the resources we expend on conservation today). In this respect, archaeological interpretation is different from other forms of environmental interpretation, and requires special skills. Our interpretations should focus on real people from the past, and should seek to generate an emotional response from the public in the manner of a good film or novel, rather than simply to present a series of facts, however interesting those facts might be.

Second, we must not worry about seeking to present the public with clear cut interpretations when we don't know the full story ourselves. Indeed, we should avoid falling into the trap of presenting any particular theory as fact. I was once told by a respected interpretation officer that 'members of the public will never appreciate something unless they understand it'. This I fundamentally disagree with. I believe that much of the public fascination with prehistoric rock carvings, and even Hadrian's Wall, stems from the fact that even the 'experts' do not understand exactly what they were all about. It should be explained to the public that archaeologists have developed, and will continue to develop, new interpretations on the basis of the currently available evidence. The old adage that two archaeologists will always come up with at least three opinions should be presented to the public as a strength of the discipline rather than simply dismissed as a joke. People should be presented with alternatives and invited to form their own views, even to formulate their own personal interpretations which they may find more satisfying than those offered by the experts.

Third, we must avoid the temptation to 'dumb down' complex situations in the attempt to present a non-specialist audience with simple and straightforward explanations. We must remember that all archaeology is interpretation, and the basic difference between an academic report and a public leaflet lies essentially in the level of detail. Whatever the level of detail being provided in a particular case, the intelligence of the audience should not be underestimated and the message should be informative and challenging. Ideally, it should stimulate people into wanting to find out more. There is clearly a need to provide appropriate information at a number of different levels, but none of these levels is necessarily any more important, or any less difficult, than the others. Identifying the different audiences to be targeted, then finding suitable messages and approaches by which to reach each audience, is a complex task for which few professional archaeologists are qualified.

In some cases, the bringing together of an environmental interpretation consultant and an archaeologist may hit the jackpot, but I am aware of many projects where such an arrangement has resulted in much frustration, wasted time and resentment in both camps. I suspect that this resentment occurs because neither the archaeologist nor the interpreter, each of whom may bring years of specialist experience to the table, is capable of fully understanding and appreciating the concerns of the other. I believe that we now have a growing need for specialist archaeological interpreters who can combine a sound working knowledge of archaeology, at the local or regional level, with an ability to experiment effectively with new interpretive techniques. Such practitioners could be archaeologists prepared to learn the rudiments of interpretation, or environmental interpreters with a sound basic understanding of the theory and practice of archaeology: either way, they could have a potentially crucial role to play in the provision of effective archaeological interpretation in an infinite range of contexts. As archaeologists, if we are unable to provide effective interpretation then our subject will lose out to the marketing professionals whose main aim is to sell things, including the heritage, regardless of the accuracy or authenticity of their message. It has already been observed that '*the heritage has been sucked in by tourism, public relations and marketing professionals, redefined, reconstituted and repackaged to become an exercise in trivia*' (Uzzell 1994, 293). The future of archaeology depends on the maintenance and development of public interest in the subject, and such interest can best be guaranteed through the provision of more effective, challenging and meaningful archaeological interpretation. It is a fundamental duty of the archaeological profession, working with partners as necessary, to provide this service and thus counter the constant threat to trivialise and 'dumb down' our subject in the name of marketing or tourism.

The basic aim of the archaeological interpreter should not be to present the public with facts or definitive interpretations. It should be to stimulate interest in the heritage by encouraging individuals to think for themselves about what it might have been like to have been alive in the past. Such an approach does not dismiss people simply as passive consumers of a 'manufactured heritage', provided for them by experts, but sees them as active participants in the creation of their own, individual interpretations of the past. The contributors to this volume present some recent initiatives whereby people have been encouraged to think for themselves in this way, which must surely be the way forward for archaeology and interpretation in the early 21st century.

Note

The above account is based on my own personal views and opinions. It certainly should not be taken as in any way representative of the views or official policies of my employer, the Northumberland National Park Authority.

Acknowledgements

I would like to thank everyone who attended the IFA conference session for enduring the presentation of the original draft of this paper, especially those delegates who discussed elements of it with me, both at and after the conference. Thanks also to Sarah Stuart-Nash of Southampton University for providing me (several years ago) with a copy of her unpublished research on North American rock art. Finally, for their constructive criticism of a draft of this paper, I would like to thank my colleagues Rob Young and Jonathan Mullard: several improvements to the text were made as a direct result of their suggestions. Responsibility for all remaining errors and shortcomings must rest, as ever, with the writer.

References

Barrett, J. C., 1994. *Fragments from Antiquity: An Archaeology of Social Life in Britain, 2900-1200BC*. Oxford: Blackwell.

Beckensall, S., 1999. *British Prehistoric Rock Art*. Stroud: Tempus.

Birley, A. R., 1997. *Hadrian: the Restless Emperor*. London: Routledge.

Bradley, R. J., 1997. *Rock Art and the Prehistory of Atlantic Europe: Signing the Land*. London: Routledge.

Breeze, D. J., 1996. *Roman Scotland*. London: Batsford.

Breeze, D. J. & Dobson, B., 2000. *Hadrian's Wall*. London: Penguin.

Brown, D., 1971. *Bury my Heart at Wounded Knee. An Indian History of the American West*. London: Barrie & Jenkins.

Cole, S. J., 1990. *Legacy on Stone: Rock Art of the Colorado Plateau and Four Corners Region*. Boulder, Colorado: Johnson Books.

Day, D., 2001. *Tolkein's Ring*. London: Pavilion.

Divine, D., 1995. *Hadrian's Wall: the Northwest Frontier of Rome*. New York: Barnes & Noble.

Fowler, A., 2001. The Ring Masters. The Mail on Sunday *Night & Day* magazine: Lord of the Rings souvenir issue, December 2nd, 2001. 30-31.

Frodsham P., 1995. Monuments in the Landscape: Some Thoughts on the Practical Management of the Historic Environment. *Northern Archaeology* vol 12, 79-89.

Frodsham, P., 1996. Spirals in Time: Morwick Mill and the spiral motif in the British Neolithic, in Frodsham, P. (ed) *Neolithic Studies in No-Man's Land: Papers on the Neolithic of Northern England, from the Trent to the Tweed* (= *Northern Archaeology* vol 13/14), 101-138.

Frodsham, P., 1999. Forgetting Gefrin: elements of the Past in the Past at Yeavering. In Frodsham, P,

Topping, P. & Cowley, D. (eds) *'We were always chasing time.' Papers presented to Keith Blood.* (= Northern Archaeology 17/18). Newcastle.

Frodsham, P., 2000. Worlds Without Ends. Towards a New Prehistory for Central Britain. In J. Harding & R. Johnson (eds) *Northern Pasts: Interpretations of the Later Prehistory of Northern England and Southern Scotland* (BAR British Series 302) Oxford: BAR Publishing.

Frodsham, P., Miller, A. & Weir, A., 1995. Lordenshaws: A Management Agreement for an Historic Landscape, in Berry, A. Q., & Brown, I. W. (eds) *Managing Ancient Monuments: An Integrated Approach.* Mold: Clwyd County Council.

Frodsham, P. (in press) *Archaeology in Northumberland National Park.* York: CBA.

Gates, T., 1999. *The Hadrian's Wall Landscape from Chesters to Greenhead: An Air Photographic Survey.* Unpublished report for Northumberland National Park Authority, Hexham.

Grant, C., 1967. *Rock Art of the American Indian.* New York: Promontory Press.

Grant, C., 1983. *The Rock Art of the North American Indians.* Cambridge: Cambridge University Press.

Heaney, S., 1999. *Beowulf.* London: Faber & Faber.

Hedley, I., 2001. The Discovering our Hillfort Heritage Project. In *Archaeology North* 18 (Summer 2001), 14-15.

Hingley, R., 2000. *Roman Officers and English Gentlemen.* London: Routledge.

Hodder, I., Shanks, M., Alexandri, A., Buchli, V., Carman, J., Last, J. & Lucas, G., 1995. *Interpreting Archaeology: Finding meaning in the past.* London: Routledge.

Hoff, B. 1982. *The Tao of Pooh.* New York: Dutton.

Maxfield, V.A., 1990. Hadrian's Wall in its Imperial Setting. *Archaeologia Aeliana* 5th series, volume XVIII. 1-27.

McCann, J., 1980. *Riddles of the Stone Age: Rock Carvings of Ancient Europe.* London: Thames & Hudson.

Morris, R. W. B., 1979. *The Prehistoric Rock Art of Galloway and the Isle of Man.* Poole: Blandford.

Morris, R. W. B. 1989 The Prehistoric Rock Art of Great Britain: A Survey of all Sites Bearing Motifs more Complex than Simple Cup-marks. *Proceedings of the Prehistoric Society* 55, 45-88.

Munn, N. R., 1973. *Walbiri Iconography, Graphic Representation and Cultural Symbolism in a Central Australian Society.* Chicago: University of Chicago Press.

Northumberland National Park Authority 2000 *The Lost Palace – pupils' shared text* (part of Yeavering education pack). Hexham.

Simpson, J. Y., 1864. On the Cup-Cuttings and Ring Cuttings on the Calder Stones near Liverpool. *Transactions of the Historic Society of Lancashire and Cheshire,* vol 7, 257-262.

Simpson J. Y., 1867. *Archaic Sculpterings of cups, circles, rings &c upon Stones and Rocks in Scotland, England and other Countries.* Edinburgh: Edmonston & Douglas.

Speller, E., 2002. *Following Hadrian: A Second-century Journey through the Roman Empire.* London: Review.

Stuart-Nash, S., 1996. *Conflicting Images in Stone: Archaeology and Rock Art in the Colonial Landscapes of the American West.* Unpublished thesis, University of Southampton.

Tilley, C., 1993. Interpretation and a Poetics of the Past, in Tilley, C. (ed) *Interpretative Archaeology.* Oxford: Berg.

Uzzell, D.L., 1994. Heritage Interpretation in Britain Four Decades after Tilden: An Assessment. In R. Harrison (ed.). *Manual of Heritage Management.* Oxford: Butterworth-Heinemann, 293-302.

Williams, J. T., 1995. *Pooh and the Philosophers.* London: Methuen.

Young, M.J., 1988. *Signs from the Ancestors: Zuni Cultural Symbolism and Perceptions of Rock Art.* Albuquerque: University of New Mexico Press.

2

Sowing the seeds of doubt.
The presentation of the past to the public.

Emma Carver

This paper initially discusses some of the methods used by Historic Scotland to interpret the monuments in its care. Thereafter attention is focussed on archaeological sites in particular because the writer believes that there is a unique set of problems associated with the interpretation of these sites which is not applicable at historic (meaning extant remains in this case) or environmental sites. Even more specifically, the <u>content</u> of the interpretation will be discussed and the issues that this raises in relation to the archaeology and the subject itself, rather than managing or conserving sites for the public.

Traditionally, as Alain Schnapp has recently reminded us, the subject of archaeology has had three tools - *typology*, *technology* and *stratigraphy* (Schnapp 1997). These have allowed us to ask and at times answer the questions <u>what</u>, <u>how</u> and <u>when</u>. To this list we can now add *theory* which gives us the framework to ask <u>why</u>; for example, why did people appear to do certain things at certain times, adopt distinct technologies or move from A to B. Over the last thirty or forty years archaeologists have looked at subsistence strategies, economic and commercial effects and more recently at expressions of ritual, religion, funerary practice and spirituality. The level of data available to us now means we have the opportunity to bring together, rather than separate out, these elements of human life. This in turn enables us to paint an altogether more complex and more recognisable picture of the past. However, as the subject grows richer we move further away from the comfort and ease of mono-causal explanations.

Running parallel to these developments is an increased responsibility to convey our findings, not just because we want to, which we do, but because it is necessary to insure and justify the future of the subject. As McGimsey and Davis (1977, 89; quoted in Jameson 1997, 9) stress:

> '*While it will always be true that archaeologists need to communicate effectively among themselves, it is now abundantly clear that unless they also communicate effectively with the general public ... all else will be wasted effort.*'

Communication

Archaeologists need to communicate with three distinct audiences and there are therefore three demands on the writer. Firstly, we have a moral and intellectual obligation to those within the archaeological community to lodge the results of fieldwork in the public domain. The subject is essentially built on case studies, each one contributing to the next. This usually takes the form of a fairly standardised site report. Recent departures from this format can be seen in the journal Internet Archaeology[1] where we see imaginative uses of the technology to convey information and the recent monograph on Cadbury Castle (Barrett, Freeman & Woodward 2000) which uses a thematic approach.

Secondly, almost any commissioned archaeological work will require a report of some sort to be presented at the completion of a contract. The complexity and approach of this will depend on the commissioner whether that be a developer or an agency. These documents are often largely technical essays with little interpretation or synthesis of the subject matter.

Finally, increasingly we need to explain our findings to a more general audience and this is what is under discussion in this paper. This need comes from a variety of motives. At Historic Scotland, for example, we have a public duty to provide information on the properties which have been entrusted to the care of the state. There are no hard and fast rules as to how this should be done, but on the whole this is a straightforward relationship. The same could be said for museums holding archaeological collections, particularly those that receive public money. In other areas the relationship is not so clear-cut. For example, do universities have an obligation to present the findings of a research excavation to the general public? What is the position in the commercial sector - is the obligation simply to the developer who has funded the work?

Faced with these new demands, archaeologists at times seem poorly equipped to deal with them. The

---

[1] Internet Archaeology (http://www.intarch.org.uk)

dissemination of the results of developer-funded excavations to a wider audience is beginning to be the subject of concentrated attention as the sheer quantity of information gathered in the last 10 years is recognised. But how are we coping with the increasing demands of the cultural tourist? Archaeologists have long realised that archaeology is a subject which captures the imagination of a great number of people. But at several archaeological sites and museums in Britain now it is clear that the interpretation has not been prepared by archaeologists.

A new set of skills

Does this matter? There are some who believe that as long as some original input remains, whether that be providing a framework or retaining editorial control, others, professional interpreters for example, are better placed to create meaningful text for display or other purposes. Whilst in some circumstances this is undoubtedly true, does it mean that the profession as a whole is prepared only to <u>oversee</u> what is presented to the public? This is not only an arrogant position but it is also short sighted, as it assumes that archaeologists will retain the position they hold now where they are actually consulted.

If we are to take our relations with a wider audience more seriously then we must learn to speak with them. The following is an example of how we might go about this and is the solution that has been adopted by Historic Scotland. The agency defined its policy on interpretation only fairly recently.[2] There are two threads to the policy, one is to promote the understanding and enjoyment of the monuments in Historic Scotland's care - this is actually part of our mission statement - and the second the beneficial spin-off from that which is to instil a desire to <u>conserve</u> the heritage.

Following archaeological tradition we have borrowed ideas from others. Our policy on interpretation is heavily influenced by the work of Freeman Tilden, an American playwright and philosopher writing in the 1950s and Sam Ham, Professor at the Department of Resource Recreation and Tourism at the College of Forestry, Wildlife and Range Sciences at the University of Idaho. Tilden not only defined interpretation as he saw it but he also set out six principles of Interpretation in his seminal work *Interpreting our Heritage*, first published in 1957. His definition of the practice of interpretation is as follows:

> *An educational activity which aims to reveal meanings and relationships through the use of original objects, by firsthand experience, and by*

illustrative media, rather than simply to communicate factual information.

and this was his oft repeated message:

> *Through interpretation, UNDERSTANDING*
> *Through understanding, APPRECIATION*
> *Through appreciation, PROTECTION*

Tilden's book has been the building block on which the practice of interpretation has developed and become a recognised profession in its own right over the last forty years. Sam Ham, following in Tilden's footsteps, has done much work on the nature of audiences, defining for example a key characteristic of the visitors who come to heritage sites, whether that be archaeological or the so-called 'natural world'. He describes them as a non-captive audience meaning one 'that has the option of ignoring the information without punishment or loss of a potential reward' (1992:7).

Using these principles we now have a rolling programme to produce Interpretation Plans for each property. These establish what we wish to interpret and why, how we wish to interpret and where, who we wish to communicate with, and finally what are the appropriate resources required to achieve these aims. It is a process that forces us to think about issues relevant to each site individually and to tailor the presentation appropriately.

Fig. 2.1 shows an example of a panel we recently produced for the excavations at Cadzow Castle in the Clyde Valley. This is indicative designwise of the kind of external panel we produce now. The information is provided in a hierarchy which is common practice, but in addition we endeavour to interpret the facts by writing theme statements thereby adopting the principle that visitors remember ideas not facts. You might, for example, introduce a topic on Medieval Abbeys: *No single person ever saw a medieval abbey built from start to finish.* Or introducing the coastal defences at Fort Charlotte in Shetland: *The fortifications you can see today were not the first on this site.*

The approaches discussed here are essentially liberating but also challenging. The writer is forced to ask the questions that the reader might ask rather than presenting what the writer knows.

In addition there is the hope that by providing interpretation which inspires an interest in the past, a visitor will want to visit other sites and this is where an integrated interpretation policy really comes to the fore. In its most extreme form this kind of approach can be developed into a marketing tool and is presented as such by some American practitioners. (See for example John Veverka's publications and website.)

---

[2] It is essentially the work of Chris Tabraham, Principal Inspector of Ancient Monuments.

CADZOW CASTLE

These ruins are all that is left of Cadzow Castle.

They are now the subject of a programme of consolidation works so that the castle can be opened to visitors. To this end Historic Scotland have commissioned AOC Archaeology Group to carry out preliminary archaeological investigations between December 2000 and March 2001. These assessment works will incorporate topographic survey, geophysical survey and trial excavations within the grounds of the castle.

We will try to find out who built Cadzow Castle, what it looked like, who lived in it and finally, who destroyed it.

It may be that Sir James Hamilton of Finnart, who had already built Craignethan Castle (8 miles south-east of here), may have instigated building work here in the 1530s. Craignethan and Hamilton Castles were demolished in the early summer of 1579 following their seizure by the Crown. Cadzow Castle may have suffered a similar fate at the same time.

We will also be looking at how the castle was built and what happened to it after it was abandoned.

During the 18th century what was left of the castle was "tidied-up" and romanticised as a feature within the designed landscape of the High Park. Yet further disruption was caused by the construction of the Duke's Bridge and associated roads in the 1860s.

Avon Water.

You Are Here

Modern road which has divided the castle in two.

West Range and Outer Ward.

Inner Ward with circular towers.

Châtelhéraut.

Aerial photograph showing the location of the remains of Cadzow Castle in relation to Châtelhéraut.

Cadzow Castle is cared for by Historic Scotland on behalf of Scottish Ministers.

HISTORIC SCOTLAND

Fig. 2.1 A temporary panel for the excavations at Cadzow Castle.

The presentation of the unknown

However, this brings us to a problem touched on earlier, a problem particular to archaeological sites, and that is the presentation of the unknown. Archaeologists are used to wrestling with the unknown; indeed they are trained to wrestle with it. But how do we pass on a willingness to accept this on a simple interpretation panel at a monument? Drawing on comparisons with the interpretation of the natural environment the problem is illustrated below - which would you find more arresting?

The Red Admiral lives here and this is what it looks like.	We think the Red Admiral once lived here.

or an example from an historical site:

This castle was built in 1549, as you can see in the inscription on the door lintel.	This building was probably erected in the middle of the second millennium AD.

Thinking now of a stone circle or a crop mark site, or simply the consolidated remains of an excavation, the interpreter, when faced with what visitors will want to know about this site, can quickly become overwhelmed by the unknown. This is why the subject needs special thought. Archaeologists need to think creatively about explaining their findings in a way that is accurate and acceptable to the profession, whilst being palitable to our audience.

Archaeology consists of two parallel worlds; the representation of <u>what</u> has been found and its context, together with <u>how</u> archaeology is done. Very often in an exhibition there will be a whole section on 'archaeology the discipline' - in some respects this makes it very exciting and honest - in some perhaps it is a false assumption that people care how you did it - might they just want to know what you did? Playing devil's advocate, does a poet tell you about the pen he used - a chewed black biro on foolscap? No, he doesn't, but to a scientist methodology is paramount and herein lies the dichotomy present in every aspect of the subject.

Perhaps in order to develop this further, just as we have freely borrowed from other disciplines to enhance our battery of theoretical approaches we need to look further afield at the methods being employed by other disciplines who have already thought of new ways of presenting their findings.

One very exciting area is the application of virtual reality to archaeology. Mark Gillings has argued that 'for developments in Virtual Reality to be truly useful to archaeology, they must be firmly grounded in archaeological theory and accessible and applicable at all levels of archaeological practice' (Gillings 2000). He sees this as another tool in the way that a plan or map is used to present archaeological information.

Maurizio Forte, another practitioner in this area, has pointed out that 'above and beyond its strong popular impact [which nobody can deny], computer reconstruction allows the presentation of complex information in a visual way that enables it to be used to test and refine the image or model that has been created' (Forte 2000). So might this be the tool that can successfully bring together visually the two themes in archaeology - not only the story but how the story was written?

Interactive virtual archaeology presentations can be used to show, by way of example, what was found on an excavation and why that means that a whole building once stood here. This is a simplistic example, but for the technology to work for archaeology and not to its detriment you can't have one without the other. Simulated architectural drawings of ancient buildings do not mean anything without the layers of archaeological data which led to their reconstruction. But the beauty of the technology is that you can literally peel away or build up those layers visually before your very eyes.

Another area with much potential is the development of multicultural approaches in the presentation of archaeology. Pioneering work on cultural identity in the subject itself by Siân Jones amongst others has paved the way, but the art of reflecting different communities' histories, and in so doing encouraging a wider spectrum of the population to become involved in archaeology, is in its infancy (Jones 1997; Graves-Brown, Jones & Gamble 1996). In many ways museums are taking the lead in this area through a series of access programmes as illustrated

in a recent edition of *Museum Practice* (17:52-78, especially 'Digging for Dreams' *ibid*. 67-70). In the lead article Judy Ling Wong, the director of the Black Environment Network[3], writes on an encouraging note 'Multicultural interpretation should not be seen as a threat to the heritage sector, but rather an opportunity to expand interpretation and replace divisive, monocultural viewpoints with a stimulus for revelatory experiences, discovery and personal transformation'. (It is interesting to note also that English Heritage's publication *Power of Place* was welcomed in this quarter.[4]) However, whilst applauding this and other practical initiatives[5] we need to ensure that the will to broaden our vision filters through the system to influence the way practitioners write and think about archaeology.

In conclusion, we need to come to terms with the skills and ideas touched upon in this short paper as a matter of course if the transmission of archaeological information to a wider audience is to remain in archaeologists' hands. More is required of us than ever before and our response is judged - evaluation is increasingly being written into even the simplest of project designs. One way of responding to these demands is illustrated by that adopted by Historic Scotland which has provided us with a framework within which to develop our new skills. But we also need to be receptive to new technologies and new approaches and think carefully how we can use these to communicate our ideas and our results to a broader audience.

There is a real danger that if field archaeologists and curators alike do not rise to these challenges we will simply become the primary source, occasionally dipped into and often ignored.

Note: The views expressed in this paper were current when this paper was given in Spring 2001. Since then, Historic Scotland has set up its own interpretation unit with a remit to place greater emphasis on communication with the general public.

References

Barceló, J.A., Forte, M. & Sanders, D.H. (eds.), 2000. *Virtual Reality in Archaeology Computer applications and quantitative methods in*

---

[3] See http://www.ben-network.co.uk/ for further information.
[4] This document is available on the English Heritage website (http://www.english-heritage.org.uk/).
[5] Such as the adoption of Black History Month by English Heritage and other major cultural organisations, for example, the National Maritime Museum.

archaeology. Oxford: British Archaeological Reports/BAR Publishing.

Barrett, J.C., Freeman, P.W.M. & Woodward, A., 2000. *Cadbury Castle, Somerset The Later Prehistoric and Early Historic Archaeology.* London: English Heritage.

Cultural Diversity Feature, 2001. *Museum Practice* (17: 52-78).

Forte, M., 2000. 'About Virtual Archaeology: disorders, cognitive interactions and virtual reality. In Barceló, Forte & Sanders (eds.).

Gillings, M., 2000. 'Plans, Elevations and Virtual Worlds: the development of techniques for the routine construction of hyperreal situations'. In Barceló, Forte & Sanders (eds.).

Graves-Brown, P., Jones, S. & Gamble, C., 1996. *Cultural Identity and Archaeology The construction of European Communities.* London: Routledge

Ham, S.H., 1992. *Environmental Interpretation. A Practical Guide for People with Big Ideas and Small Budgets.* Golden, Colorado: North American Press.

Jameson, J.H. (ed.), 1997. *Presenting Archaeology to the Public.* Walnut Creek, California: AltaMira Press.

Jones, S., 1997. *The Archaeology of Ethnicity: constructing identities in the past and present.* London: Routledge.

McGimsey & Davis, 1977. Quoted in Jameson, J.H. (ed.) 1997, page 9.

Schnapp, A.,1997. *The Discovery of the Past. The Origins of Archaeology.* London: British Museum Press.

Tilden, F., 1957. *Interpreting our Heritage.* Chapel Hill, NC: University of North Carolina Press.

Veverka, J. A., 1994. *Interpretative Master Planning.* Montana: Falcon Press Publishing Co. (or http://www.heritageinterp.com)

3

Virtually the Ice Age.
Interpreting the Palaeolithic Archaeology of Creswell Crags.

Ian Wall

Introduction

This article presents a reworked version of a paper given at IFA conference 2001 in a session entitled Interpreting the Ambiguous. Key points of the paper highlighted that:

- Interpretive projects should be considered as a part of research based projects whenever practical, rather than as a bolt on to research. After all, why is the research being done in the first place?
- The internet provides a valuable media form for archaeological interpretation although like any interpretive media it's relative advantages and disadvantages need to be critically assessed.
- Any interpretive project should involve the establishment of a project team which reflects theoretical stances from both fields of interpretation and archaeology to avoid criticisms of dumbing down, poor or inaccurate messages and accusations of irrelevance.

The project 'Virtually the Ice Age', set out to develop on-line resources which focussed on the Pleistocene archaeology of Creswell Crags and was used as a case study to explore these issues. The conference paper did not explore in detail the technological framework and the host of emerging standards but rather reflected specific approaches and issues concerned with interpreting ambiguous archaeology from the Ice Age via the internet.

The paper concluded that the internet does provide a valuable tool for archaeological interpretation. However the use of this media is just one of a number of techniques which requires careful planning, evaluation and critical assessment.

The Archaeology of Creswell Crags and Area

Creswell Crags is located five miles south west of Worksop, Nottinghamshire, and comprises a natural gorge and cave system. The Creswell Gorge (fig. 3.1) cuts through the low plateau of the Southern Magnesian Limestone (one of Britain's rarest rock types) which runs approximately north-south from Mansfield to County Durham. Creswell Crags is one of a number of gorges in the area, which collectively represent one of the largest clusters of Pleistocene remains in the country (Wall and Jacobi 2000; Jenkinson 1984; Campbell 1977) and characterise the Creswell area as an outstanding cultural and natural landscape (Mills 2001).

Scientific archaeological research began in earnest in the 1870s. The caves at Creswell Crags appear to be some of the first excavated by Victorian antiquarians (Mello 1875, 1876; Heath 1879; Dawkins 1876, 1879) with subsequent periodic excavation carried out by numerous researchers throughout the 20th century. This work created a substantial and significant archaeological archive comprising Mousterian quartzite, flint and ironstone tool assemblages, as well as Early Upper and Late Upper Palaeolithic material (Campbell 1977). The Late Upper Palaeolithic assemblage, or Creswellian, also included bone and ivory tools as well as some of the most prestigious bone art engravings in the country (Sieveking 1987, 1992, Dawkins 1925). In addition to the archaeology, excavation recovered some of the most important Devensian and Ipswichian mammal and small mammal faunas.

The significance and value of these assemblages to archaeological research lies in the opportunity of using the evidence to answer fundamental questions about the colonisation and recolonisation of the Midlands by human groups. These included Neandarthal populations 40,000-60,000 years ago and Modern humans approximately 30,000 years ago and 12,500 years ago. Further, the northerly location of Creswell has resulted in the creation of a fossil record influenced by dramatic climatic and environmental shifts, resulting in the possibilities for studying environmental change and the strategies used by people who were recolonising these landscapes.

Why interpret Creswell Crags and why use the internet?

At face value, the archaeology of Creswell Crags has little relevance today. The events and stories associated with the site took place more than 10,000 years ago and as such could be conceived as not relevant either to the communities living close to the site or within the UK, let alone internationally. The results of earlier surveys

Fig. 3.1. Aerial view of Creswell Crags.

(Merriman 1991) if conducted today may still suggest that archaeology is perceived as high brow and 'closed' to people outside the profession (Pearson 1993, 227). This is in part down to archaeologists who possibly fail to see the alternative values people place on sites and remains. Creswell is a rare and finite resource and one of the most important clusters of Palaeolithic remains for a whole host of reasons. However, we need to be able to understand the values and relevance other people place on the site, a process which should guide the process of interpretation moving away from an archaeo-centric perspective.

Archaeologists have argued for a more inclusive archaeology, enabling people to reflect on their own lives, to compare differences and similarities with people in the past; to do an archaeology of us (Pearson 1993; Shanks and Tilley 1987a ; Gould and Schiffer 1981).

Once visitors to archaeological sites, actually or virtually, are engaged in that process, it is possible to provide alternative interpretations and make a case for the preservation of sites. Engaging with visitors in this way allows additional connections to be made which relate to our behavior today, how we are threatening the long term future of the planet, issues of sustainability, and questioning stereotypes and racist attitudes towards pre- or non-industrial societies (Stone and Mackenzie 1990).

Archaeologists should embrace interpretation as a tool to enable a whole range of different audiences to self reflect through the creation of their own narratives rather than presenting an interpretation which is closed and known. The internet, in particular presents a huge opportunity for archaeologists to reach out to new audiences who are turned off by a past which is presented as 'closed'.

Prior to the development of Creswell Crags Museum and Education Centre in 1984 (formerly Creswell Crags Visitor Centre), the site was not interpreted. Following the development of the museum access to the story of human colonisation and past Ice Age environments has improved. Displays, events and activities on the site today are used to help visitors experience and engage with a story in the atmospheric setting of the gorge. However, despite the work of the museum, there are still obstacles which limit access to the archaeology.

Much of the recent research remains unpublished and when articles are published they are often in technical publications where it is difficult for non-specialists to contextualise the information. Physical access is equally difficult. Archives generated through over 100 years of research work have become dispersed. Anyone wishing to study the objects and associated excavation archives has to visit more than 30 different museum departments (Wall and Jacobi 2000). Access to the caves, despite recent major improvements in access around the site, remain difficult.

The project 'Virtually the Ice Age' developed as a direct need to create an interpretive resource which overcame these access issues. This was a partnership project involving Creswell Heritage Trust, The British Museum and Derby Museum and Art Gallery.

Creswell Crags and Virtually the Ice Age

The key objective was to create a resource which brought together the objects and the sites and made these accessible to a wider audience as possible via the internet. Further adaptations of the content would then enable the resource to be delivered as a CD ROM and via touch screen installations at appropriate museums. The web based resource is online (www.creswell-crags.org.uk/virtuallytheiceage).

In summary the aims of the project were:

- To tell the Creswell story well in an accessible way.
- Promote Creswell Crags and the Creswell landscape as an outstanding and internationally significant resource for understanding the Ice Age
- Attract new audiences and encourage people to visit Creswell Crags
- Assist with the process of regeneration of the former North Nottinghamshire and North East Derbyshire Coalfield
- Encourage visitors to explore the Creswell collections housed in museums across the country
- Engage local communities in their local heritage, providing opportunities for them to present their own narratives and explore their own views about the past.

- Broaden the link between the Creswell evidence and evidence from sites at a global level.
- Create a high quality life long learning resource to interact with and challenge the visitor to solve problems or respond to specific presentations.
- Broaden the skills base of museum staff.

These aims were achieved through:

- The development of a catalogue of selected objects excavated from the caves
- The development of a series of themed interpretive sections which link objects, sites and excavation archives and associated stories. Themes developed included 'Stone Age People', 'The Natural World', 'Discover the Past'.
- Providing virtual physical access to the sites through a Virtual Tour
- Providing a forum for local communities to present their histories and research as well as providing a means of interacting with specialists in museums and universities via a message board, news section, and community pages.
- Providing training for staff at Creswell on web authoring in order that pages can be updated and created.

Content and Structure

A number of guiding principles influenced the development of the web site structure and content.

Interpretation delivered through the internet needs to consider carefully the whole process of how users access and navigate through the content. One advantage of new media is that it allows content to be packaged and accessed in a multitude of ways. The development of multiple access routes through content helps to respond to different user needs. Recent surveys relating to museum web sites highlight the need to reassess traditional boundaries between researchers and users because the web presents a far more fluid model where users search for, find and consume information (Morris Hargreaves McIntyre 2000, 9). This is one of the major advantages of this technology where content should be carefully structured so that users are in control of their own learning by being enabled to follow particular pathways and select appropriate content. Evidently the links through text and images need to be planned for this to take place. There is a balance here between too many links which may well disorientate users who when lost just give up and leave the site, and not enough links, which limit possibilities for users to follow a desired learning thread.

The various sections of content accessible from the home page www.creswell-crags.org.uk/virtuallytheiceage (fig. 3.2) are described:

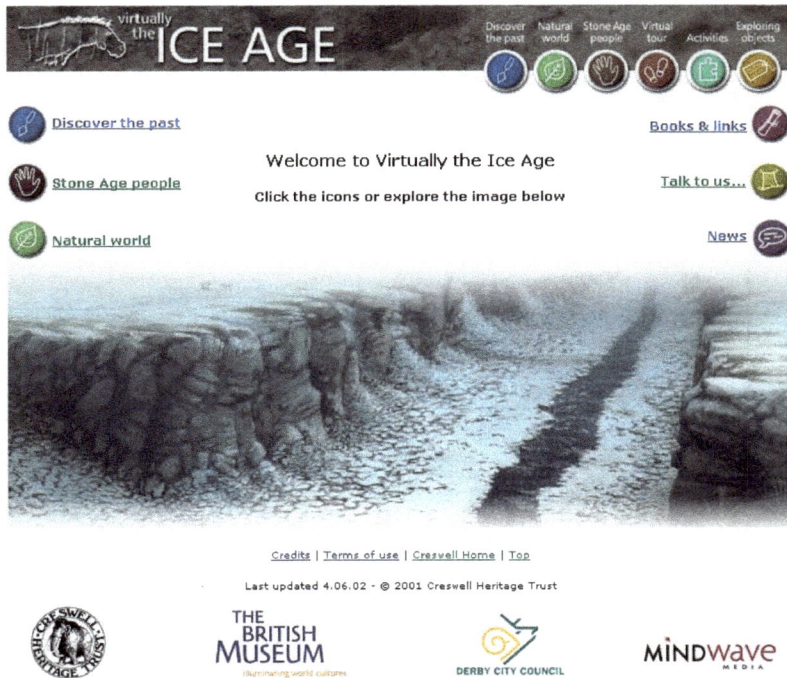

Fig. 3.2. Virtually the Ice Age home page.

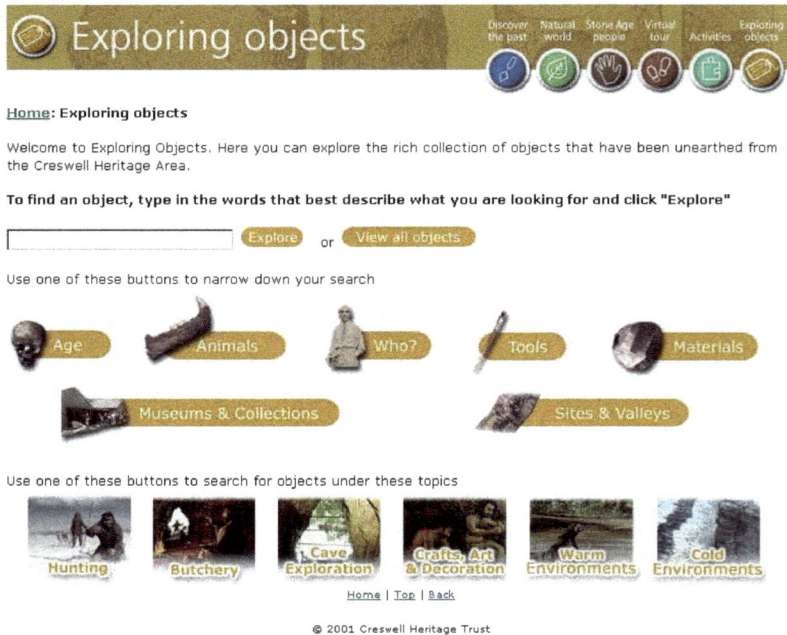

Fig. 3.3. Search screen for Object Catalogue.

Object Catalogue

The catalogue of objects, accessible through the 'Exploring Objects' icon, represents at one level the raw archaeological archive. The format presents an image of the museum object accompanied by text. Occasionally multiple views of the object are provided in addition to the option of enlarging the image to full screen.

Presenting images of the objects makes it possible for visitors to interact with them as objects in their own right. Non-contextualising objects presents an open book where audiences can appreciate and interact with items on their own terms rather than being presented with an explanation of context. Selection from the range of material including faunal remains, stone, bone and ivory tools, excavation archive plans, notebook extracts, and photographic material, was based on their visual quality, the significance in an archaeological context and the contribution the object provided to a particular theme and story. Further projects which may involve developing the object catalogue will have an opportunity to be more enabling and involving audiences more fully in the process of object selection.

Text adjacent to the object images provides an archaeological interpretation of that object. This describes characteristics such as the age, what it is made of, where it was found, and what it may have been used for. This presents an extended museum label and was designed to give the academic view. The text was structured into a title and headline followed by a detailed description. The use of archaeological language and jargon was kept to a minimum and where used was supported by a glossary.

The process of scripting for each object involved a series of editorial cycles. A specialist authored initial text. This text was subsequently edited to reflect the information

hierarchy format and remove any potential ambiguous terms. Once edited, the specialist carried out a final check to ensure that the original intended meaning had not been corrupted.

A user is given a choice of accessing the information from the catalogue using three different routes (fig. 3.3). For users who know what they want to find, a free text search is possible. For users who require help to narrow down a search, a series of categories are presented under age of object, animal types, archaeological researchers, tool types, types of materials, museums where the objects are stored, and the sites where the objects were found. A final tier of search is provided for the younger user through specific topics 'Hunting', 'Butchery', 'Cave Exploration', 'Crafts, Art and Decoration', 'Warm Environments' and 'Cold Environments'. Objects are pre-selected for this final category search.

Sustaining and building on this resource is of paramount importance. The entire catalogue is database driven and served on the site through active server pages. This facilitates the opportunity to add to and extend the catalogue relatively easily in future projects.

Themed Sections

In addition to the object catalogue, the site develops three themed sections where the objects are contextualised into on-line exhibitions. These provide journeys into archaeological discovery in 'Discover the Past', the

people who visited Creswell Crags during the Ice Age in 'Stone Age People', and the climate and environment during the Ice Age in 'Natural World'. Packaging the material into themes is a fundamental principle as visitors will often remember the theme and the story but will forget detailed information (Binks *et. al.* 1988, 29).

The development of content for these sections relied on the information contained within the object catalogue using the most recent research so that these sections were not merely a restatement of what we thought before we began (Hills 1993) but are a careful reworking of the evidence. The input of specialist archaeologists here was vital in order that the interpretation did not misrepresent the evidence nor generalise it into a meaningless statement.

Virtual Tour

The presentation of a virtual tour was critical if we were to address issues involving access. From a visitor perspective access around the site, particularly for people who have mobility difficulties, is hazardous. The routes up to the caves often have steep gradients and are stepped, while access inside the caves is restricted. In addition, access to the caves remains a sensitive preservation issue. *In situ* archaeological deposits are, in some cases, substantial and vulnerable to visitor pressure. For example Pin Hole has a 3 metre high section spanning approximately the last 50,000 years. Access to this cave is restricted to special interest groups and visitors on special event days such as National Archaeology Days. The virtual tour opens access to new audiences who are either not permitted to enter into the caves or are not physically able to visit or move around the site.

A total of 14 view points are available within the limestone gorge and within three of the larger caves, Robin Hood Cave, Pin Hole (fig. 3.4) and Church Hole. Viewing the tour through the internet requires the user to have installed *QuickTime* software. This is the only plug-in which the web site requires.

Intellectual access to the stories about archaeological discovery can be addressed far more satisfactorily by taking visitors around the site. The virtual tour helps increase understanding of the physical form of the caves and can help visitors empathize with the whole process of excavation through an understanding of the cave environment. Opportunities also exist for placing objects back into their archaeological context. The next logical step, which was beyond the scope of this initial project would be to reconstruct the site stratigraphy, to replace objects into the layers and to engage visitors in the process of excavation through a virtual re-excavation of the cave. The whole process of interpretation becomes far more immediate as objects are lifted from the cave earth and reinterpreted.

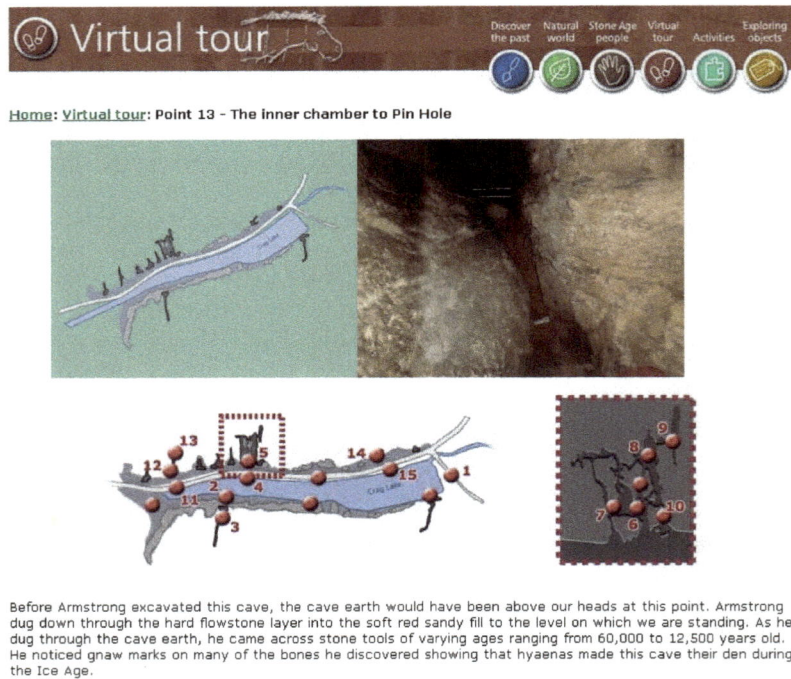

Before Armstrong excavated this cave, the cave earth would have been above our heads at this point. Armstrong dug down through the hard flowstone layer into the soft red sandy fill to the level on which we are standing. As he dug through the cave earth, he came across stone tools of varying ages ranging from 60,000 to 12,500 years old. He noticed gnaw marks on many of the bones he discovered showing that hyaenas made this cave their den during the Ice Age.

Fig. 3.4. Virtual tour Pin Hole screen shot.

Activities

The design and development of the 'Activities' area of the web site went through several stages. The intention was initially to create a series of interactives and games such as a re-excavation of the cave which lived up to user expectations of other computer games. This was totally unrealistic in terms of budget. Discussions also considered removing this section altogether because the title 'Activities' may have raised expectations and led to disappointment.

Principles concerning access to the content finally drove the development of activities which provided interaction within the scope of low end web browsers and slow internet connections. Currently within this section it is possible to explore the evidence behind two reconstruction paintings of the gorge as well as capturing line drawings of these images to print and colour-in. Far more development is anticipated here, underlining the principles that it is not necessary to do it all at once and the flexibility of the internet as a resource with which to add and experiment with different ideas at a later stage.

News and Views

An important consideration for web sites is the process of creating and presenting new information at regular intervals. Not only does this encourage visitors to come back to the site but provides an opportunity to respond to

new research information. The New and Views section was designed specifically with this in mind, providing a noticeboard which could be changed quickly and easily when other areas of the web site were designed to be more static and non-changing.

In addition to presenting new information, this area presents an opportunity to respond to visitors expectations by creating content based on the discussion taking place on the message board.

Message Board

Access to people is as important as access to content. The message board creates that opportunity for visitors to engage with specialists within museums as well as with each other.

Books and Links

The potential number of different visitors prompted the development of pages which signposted further information. Extensive bibliographies are available on Creswell Crags as well as more general archaeological texts. This section is also used to promote links to other sites as well as indicating in which museums the collections excavated from the Creswell sites are stored and displayed.

Community Pages

Community pages, accessed from the Creswell Crags homepage, were developed to present the outreach work of the museum and provide a platform for the different communities within the immediate area to express their own versions and values relating to the historic landscape. As with the 'Activities' pages, these areas are seen as open ended, responding to different projects and developing different views on the historic and natural environment.

The school community have already been represented here through a project creating Ice Age images revolving around the stories at Creswell Crags. The local history group in Shirebrook is one of a number of groups who have been developing trails through these historic landscapes. These pages are a way of creating exhibition space where other interpretations are presented and which reflect local values and other interpretations of the archaeology.

Interpretation

Interpretation has been defined differently by different people (see for example Tilden 1977). Probably the most succinct is by the Centre for Environmental Interpretation who described interpretation as 'the art of explaining the meaning and significance of sites visited by the public'. Tilden also states information on its own is not interpretation but that interpretation is revelation based on information. The emphasis is on engaging audiences through their own experiences and through different media to discover and self explore the significance of sites and landscapes. Interpreting the often ambiguous past is made accessible by placing audiences within the particular time frame.

What techniques and principles should online resources follow if they are to fulfill these interpretive objectives?

The success of web sites and on-line resources in delivering interpretation is generally largely unknown. Recent surveys provide an index of user expectation but admit that further surveys are required to assess their effectiveness for delivering interpretive objectives (Morris Hargreaves McIntyre 2000). Consequently Virtually the Ice Age took guideline principles used in off line resources and translated them into an on-line context. Particular challenges lay behind the need to develop content which was accessible by as wide an audience as possible regardless of types of web browsers, band width and modem speed, and the availability of software plug-ins.

The following examples are described to illustrate how we approached interpretation within the themed sections on 'Stone Age People', 'Natural World' and 'Discover the Past'.

Content needs to be interactive and engaging so that the imagination of visitors to the web site is sparked. Provocation is a key tool. Within the section 'Stone Age People' visitors are confronted with the question 'Could you have survived the Ice Age?' Immediately this is all about the user and people relating their own experiences and comparing themselves to hunter gatherers. Rather than being told that people in the Ice Age were technologically and culturally advanced they may arrive at that interpretation by looking at themselves. In a subsequent section users are challenged by five simple questions about the Ice Age. Again the emphasis is on approaching the subject from the audience perspective.

Another example from 'Stone Age People' uses the Palaeolithic art from Creswell as a provocative tool. Visitors to the subsection 'Culture and Creativity' are presented with the horse engraving and asked 'What would this engraving of a horse have meant to you 12,000 years ago?' Equally powerful would have been the question 'What would **you** have drawn 12,000 years ago?' Both engage users in the resource and in the process of interpretation. Opportunities exist to explore intricate human traits such as creativity, sensitivity, personal possibly treasured possessions. These objects, as well as providing an understanding of past cultures enable us to reflect on our own lives and experiences, they provide a point of reference. Consequently, although the object could be found in the catalogue with a more traditional museum-type label, it's use in 'Stone Age People' invites users to reflect.

Interpreting the ambiguous also presents us with opportunities to say **your** interpretations are just as valid as **ours**. Objects will mean different things to different people today as they would have in the past. As many different audiences as possible should be given the opportunity to create their own stories. Interpretation is as much about engaging and exploring what we don't know as about engaging with what we think we do.

The process of questioning is also used within the section 'Natural World' to test assumptions and stereotypes about Ice Age climates and environments. These assumptions are not helped through the use of the term Ice Age. Visitors to the page are asked to select one of three types of environment which they think existed during this period. The response tells them that all answers are possibly correct, an answer which confirms that the Ice Age spans an incredible amount of time and witnessed dramatic shifts in climate. Again the content is engaging and more fun than merely describing a climatic graph.

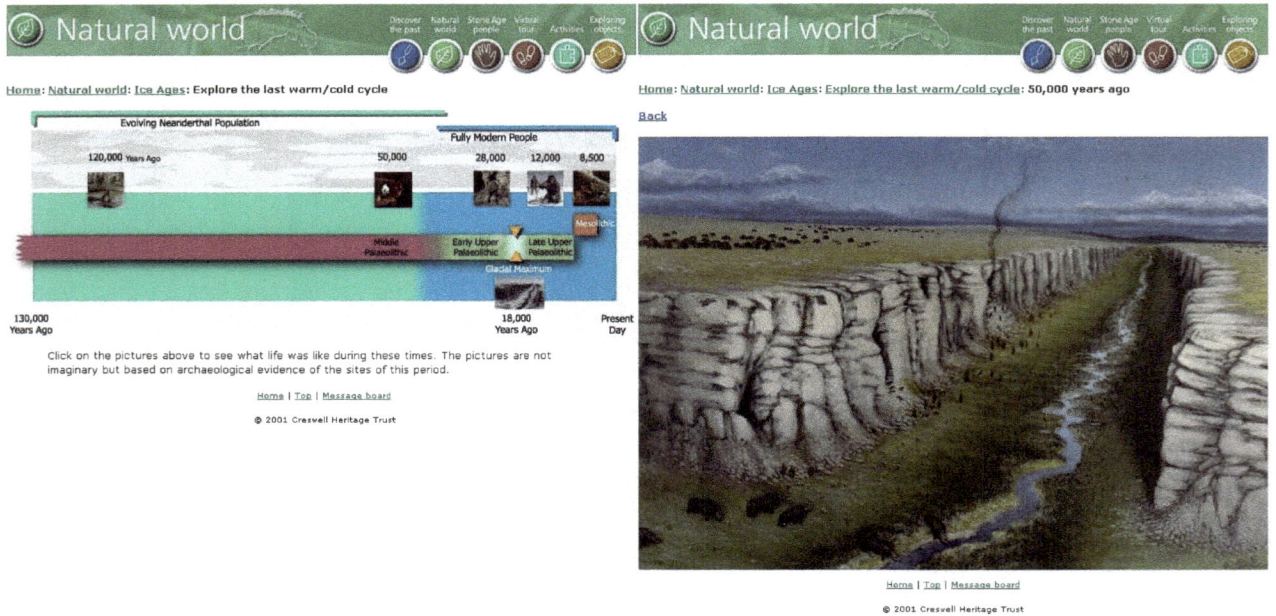

Fig. 3.5. Time line and landscape reconstruction at 50,000 years ago.

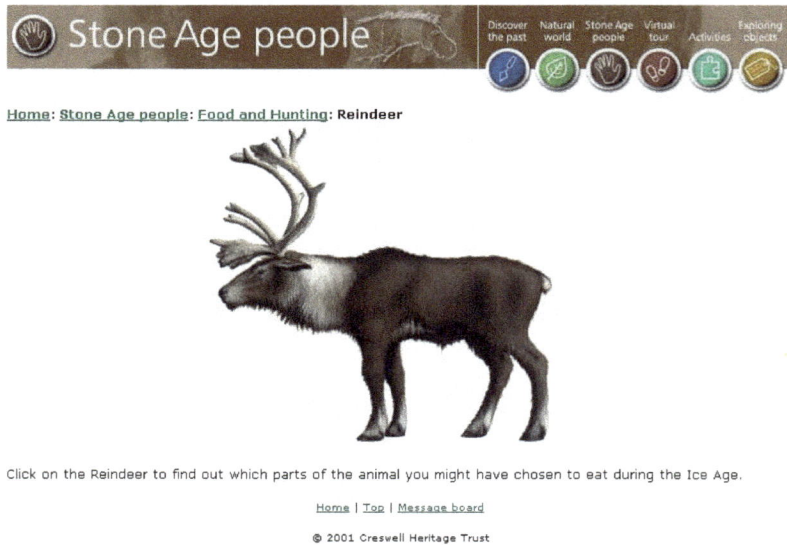

Fig. 3.6. The interactive reindeer.

Within the section on the 'Natural World' reconstruction drawings play a valuable role. A series of illustrations present the same view of Creswell Crags at different times in the past; 8,500, 12,000, 18,000, 28,000, 50,000 and 120,000 years ago (fig. 3.5). A further set of illustrations provide close up detail of scenes within five of those pictures. Extreme care was taken in writing the brief for these paintings with research involving detailed discussion about the clothing, artefacts, events, vegetation, animals, geomorphology and climate. Although these reconstructions create a landscape which

potentially did not exist and is our best guess using the available evidence, they present an opportunity to communicate complex evidence with different audiences as well as portraying the atmosphere of the site. Furthermore, in a multimedia context, the use of images like these provide scope for introducing multiple interpretations and investigating the evidence which lies behind the image. For example it is possible within 'Activities' to explore the evidence which helped picture the environment and events in a particular way. Also the accompanying text which describes 'Creswell Crags as it might have been...' leaves the visitor in no doubt that this is our best guess and provides an opening for debate and questioning as to why we have shown it like this.

First person interpretation is one of the most effective forms of interpretation. Within the section 'Discover the Past' we have attempted to recreate this interpretive form by developing a series of first person narratives which reflect and provide a comparison of the methodologies and thoughts of past archaeologists who have worked at Creswell Crags. These narratives are presented as a series of letters from 1999, 1936 and 1879 and have been created from an understanding of the historical context in which these people were working.

Finally, new media has the opportunity to create interpretation which is fun and enjoyable to use. The interactive reindeer (fig. 3.6) and horse within 'Stone Age People' allows visitors to select portions of the animal and to explore the edible and the most useful parts for tools and equipment.

Conclusion

Archaeological interpretation delivered through the internet offers a number of opportunities. The relative ease with which interactive pages with minimal programming skills can be created and quickly updated makes this an appropriate medium to present archaeology to a non-specialist audience. Principles of interpretation can be applied in the same way as used within traditional museum exhibitions although the content can be structured in a particular format that allows visitors to control the way they access and absorb information. Furthermore visitors are able to return time and time again to rich and imaginative content in the comfort of their homes as well as in schools or libraries. In this way internet resources can help to prepare people for an actual visit to the site by introducing the site's themes. In addition, the use of quizzes and games provoke visitors to explore and self discover content. Through features such as message boards and news pages interpretation can keep pace with new discoveries, visitors can talk and discuss their own interests with archaeologists and museum staff, and the interests which people have in archaeology can be extended.

At a more pragmatic level digital resources help to solve difficulties over access and this was a prior aim for Virtually the Ice Age to bring together and make accessible dispersed collections as well as developing virtual access to the gorge and caves.

Ultimately the success of any interpretive project requires the development of a team who understand the nature of archaeology and interpretation. This will ensure that both disciplines are not compromised and that audiences are provided with an opportunity to engage as fully as

possible with the interpretation of sites and their associated remains.

References

Binks G., Dyke J. and Dagnell P., 1988. *Visitors Welcome: A Manual on the Presentation and Interpretation of Archaeological Excavations.* London: HMSO.

Dawkins, W.B., 1876. On the mammalia and traces of Man found in the Robin-Hood Cave. *Quarterly Journal of the Geological Society of London*, 32(3), 245-258.

Dawkins, W.B., 1879. On the bone caves of Derbyshire. *Report of the British Association for the Advancement of Science (Sheffield 1879)*, 337-338.

Dawkins, W.B., 1925. Late Palaeolithic art in the Cresswell Caves. *Man*, 25, 48.

Campbell, J.B., 1977. *The Upper Palaeolithic of Britain: a study of man and nature during the Late Ice Age.* Oxford: Clarendon press.

Gould R.A. and Schiffer M.B. (eds), 1981. *Modern Material Culture: The Archaeology of Us.* New York: Academic Press.

Heath, T., 1879. *An abstract description and history of the Bone Caves of Creswell Crags.* Derby: Wilkins and Ellis.

Hills, C., 1993. The Dissemination of Information. In Hunter, J. and Ralston, I. (eds), *Archaeological Resource Management in the UK an introduction.* Stroud: Alan Sutton/Institute of Field Archaeologists.

Jenkinson, R.D.S., 1984. *Creswell Crags: Late Pleistocene Sites in the East Midlands.* Oxford: British Archaeological Reports British Series 122.

Mello, J.M.. 1875. On some bone-caves in Creswell Crags. *Quarterly Journal of the Geological Society of London*, 31(4), 679-683.

Mello, J.M., 1876. The bone-caves of Creswell Crags. – 2nd paper. *Quarterly Journal of the Geological Society of London*, 32(3), 240-244.

Merriman, N., 1991. *Beyond the Glass Case: The Past, Heritage and the Public.* Leicester: Leicester University Press.

Mills, N., 2001. *Creswell Crags Conservation Plan.* Creswell Heritage Trust unpublished report

Morris Hargreaves McIntyre, 2000. *Great Expectations: Virtual Collections Access in the Information Age.* A study commissioned by: Museum of Science & Industry in Manchester, National Museum of Labour History, The Petrie Museum of Egyptology, Manchester City Art Galleries, The Whitworth Art Gallery, The Manchester Museum. Unpublished report.

Parker Pearson, M., 1993. *Visitors Welcome.* In Hunter, J. and Ralston, I. (eds), *Archaeological Resource*

Management in the UK an introduction. Stroud: Alan Sutton/Institute of Field Archaeologists.

Shanks M. and Tilley C., 1987. *Reconstructing Archaeology: Theory and Practice.* Cambridge: Cambridge University Press.

Sieveking, A., 1987. *A Catalogue of Palaeolithic Art in the British Museum.* London: British Museum Publications.

Sieveking, A., 1992. The continental affiliations of two Palaeolithic engraved bones found in England. *Antiquaries Journal,* 72, 1-17.

Stone P. and MacKenzie R. (eds), 1990. *The Excluded Past: Archaeology in Education.* London: Unwin Hyman.

Tilden, F., 1977. *Interpreting Our Heritage.* Chapel Hill, NC: University of North Carolina Press.

Wall, I.J and Jacobi, R.E.M., 2000. *An Assessment of the Pleistocene collections from the cave and rockshelter sites in the Creswell Area.* Creswell Heritage Trust unpublished report.

4

Telling stories.
Archaeology, interpretation and the National Trust at Avebury.

Ruth Taylor

Introduction

The National Trust is the largest owner of archaeological and historical places in England. Over 11 million people visit our pay-for-entry properties and many more visit the countryside. Interpretation has a key role to play in the Trust's commitment to lifelong learning and furthering peoples' understanding of the historic and natural environments. Indeed our vision in the National Trust Strategic Plan is:

'*To inspire present and future generations with understanding and enjoyment of the historic and natural environment through exemplary and innovative work in conservation, education and presentation.*'

Our aim is to have a learning programme at the heart of the Trust which not only provides inspirational learning opportunities for those who come to the Trust but can also reach out to communities and individuals who currently see us as remote and irrelevant to their lives. While sustaining and reinforcing the Trust's emphasis on scholarship and excellence, we aim to re-present, explain and re-interpret our heritage in fresh and appealing ways that will deepen and widen support, and help us win new audiences.

So what do we actually mean by interpretation? There are many different definitions, the simplest being 'provoke, relate, reveal'. A useful definition, because it holds the key elements, is that provided by the Association for Heritage Interpretation:

'*Interpretation is the process of communicating to people the significance of a place or object so that they can enjoy it more, understand their heritage and environment better, and develop a positive attitude to conservation.*'

This definition encompasses the three main elements of interpretation: **people,** whether visitors or a local community; **a site** of natural, historical or cultural value; and the **communication** of a message.

To illustrate the National Trust's approach to interpretation I shall describe an exhibition project we

carried out at Avebury. This illustrates how we plan interpretation and the importance of good planning, the interdisciplinary nature of the work between archaeologists and interpretation professionals and the importance of knowing about our visitors.

Avebury World Heritage Site

The henge at Avebury, Wiltshire, is one of the greatest achievements of prehistoric Europe. The great stone circles, encompassing part of the village of Avebury, are surrounded by a massive bank and ditch built 5000 years ago. Many of the stones were re-erected in the 1930s by the archaeologist Alexander Keiller. In the surrounding countryside are further monuments: West Kennet Avenue, The Sanctuary; West Kennet Long Barrow, Silbury Hill and Windmill Hill.

Interpretation planning

Each National Trust property has embarked on writing an interpretation plan, linked to the property management plan. This then drives forward improvements in the interpretation at the property. Interpreting archaeological sites such as Avebury is a complex task. Visitors may not have an understanding of the time scales involved, much of the evidence of the past way of life is hidden, and what evidence there is can be interpreted in different ways. How do we explain the ambiguities without confusing the visitor? There are many stories to tell - which do we choose?

We know from our research that people are interested in people. They want to know how people lived in the past; who built the stone circles at Avebury and why they were built. Some of these questions cannot be answered with simple answers and results are based on conjecture. However in planning the interpretation at Avebury we investigated what visitors wanted to find out about and then chose themes which helped to answer some of these questions. These also aided visitor's understanding of the archaeology and the development of the landscape.

Statement of significance

A key part of the management and interpretation planning process is the statement of significance for the site which describes what matters about the place and why. It expresses the 'spirit of place' and summarises the key features and attributes which are considered at the time of writing to be the most significant and which the National Trust should seek to conserve. Views on significance are actively gathered through a dialogue with the many communities who have an interest in the place. Significance can cover archaeological features but there might also be social and cultural records associated with the place like folklore and tradition. There might be particular aesthetic responses such as peace and tranquillity, the intimacy or the wildness of the place. There might be certain species or habitats of interest. Significance could lie in the fact that a particular feature is missing-such as a deer park without deer. Through consultation an agreed statement of significance is drawn up for each property.   (Avebury is an unusually complicated place in that it has another tier of planning as a World Heritage Site (WHS). Each WHS has its own management plan often co-ordinated by a management-planning officer with the help of various working groups. This includes an interpretation plan for the overall World Heritage Site.)

Once the statement of significance is agreed as part of the management plan, the property manager carries out the interpretation planning process with the property staff, including archaeologists and expert advice from the interpretation officer. It includes the following key elements:-

- Market research of audiences and audit of existing interpretation
- The statement of significance
- Aims and objectives of the interpretation plan
- Themes for interpretation
- The appropriate media to use on the site
- Resources available or necessary
- Timetable
- Budget
- Project team

In the Trust our work is driven by the National Strategic plan and each region links their Regional Strategic plan and their property plans to this.

Interpretation audit

To start the interpretative planning process, existing interpretation at Avebury was reviewed and audited by a consultant. This highlighted the strengths and weaknesses of the interpretation.

There are a limited number of techniques available when interpreting countryside sites such as Avebury. One of the most popular techniques in open sites is the exterior interpretation panel. However, this needs to be used carefully if it is not to intrude and change the very nature of the site it is interpreting. The Trust removed a number of interpretation panels from the henge monument when it first took over management of Avebury in 1994 to reduce erosion which was taking place around the panels and to free the monument of clutter. Two new orientation panels were placed in the car park (fig. 4.1). One panel shows the village and henge monument and one panel has a map of the World Heritage Site, showing access routes to the outlying monuments such as Silbury Hill and West Kennet long barrow. Other interpretation on the site includes an information caravan in the car park in the summer. A site specific panel in the manor barn complex, a guidebook, walks pack (fig. 4.2), and children's guide. A small exhibition in the Alexander Keiller museum shows artefacts from the site and describes the archaeology of the monuments.

The review of interpretation highlighted that there were gaps in the historical story of Avebury, particularly the more recent past, and little information was available on the way people lived their lives in the past. We carried out extensive market research over 5 years to establish why our visitors came to Avebury and what particularly interested them about the place (see below). At the time we were reviewing interpretation, a new space came available as the Museum of Wiltshire Life moved their exhibition from the manor barn back to Lackham. This helped us decide that a World Heritage Site as important as Avebury merited the investment in an exhibition. Furthermore the information we wanted to portray was best suited to the exhibition medium.

Visitors and target groups

Prior to planning the exhibition we reviewed the market research and in particular the visitor groups. These can be segmented into six different broad groups:

- 17% local day trippers
- 15% day trippers (from further away)
- 19% archaeological/historical interest
- 18% environmental interest
- 16% spiritually motivated
- 12% casual/non specific

Also 30% of visitors came with children

We then carried out some formative evaluation using questionnaires to help decide what to include in the exhibition. All groups were interested in finding out, 'who built Avebury, how, why and when?', also, 'the construction of the stones, longbarrows, Silbury Hill etc'.

Fig. 4.1 Outdoor panels.

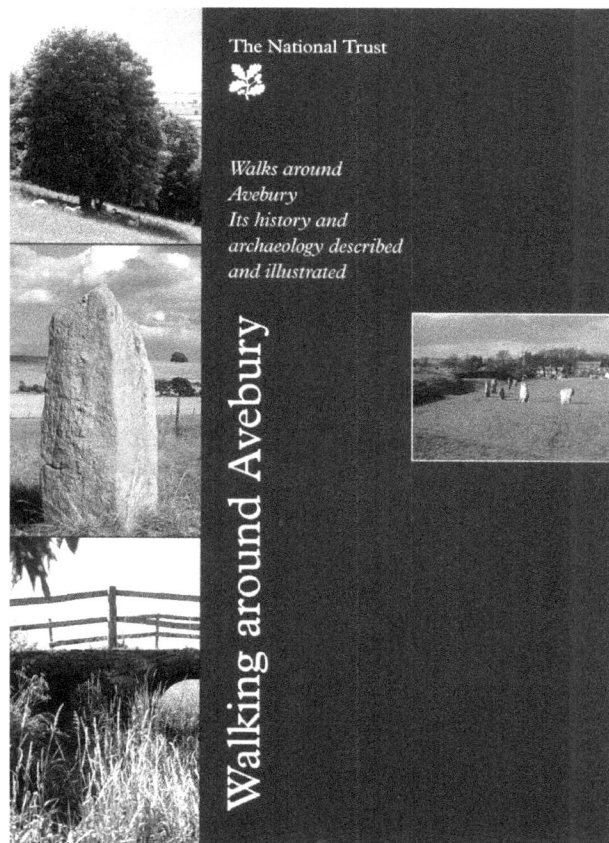

Fig. 4.2 Walking around Avebury - walks pack.

Secondary themes of interest included, 'the landscape, how it looked and how it has changed' and 'spiritual/religious explanations'. Only the day trippers and casual visitors were interested in using videos and CD Roms and both types of day trippers and casual visitors were interested in using interactives. (Interestingly respondents divided equally over whether they preferred a thematic or a chronological exhibition.) This research helped us decide the themes and stories we were going to use. We could see that a large group of our visitors were already visiting with an interest in archaeology and there was also a large group with a spiritual interest which needed accommodating. We then tested out the themes we were planning to use and understanding of key concepts such as the term 'Neolithic'. From this testing we could see that layers of interpretation were going to be needed for the different target groups.

Project team

A project team was set up to commission and install the exhibition. This included writing the brief, commissioning the designers, writing the content and testing the exhibition once the installation had taken place. The team consisted of:

Property manager
Project manager
Curator/archaeologist
Interpretation officer
Building manager
Historic buildings representative
Financial controller
Project sponsor-Area manager
Marketing and communications manager

Exhibition themes

To help visitors learn about the archaeological landscape at Avebury they need more than just facts. They need to have the facts put into context. Research in informal learning shows how people take on information in informal settings such as museums and exhibitions. Visitors learn best if information is linked in a theme or story rather than being presented as disparate bits. Using the visitor research we had undertaken we were able to choose two themes from the many stories which could have been told. These were 'The Avebury landscape' and 'Discovering Avebury' with the overall exhibition title as 'Avebury - 6000 years of mystery' (fig. 4.3):

'In the few kilometres around Avebury are some of the most spectacular prehistoric monuments to be found anywhere in the world. They were built over a 2000 year period, starting nearly 6000 years ago.'

The content for the exhibition was written by the curator, Ros Cleal, with editing from the exhibition team and designers, and consultation with a peer review group. This interplay between the curator, who was the expert on the archaeology of the site, and the interpretation team, who represented the visitor and knew very little about the site, was a valuable asset to the project. The difficult decision in any interpretation project is what to leave out, as there is never enough space to explain everything about the site. On the other hand ruthless editing of the content of an exhibition panel can lose the very story it was designed to tell. By working together, the content can be edited by the design team to enable an interested visitor to understand the content then checked by the curator to make sure the essential elements of the story are still apparent.

The two themes tell different parts of the Avebury story.

1. **The Avebury landscape.** This is a chronological theme, taking visitors on a walk through the development of the landscape, helping people to understand what all the different humps and bumps in the landscape represent. It forms an introduction to Avebury, giving an outline of the development of the landscape through time and the context of the individual monuments in the past and present. It presents a broad picture of this cultural landscape giving information on geology, natural history, conservation, World Heritage Site status and how these link together. Visitors can gain a better understanding of the henge and monuments they have come to see and an appreciation of how Avebury relates to the wider world. It includes information on the people that lived in Avebury in the past, what life was like at the time the stone circles were built and what happened to people when they died.

2. **Discovering Avebury.** This covers the more recent history of Avebury, including Roman, Saxon, medieval and more modern strands. There are stories of people who have helped to uncover Avebury's prehistoric past, eg Alexander Keiller, and the techniques of discovery. It shows that there is more to discover about Avebury than is immediately obvious and describes Avebury as a living community through the centuries, existing side by side with the monuments.

Different techniques are used to give layers of interpretation within the exhibition. A CD Rom shows eight reconstruction landscapes through time from Neolithic through to present day, painted by Jane Brayne (fig. 4.4). You can fly through the landscapes, home in on specific monuments and find out more about each one. You can find out about the techniques of discovery, what snails and pollen have been found and when archaeological investigations have taken place. Another section of the CD shows the people connected with Avebury, their lives and the discoveries they made.

Fig. 4.3 Exhibition: 'Avebury - 6000 years of mystery'.

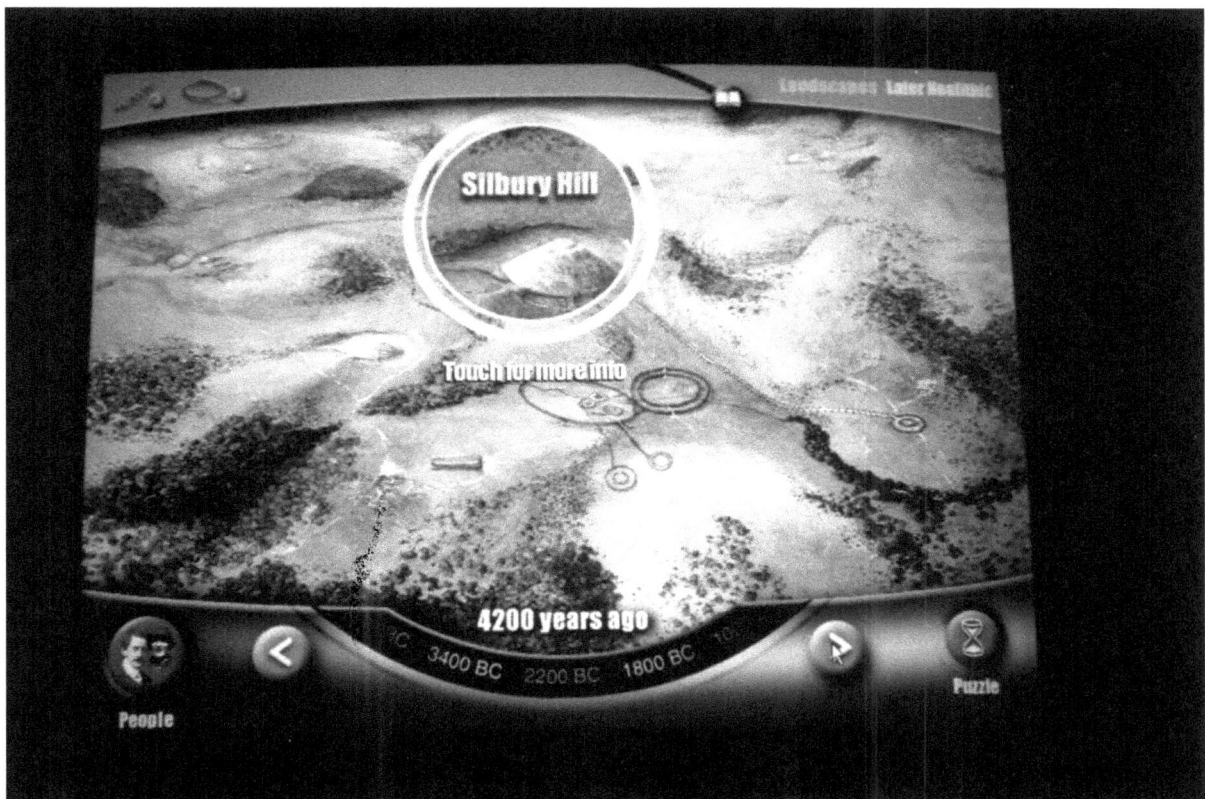

Fig. 4.4 CD-ROM interactive.

The main exhibition panels, which have a hierarchy of text so that you can choose how deeply you investigate any subject area, are supported by hands-on interactives. For instance, the bronze age section has a burial mound you can investigate and decide from the finds you unearth who was buried in the mound (fig. 4.5). The Silbury Hill section has a model you can rotate to find the different layers inside the hill. A large landscape model sets the henge in the landscape with the surrounding monuments.

A family area has jigsaw puzzles of different types of pots and illustrations from the exhibition. Children and adults can construct a magnetic time line to reinforce some of the learning points from the exhibition. Close to this is a browsing area with folios to browse. Different people connected with Avebury have been encouraged to write their thoughts about Avebury including druids, local residents a minister and archaeologists. Visitors are encouraged to contribute to the folios through a comments box.

Evaluation

We have had a very favourable response to the exhibition from visitors and the local community. We have used two methods of evaluation; the comments cards filled in at the end of the exhibition and a questionnaire. The comments cards were useful when we first opened the exhibition as they showed immediately that we had a problem with the lighting, deliberately kept low not to disturb the resident bat population but too low for visitors comfort. This was rectified and we are now finding that visitors particularly enjoy the CD Rom and the innovative interactive elements of the exhibition.

Interpretation -a magnificent conservation tool

Archaeologists need interpretation. Without it their research could remain the province of experts in dusty tomes on library shelves. If presented in an approachable format the public can be enthused and enthralled by the stories behind archaeological excavations and the information they reveal. Nowhere is this more apparent than in the popularity of television programmes about archaeology. Interpretation can stimulate curiosity and influence behaviour. In managing and preserving archaeological sites this is an important consideration. If visitors can be enthused about the value of a site and persuaded through interpretation to take certain walking routes, to avoid or lessen erosion, how much better is this than fences and prohibitive signs? If we are to encourage people to value their past, learn from it and help in its conservation then we must continue to find new and innovative techniques to enthral and enthuse.

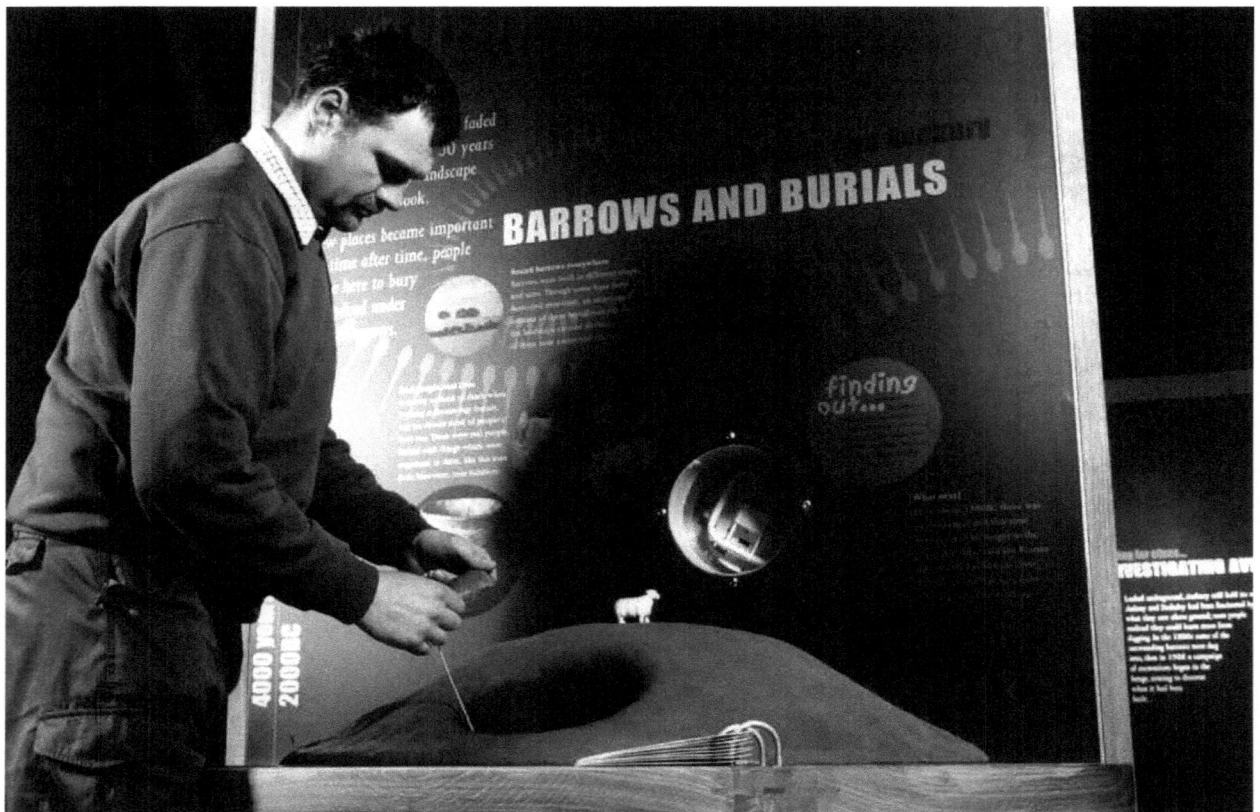

Fig. 4.5 Barrows and burials interactive.

5

The Maelmin Heritage Trail.
Archaeological research and the public.

Clive Waddington

Preamble

The trail has its genesis in a multi-disciplinary archaeology research project conducted by the author and Dave Passmore since the early 1990s. The consequence of this is that the interpretive front end of the project is ultimately grounded in university-led research and there exists, therefore, a direct link between the archaeology and its public interpretation. It was considered essential that the research archaeologists themselves played an active role in developing the interpretive material to ensure the accuracy of information presented. In addition, the personal experiences of the archaeologist could be drawn on to enliven the material rather than perpetuating an interpreter's view of what archaeologists are and what they do. By installing archaeologists within the interpretive loop it means that archaeologists have the capacity to influence and set the agenda as well as create synergies with those specialising in interpretive strategy, content and design. Furthermore, it is cost effective as it helps to keep archaeologists in employment and reduces the need for expensive interpretation consultants.

The nature of interpretation

In order to avoid any misconceptions arising from this discourse, the word interpretation is used here in the sense that Tilden (1977, 3-5) understands it, namely that it is the task of revealing to others in such a way that its 'effectiveness depends upon a regular nourishment by well-directed and discriminating research' (*ibid*, 5). This understanding of what our responsibilities are as archaeologists and interpreters is critical as it underpins the approach taken to disseminating information, as well as the type of information itself. This is an area in need of further debate, and the paper delivered at the conference was intended to be polemical in order to provoke thoughts on the imperatives that prescribe what and how we interpret. It is partly an ethical question, but it is one of crucial importance as it underpins for each of us the way we practice public interpretation. The approach that has been adopted for this project has been to inform and stimulate rather than advance deliberately tendentious or political viewpoints, as has become fashionable in some of the more extreme post-processual quarters.

This is not to assume that archaeologists deal solely with 'facts'. Far from it, we are purveyors of the fragmentary and the vague much of the time. However, unlike some caught in the more extreme positions of post-modern relativism, it is argued here that some of the data that archaeologists deal with is, without getting wrapped up in semantics and philosophical questions of truth and the like, to all intents and purposes factual. For example: '*a polished stone axe is a polished stone axe and will almost certainly date to the Neolithic period. The Neolithic period in Britain dates broadly from 4000BC to 2500BC and was a time when domestic cereal crops were grown and pottery vessels first made*'. The previous sentences serve to show how some information can be considered 'factual'. For other interpretation there is, however, less certainty as is evident in the following sentences: '*Some archaeologists view the Neolithic as a period when farmers from Europe colonised the British Isles while others view farming as being adopted by the indigenous population. Some archaeologists argue that the Neolithic was as much concerned with profound social and ideological changes as it was a practical change to farmed food production*'. In this case the subjectivity inherent in such views is made explicit to the audience and this provocation to retain or reject such views empowers readers to make their own decision. This does not need to be a problem. Rather, it gives us the opportunity to present different points of view and stimulate our audiences to think for themselves. The point that is being made is that so long as the textual interpretation is explicit as to the level of certainty with which various information is known, then this is posited as good practice. The objection comes when personal and highly subjective views are presented with the same certainty, usually as an assertion, as information that genuinely has much greater validity. This results in the mixing up of levels of proof, and unless the reader is fully conversant with the raw data they are unable to disentangle the more reliable information from the highly subjective and personal. The reason some relativists resort to such literary acrobatics is because their own intellectual position does not allow them to advance their highly personal subjective view as being more correct than those of others and so have to rely on assertion to give their view authority. However, as Fleming (1995, 1041) has pointedly observed 'Assertion, though unavoidable at times, is not a substitute for argument.'

To me, adopting *extreme* relativist positions is tantamount to legitimising the 'anything goes' book of history as it is happy to subjugate reliable information based on rigorous, systematic and sometimes testable data for opinionated perspectives and the politics of the individual, which as Saville (1999, 202) recently stated, have 'too great a concern with certain critical constituencies'. I believe that it is our duty as archaeologists to reveal the past as best we can using the factual data we have as our building blocks and then presenting our subjective views to fill in the gaps, with the caveat that it must be explicit where we depart from understanding based on empirical evidence and embark on understanding drawn from subjective viewpoints and less certain or equivocal evidence. I am not arguing for a positivist approach to interpretation, as the post-modernist critique certainly has made some highly valuable contributions to approaches and understandings of the past, but rather for the pendulum to swing back from the more extreme relativist margins towards the middle ground. This tension has been characterised by Molyneaux (1994, 3) as a conflict between the material (empirical) past and the ideological (subjective) past. In other words, it is a question of honesty and intention. This is not to condemn relativist views from archaeological interpretation but rather to make clear that such approaches are acceptable so long as the data on which they are based is referred to and the view presented acknowledges its intentionally partial foundation. Subjective views are fine so long as it is clear that is what they are, because after all much of our subject matter is indeed subjective. Subjectivity is an inevitable by-product when we deal with the more human and non-physical areas of our discipline and one that we should be at pains to be aware of. If hard-core relativists are going to opt for such approaches to the past the position adopted should be made abundantly clear to the audience.

For most of us, history in its broadest sense is about trying to find out what happened in the past. Those practitioners who do not view it as such, but rather as a canvas upon which they can map their own personal views about the world, should perhaps question whether they are in the wrong business and should perhaps present themselves as philosophers or politicians. It is argued here that the past is not the most appropriate canvas for these sorts of debates to be played out as it encourages distortion, bias and misuse for personal and political ends. The past is an extremely powerful tool as it forges and underpins notions of identity, legitimacy and perspectives on the present. The presentation of the past in places ranging from Nazi Germany to modern day Iraq (see Blockley 1999, 18) serve as examples of how the past has, or is, being used to shore up the political claims of certain groups in society. Those who intentionally politicise the interpretation of the past seem not to be archaeologists or historians but rather political/philosophical/ideological activists of one brand or another. Inevitably current debates need to be linked to the past in order to make comparisons, identify trends through time and space and so on, but intentionally subjective accounts need to be explicitly noted as being exactly that: political histories from a certain perspective. When it comes to interpreting the past to the public our responsibility weighs heavy on the presentation of that which is known rather than that which we would like people to think. If we deliberately set out to dabble with the past in such a way as to present it in our own image then we no longer become its guardians but its manipulators. We must, therefore, use our subjective views with care and make clear whence they came, and where possible present alternative views that use the available evidence in a different way. This puts the audience in control as they then have the capacity to come to their own decision based on the available evidence. By empowering the audience, peoples' engagement with the past becomes all the more stimulating as their own thoughts have a part to play and they become more aware of the contested nature of much of our archaeological knowledge base. This can only be a good thing as it encourages the audience to be sceptical, to question and to take an active part in uncovering the history of the world around them from a critical and responsible vantage. Why should we feel insecure about giving others access to the past just because the subject matter can be understood in different ways? Indeed such statements have been recently voiced by Stone and Planel (1999, 2) who state that, 'One role of archaeologists, interpreters and educators is to expose their audiences to the concept of other ways of interpreting the past while at the same time identifying and exposing any deliberate misuse of the past'. We should be positive about this as it is this sense of mystery and alternative understandings that makes our subject so appealing, and such a powerful draw for the public at large, and as mediators of those mysteries we should strive to reveal intelligently and honestly. By democratising archaeological knowledge and understanding, this can only help to avoid the various 'excluded pasts' identified by Mackenzie and Stone (1990).

Subjectivity has its place, and if utilised well can be an invaluable aid to stimulating an audience by alerting people to question the past and the world around them in new ways, as well as making people aware of different points of view. This is where the craft of the archaeological interpreter comes into play, as the line between stimulating interpretation that enriches the experience of the visitor and one-sided misinformation can be a fine one. Furthermore, the audience should not be patronised, nor led to believe that the opinions of the interpreter are the facts of the matter. Making clear to the audience where the different levels of subjectivity creep into the interpretation is indeed the art of the archaeological interpreter.

Research strategy

It is necessary at this point to provide some background on the Milfield research project itself in order to explain the approach adopted as this has directly influenced the resulting interpretation and its content. The research project is known as 'The Milfield Basin Archaeological Landscape Project' (Waddington 1999) and is multi-disciplinary in scope, with particular emphasis placed upon an integrated archaeological, palaeoenvironmental and geoarchaeological strategy. The project is directed jointly by the author and David Passmore of the Department of Geography, University of Newcastle upon Tyne. Emphasis has been placed throughout on the interactions between humans and environment and the changing nature of this relationship through time. The research is oriented around a landscape perspective that views past human behaviour as being more or less continuous across the landscape with varying degrees of intensity and types of activity taking place (Zvelebil *et al* 1992). It is intended that by adopting a landscape approach some of the shortcomings of site-based studies will be overcome, although on-site investigations also formed an important part of the work providing windows of detail at specific locales. A largescale fieldwork programme was undertaken, including fieldwalking of just under 1000ha of land, evaluation excavations on eight sites, test-pitting, an aerial photograph transcription programme, gemomorphological mapping, sediment coring and pollen analysis (see Waddington 1999 for preliminary results). The latest round of research has been funded by English Heritage and this provided match-funding for a European Union grant that was used to fund the heritage trail.

Interpretation strategy

The interpretation side of the project developed from discussions between the author and a local Milfield businessman, Peter Forrester, who is the proprietor of the Milfield Café and Countrystore. It became clear that we shared an ambition for the provision of appropriate interpretation for the public telling the story of the incredibly rich archaeological heritage of this part of Northumberland. Very few people who live locally were aware of the history and archaeology of the region and the pivotal role it has played in archaeological research. For example, the excavations undertaken by Brian Hope-Taylor at Yeavering (1977) were considered a landmark in excavation technique and publication, while the cup and ringed marked rocks of the area have formed one of the key foci for debate in British rock art studies (Beckensall 1999; Bradley 1997; Waddington 1998), and the excavations by Harding in the Neolithic ceremonial complex have provided an important contribution to the understanding of henge monuments in Britain (Harding 1981; 2000). We both felt that this fascinating story needed to be told and made easily accessible for residents

and visitors alike. We planned at this early stage the outcomes we wanted to achieve. In brief our aims were to:

1. Increase public access to the rich and diverse human and landscape history of the valley, thereby making the region's past more easily available to a non-academic audience while also providing an opportunity to increase awareness of conservation best practice at archaeological sites.

2. Enhance peoples' pleasure and understanding of the landscape, both for those residing in the region and those visiting.

3. Strengthen the tourist potential of the region, thereby safeguarding existing jobs in the tourism sector in a region otherwise suffering from a decline in the rural economy.

4. Give people residing in the region a sense of their own past and identity and, therefore, a sense of worth and confidence in an otherwise remote and declining area.

The author and Peter Forrester set about the interpretation with a wide-ranging consultation process that included discussions with representatives from the County and District Councils, the Northumberland National Park Authority, the Parish Council, local businesses, University academics and local amateur archaeological groups and individuals. This inclusive approach meant that the project secured a wide support base and that it started out as, and still remains, a joint community and university project. This situating of the interpretation partly in the hands of the local community and partly in the hands of the researchers from the very beginning means that the project is, and is seen to be, owned both by those living in the landscape and those studying it. In this way the guiding principle of the heritage trail has much in common with the ecomuseum movement (Davis 1999) and the community development approach to interpretation as most recently summarised by Blockley (1999, 24-32). Many local people and amateur groups were involved in the archaeological fieldwork over the years with important contributions from the Northumberland Archaeological Group, the Society of Antiquaries of Newcastle upon Tyne and from the Borders Archaeological Society. This added to the sense of involvement by local people as many have actively participated in finding out about their own heritage, and this has meant that the project was not an exclusive academic exercise. A programme of public talks and lectures by the author to local societies over the past five years has provided an important forum for keeping residents up-to-date with the latest discoveries and for answering questions and concerns of local people.

The project was resourced by a combination of funding partners reflecting the catholic support for the project.

The seed funding to get the project off the ground was provided by income from the booklet 'Land of Legend' (Waddington 1999a) and this allowed consents, planning permission, travel and even radiocarbon dates to be acquired. Subsequently, the land for the heritage trail was donated on a peppercorn rent basis by BG Transco, and the cash funding was secured as an Objective 5b grant from the EU with match funding coming from English Heritage for the research work. Other contributions were generously made by the Milfield Café, Milfield post-office, Forest Enterprise, Marketing Partnership 2000, Department of Archaeology at the University of Newcastle upon Tyne and through the time given to the project by a wide range of volunteers. Most recently, in 2003, English Heritage have made a further grant available for the site through the Aggregates Levy Sustainability Fund.

An interpretive plan was developed as the first stage of the project. This detailed the strategy to be followed and identified the different interpretive elements and their content. The chronological scope of the project was designed to run from the end of the last ice-age and the first humans through to the early medieval period, although in the future this could be extended to continue through to WWII as an old RAF airfield is situated immediately next to the trail on its south side. The

different interpretive elements include:

1. An Archaeological Heritage Trail
2. Trail Guide
3. Schools Pack
4. In-door interpretation at Milfield Café

The Heritage Trail

The Maelmin Heritage Trail is a free access open-air site located immediately next to the buried remains of the early medieval royal township of Maelmin and the modern village of Milfield. According to Bede, after the reign of Edwin the town of Yeavering "was abandoned by the later kings, who built another at a place called Maelmin". With the survival of a vast crop-mark complex including a great hall, palisaded enclosure and grubenhaüser (Gates and O'Brien 1988) we now know the location of this royal town and hence the name given to the heritage trail.

The heritage trail (fig. 5.1) consists of a circular walk through woodland and an open field on the southern edge of Milfield village. There is an on-site car park and it is signposted from the A697 trunk road that runs parallel to the site on its west side. One of the principal concepts

Fig. 5.1 The entrance stone at the Maelmin Heritage Trail.

Fig. 5.2 Night time view through the entrance of the reconstructed henge with the moon visible in the sky.

behind the site was to provide a central location within the valley where visitors could park and then explore the surrounding landscape either by walking or cycling. The aim of this was to promote green tourism and encourage visitors to discover the countryside for themselves. A theme which runs through the on-site interpretation is the guiding of peoples' attention outwards from the heritage trail to the surrounding landscape and the constellation of archaeological sites within it. In this way the heritage trail provides a focus that acts as a portal for accessing the surrounding environment, its archaeological heritage, as well as other sources of information such as the Northumberland National Park visitor centre at Ingram and the Cheviot Centre in Wooler. By visiting real sites in the surrounding countryside visitors develop a more intimate engagement with the landscape and are more likely to make return visits and explore on their own in the future. Repeat visits to the region are an important aspect of tourism development and will contribute to the economic well-being of the region. Details of sites to visit and information about them is included in the trail guidebook, Land of Legend, and the schools pack.

The centrepiece of the heritage trail is a full-scale reconstruction of the Milfield North henge (fig. 5.2), the site of which is located 1500m to the north. However, the Milfield South henge lies only 75m to the west of the reconstruction. The Milfield basin contains the largest concentration of henge monuments in the British Isles (Harding 2000), but all lie in arable fields and only

survive as crop-mark sites, with no obvious remains visible above ground. Therefore, it was considered that the most appropriate way of interpreting these monuments, and to provide a sensory experience of what these structures felt like, was by building a full-scale construction based as faithfully as possible on the available evidence, with some elements necessarily conjectural. The site was excavated by Harding (1981) in the mid 1970s, and this provided the information on which the site is modeled. There are subjective elements to the construction, such as the hurdling between the inner ring of posts. However, the visitor is invited to think of other ways the monument could have looked based on the ground plan of the original excavation. Currently, shrub and tree planting is underway in an attempt to create a similar environmental setting to that of the original henge, based on the available palaeoenvironmental data. The reconstruction was intended from the outset to serve the full range of purposes identified by Blockley which include: interpretation, education, tourism development, experiment/research and local/cultural identity (Blockley 1999, 15).

The henge reconstruction was built by a diverse group of volunteers as part of an archaeological experiment. The group dressed, ate and slept using the same types of clothes, food and tools that were known, or thought to have been available, to Neolithic people, and the various aspects of this work were recorded by a post-graduate

Fig. 5.3 Two of the henge-building team preparing food.

Fig. 5.4 Moving one of the carved entrance timbers while being filmed by a TV Crew.

student whose MA dissertation was devoted to the study (Drake 2000). This experiment was useful in a number of ways. For example, it was able to demonstrate that the relatively shallow post-holes in the interior of the monument could hold substantial posts – an interpretation originally thought unlikely by the excavator (Harding 1981). Also, by constructing the monument in 3D it allowed a more palpable understanding of the architecture and its effect on bounding space and creating a sense of mystique, separateness from the outside world and raising of spiritual awareness. Looking at plans in academic journals does not convey the power of such architecture on the senses, particularly as such plans are unable to reconstruct the landscape setting around the sites, which in the case of henge monuments is thought to form part of the key to their impact on the human faithful who used them (e.g. Pollard 1992; Richards 1996; Waddington 1999; A. Harding 2000; J. Harding 2000). In this way the reconstruction assists in providing a phenomenological experience and understanding of the monument. In addition, the experimental approach allowed a wealth of photographs and film footage to be taken over the fortnight during which it took place (figs. 5.3 and 5.4). This corpus has been particularly useful as a source of interesting and evocative images that stimulate visitors and provide a human angle to the past with which people can immediately relate. In other words these images provide a useful medium for making often obscure and remote periods such as the New Stone Age (Neolithic) more readily accessible to a non-specialist audience. By the end of the fortnight 10% of the monument had been constructed by hand using 'stone-age' tools and techniques with the other 90% of the monument constructed using a machine and modern tools (due to time constraints and the costs involved). The experiment created a good deal of publicity for the project and the archaeology of the region, and this had a very positive effect in publicising the site and the region. The publicity ranged from pieces in local newspapers through to a full feature in *The Times*, together with daily radio bulletins and local television news updates. The site was formally opened in June 2000 by David Miles, the Chief Archaeologist at English Heritage.

The trail includes a series of information panels (figs. 5.5 and 5.6) arranged in chronological order with each dealing with a different period. Each panel was designed with a title indicating the period, a subtitle capturing something that defines the lifestyle of the time, a full colour scene with accompanying text and timeline across the base of the board. The heritage trail logo is pictured in the bottom left-hand corner with the wavy line representing the twin peaks of Yeavering Bell and ending in a cup and ring motif, representing conspicuous natural and human features distinctive to the region. The colour scenes were created by a Northumbrian artist, Dave Hall, in conjunction with the author who was able to advise on content and ensure archaeological consistency. However, as any images of the past can never be accurate (Stone and Planel 1999, 10-11) the scenes were deliberately designed to be unrealistic in style, but at the same time contain authentic archaeological detail. In effect the pictures were deliberately stylized so that the viewer can instantly realise that what they are looking at is an *idea* of the past that includes artistic images to prompt the imagination, providing something of the flavour of the time rather than a *realistic* image of the past. The panel layouts and the site logo were designed by Peter Forrester and the text was provided by the author. The text explains both archaeological and environmental history. A thread running throughout the boards is the interaction between humans and environment and the way each has been influenced by the other through time. The text provides basic information, but also poses questions to the viewer, and makes it clear when a plurality of views exist amongst archaeologists. In this way the text is not simply intended as instruction but also as 'provocation' as Tilden (1977, 9) advocates.

Since opening the site has attracted a variety of visitor types including local visitors, tourists, day-trippers on planned visits, educational groups of school and university age, together with new-age visitors and professional archaeologists. Milfield was affected by the foot and mouth crisis and this had the inevitable impact of reducing visitor numbers over much of 2001. However, further work to enhance the heritage trail is now under way and this includes planting of new trees and shrubs, more signage, an advertising leaflet, a nature trail, a new reconstruction of a Mesolithic hut (excavated on the Northumberland coast at Howick), marked paths to archaeological sites and two popular books on archaeology and walks in the area. Over the next few years, as the site continues to develop, it is intended to monitor visitors and their feedback more closely with the aid of postgraduate student input from the International Centre for Cultural Heritage Studies at the University of Newcastle upon Tyne. It is hoped that over the coming years the site will serve as a stimulus for local, as well as visitor, interest in this special region.

Acknowledgements

There are many archaeologists who, at various times over the last four decades, have devoted much of their time and energies to elucidating the archaeology of north Northumberland and without whom our knowledge of the area would be the poorer. In particular these include the late Brian Hope-Taylor and George Jobey as well as Colin Burgess, Anthony Harding, Roger Miket, Stan Beckensall, Pete Topping, Chris Tolan-Smith and Colm O'Brien. The many volunteers who have worked on the various fieldwork projects are also deserving of thanks, as without them little of this work would have been possible. The interpretation project owes a great debt to the thirteen hardy souls who stuck it out as Neolithic men and women during the wettest fortnight since records began and for their stoic persistence in the face of hard living. Thanks are also due to Peter Stone and Don Henson for their advice and support with the interpretive material and to the Department of Archaeology, University of Newcastle upon Tyne and the Archaeological Practice for adminstrative support. I am grateful to my project co-director Dave Passmore for his stirling work on the project and for assisting with the text on environmental topics and nature trail. Dave Hall must be congratulated and thanked for the superb illustrative material and all the extra effort that was put in above and beyond the call of duty. Peter Forrester, my partner in crime on this venture, deserves a special thankyou for his fundamental input to the project, breadth of vision and months of hard unpaid work, and to him I offer my greatest thanks. Other organisations who have made contributions to the project to whom I am most grateful include English Heritage, BG Transco, Forest Enterprise, Tarmac, the EU and Government Office North-East. There are a host of other individuals and organisations who have contributed to this project in a wide variety of ways but are too numerous to mention here and I hope they will accept my apology for not mentioning them all in person. However, this in no way diminishes the debt of gratitude that I extend to them all for their much needed support. Finally my thanks are due to Peter Stone for his

Hunter Gatherers

Life on the Move

The Mesolithic (10,000-4,000BC) is the period between the last ice age and the beginning of farming when hunter-gatherers inhabited the British Isles.

In the Milfield basin people moved around the landscape on a seasonal basis taking advantage of resources available at different times of the year such as hazelnuts in the autumn, forest fruits in the summer and salmon during Spring and Summer. Groups also managed the landscape by burning off areas of woodland to promote the growth of plant shoots. These attract grazing animals, such as red deer, which could be hunted with bow and arrow.

Settlement
The collection of flints from ploughed fields has shown that most people lived on the flat gravel terraces, probably in skin-covered tents, as family groups. Upland hunting camps, known as rock shelters, have been discovered along the face of the sandstone escarpments.

The Early Environment
The key feature of the Mesolithic environment is the rapid change from a cold grass dominated 'tundra' environment to a warm wooded landscape. By 6500BC Britain was completely separated from the continent by rising sea levels and the climate was at its warmest. This 'climatic optimum' encouraged the spread of vast broad-leaf forests across the hills as well as the lowlands.

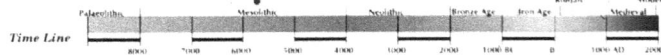

Fig. 5.5 The Mesolithic display board from the trail.

The Henge Monuments

Places for People and Gods

Reconstruction
The henge in front of you is a reconstruction not a real site. It is based on the ground plan of the Milfield North henge situated next to the barn in the distance to your right. Another henge is located less than 100m away on the other side of the main road in a cultivated field. Like all the other henges in the valley it survives as a buried monument with no traces visible on the surface. There are at least seven henges in the Till valley and three other related sites.

Milfield North Henge
The Milfield North henge was excavated during the 1970's and radiocarbon dated to around 2300BC. In the central area of the henge were three pits, the middle one of which contained a food vessel pot and possibly a wooden coffin for a burial. The other two pits were also thought to be grave pits but the acid nature of the soil has meant that bones do not survive. The stone-lined grave, or 'cist', situated inside the entrance to the inner sanctum was probably a 'threshold' deposit - deliberately positioned so that any individual entering would have to walk over the grave. In the early Anglo-Saxon period the henge was reused for burial of the dead.

Q. What is a henge?
A. A circular open-air temple formed by an outer earthen mound and inner ditch with a setting of stone or wooden uprights.

The reconstruction you see today is one possible way the monument may have looked. However, the inner ring of posts is not certain, as are the hurdles between them. Perhaps the outer ring of posts were connected to each other by wooden lintels.

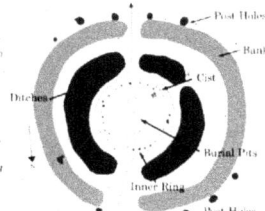

Milfield North henge (excavated elements shown).

Fig. 5.6 One of the henge display boards from the trail.

56

helpful comments on a draft of this paper. As ever, I alone am responsible for the views put forward in this paper and they do not necessarily represent those of my colleagues.

References

Beckensall, S., 1999. *British Prehistoric Rock Art.* Stroud: Tempus.

Bradley, R., 1997. *Rock Art and the Prehistory of Atlantic Europe.* Signing the Land. Lond. London: Routledge.

Blockley, M., 1999. Archaeological reconstructions and the community in the UK. In Stone, P. G. and Planel, P. G. (eds.) *The Constructed Past. Experimental Archaeology, Education and the Public.* London: Routledge. 15-34.

Davis, P., 1999. *Ecomuseums. A Sense of Place.* Leicester: Leicester University Press.

Drake, E. 2000., *The Potential of Experimental Work Within Archaeology: Maelmin – a Case Study.* Unpublished MA Dissertation, University of Newcastle upon Tyne.

Fleming, A., 1995. A tomb with a view. *Antiquity* 69: 1040-1042.

Gates, T. and O'Brien, C., 1988. Cropmarks at Milfield and New Bewick and the Recognition of Grubenhauser in Northumberland. *Archaeologia Aeliana* 5ᵗʰ series, 16: 1-9.

Harding, A., 1981. Excavations in the prehistoric ritual complex near Milfield, Northumberland. *Proceedings of the Prehistoric Society* 46: 87-135.

Harding, A., 2000. Henge monuments and landscape features in Northern England: monumentality and nature. In Ritchie, A. (ed.) *Neolithic Orkney in its European Context.* Cambridge: McDonald Institute for Archaeological Research. 267-274.

Harding, J., 2000. Later Neolithic ceremonial centres, ritual and pilgirmage: the monument complex of Thornborough, North Yorkshire. In Ritchie, A. (ed.), *Neolithic Orkney in its European Context.* Cambridge: McDonald Institute for Archaeological Research. 31-46.

Hope-Taylor, B., 1977. *Yeavering. An Anglo-British Centre of Early Northumbria.* London: H.M.S.O.

Mackenzie, R. and Stone P. G., 1990. Introduction: the concept of the excluded past. In Stone, P. G. and Mackenzie, R. (eds.), *The Excluded Past. Archaeology in Education.* London: Unwin Hyman Ltd. 1-14.

Molyneaux, B. L., 1994. Introduction: the represented past. In Stone, P. G. and Molyneaux, B. L. (eds.), *The Presented Past. Heritage, Museums and Education.* London: Routledge. 1-13.

Pollard, J., 1992. The Sanctuary, Overton Hill, Wiltshire: a re-examination. *Proceedings of the Prehistoric Society* 58: 213-226.

Richards, C., 1996. Henges and Water. Towards an Elemental Understanding of Monumentality and Landscape in Late Neolithic Britain. *Journal of Material Culture* 1 (November): 313-336.

Saville, A., 1999. Thinking things over: aspects of contemporary attitudes towards archaeology, museums and material culture. In Merrimen, N. (ed.), *Making Early Histories in Museums.* Leicester: Leicester University Press. 190-209.

Stone, P. G. and Planel, P. G., 1999. Introduction. In Stone P. G. and Planel P. G. (eds.), *The Constructed Past. Experimental Archaeology, Education and the Public.* London: Routledge. 1-14.

Tilden, F., 1977. *Interpreting our Heritage.* Chapel Hill, NC: University of North Carolina Press.

Tilley, C., (ed.) 1993. *Interpretative Archaeology.* Oxford: Berg.

Waddington, C., 1998. Cup and ring marks in context. *Cambridge Archaeological Journal* 8(1): 29-54.

Waddington, C. 1999. *A Landscape Archaeological Study of the Mesolithic-Neolithic in the Milfield Basin, Northumberland.* British Archaeological Reports British Series 291. Oxford: BAR Publishing.

Waddington, C., 1999a. *Land of Legend. Discovering Ancient Northumberland.* Wooler: Country Store Publishing.

Waddington, C., 2001. *Maelmin. An Archaeological Guide.* Wooler: Country Store Publishing.

Zvelebil, M., Green S. W., and Macklin, M., 1992. Archaeological Landscapes, Lithic Scatters, and Human Behaviour. In Rossignol, J. and Wandsnider, L. (eds.), *Space, Time and Archaeological Landscapes.* New York: Plenum Press. 193-226.

6

Drama on Gardom's Edge.
The use of theatre groups in public interpretation of prehistory.

Bill Bevan

Prologue – The Scene is Set
curtains part to reveal backdrop depicting a rural idyll in muted tones.

Gardom's Edge forms part of an intermittent gritstone escarpment which runs north to south along the eastern side of the Derwent Valley in the Derbyshire Peak District (fig. 6.1). The Edge rises from the forested, boulder-strewn, slopes of this part of the valley as a vertical cliff nearly a kilometre long. Above it, the ground is relatively level and covered in a mix of course grasses, heather and birch woodland. At approximately 300 metres above sea level, this plateau should be covered in deep blanket peat as are neighbouring moors. Intense moorland fires in the 1950s burnt much of this peat away. While potentially catastrophic at the time they would prove to be advantageous to future archaeologists, increasing the visibility of thousands of prehistoric features otherwise part buried in the peat. For five years between 1994 and 1999 the Department of Archaeology and Prehistory at the University of Sheffield and the Peak District National Park Archaeology Service ran a field project on this moorland shelf (Barnatt, Bevan and Edmonds in press).

The visible archaeology predominantly comprises stone banks and cairns forming enclosures, field systems and cairn fields. A pit alignment, linear dyke, standing stone, ring cairns and long house also survive forming relict landscapes dating from the Neolithic to the Medieval period. Surviving at trip-hop-able height amongst the heather they have been passed unnoticed by many walkers on the moors. They easily merge into the background and even when seen do not immediately have the appearance of archaeology to the untrained eye. In effect, the archaeology is little more than prosaic piles of stone with none of the obvious grandeur of Stonehenge, controversy of Seahenge, war scars of Battle or human stories of Hampton Court to create palpable interest. This did not prevent thousands of people from visiting the site during the excavations, whether to have a tour, participate in digging or make television news. In Britain and elsewhere, there is a strong interest in the past and in the discovery of lost places. How much this interest can be galvanised is not so much due to the grandeur of the remains but to how well the archaeologists, interpreters and site managers can, or are prepared, tell a good story based on the archaeology.

Act 1 – Life's a Stage
audience sees archaeologists at work

Look at them over there, what do you think they're doing in all that dirt?
Looks like they're archaeologists, like the ones on the telly.
Should know better at their age.

Since the project's inception the directors, John Barnatt, Mark Edmonds and myself, have had two fundamental and interrelated aims: to interpret prehistoric life in the area and to enable as wide a group of people as possible access to the archaeology. Our research aims and interim results from the field seasons are published elsewhere (Barnatt, Bevan and Edmonds 2001, in press), as are the results of previous surveys (Ainsworth and Barnatt 1998; Barnatt 1987; Beswick and Merrills 1983), so we will not re-present them here. Both the research and public aims are grounded in our definition of landscape archaeology – the study of how people live their lives in the world, inhabiting places and times, constructing understanding based on experience and social tradition (cf Bender 1993; Gosden 1994; Tilley 1994). By actively populating the landscape, this 'people-centred approach' is simultaneously able to address heavyweight issues and theories of social interpretation while making the past interesting and stimulating to those living in the present who are able to participate in giving their own interpretations. Many issues, such as individual perceptions of phenomena, or relationships between individual and community, easily cross-between social theory and public archaeology. People relate to people better than they do to abstract ideas of site catchment or the mundane piles of stones (cairns to you and me). So it seems somewhat surprising that so many archaeological students new to social theory are turned off it while preferring the pragmatic or environmentally deterministic. But that is more a matter of communication and minding your language………

Fig. 6.1. Aerial view of Gardom's Edge from the south. The perimeter of the Neolithic enclosure, at the centre of this view, is highlighted in solid line. Surrounding field systems and cairn fields are shaded. (Photo. Ray Manley, copyright PDNPA.)

We employed a variety of interpretative approaches and media to enable as wide a range of people from different backgrounds and with different archaeological knowledges to engage with the prehistoric landscape above Gardom's Edge. These included trench tours, lectures, museum displays, publications, landscape tours, flint-knapping and pot-firing demonstrations, schools discovery days, artists in residence, photographers, theatre groups, video, an interactive website, access for different special-needs groups and direct participation. Some are still ongoing, such as the website, displays and talks. These approaches are reviewed elsewhere (Bevan, Barnatt, Edmonds, Dymond and McElearney in press; Dymond 1998; Edmonds and McElearney 1998, 1999). Here, I will concentrate on the more theatrical side, darling, and the involvement of the *State of Flux* theatre group in educational visits and public open days.

Act 2 – Discovery
hunter enters stage left pursued by farmer

There is a movement in the bracken to one side, one child notices it and nudges his friends. As they look up another movement, a call, and a strangely dressed woman runs out of the cover chased by another, equally curiously attired. Some of the children look worried, others laugh. One even shouts 'Braveheart' at them but looks more sheepish as he realizes they are coming towards him, and coming fast. Then they are gone into the trees and none of the children dare follow.

In 1999 *State of Flux* were made integral to schools Discovery Days which were provided for primary schools

from Derbyshire and South Yorkshire (Dymond 1998). The Days aimed to provide a dynamic opportunity for both pupils and teachers to see archaeology at work (fig. 6.2), and to teach some of the skills of landscape archaeology and interpretation. These stress observation and identification of the surviving prehistoric and historic remains, and encourage pupils to make their own interpretations based on the available evidence. We emphasized the interpretative nature of archaeology and students were encouraged to discuss different options and the problems of interpretation (fig. 6.3). They were asked to make their own interpretations of features, based on the material evidence they could see, instead of passively receiving given facts from an authority figure. Sometimes pupils were asked to give their own interpretations while at others they were presented with different interpretations, and were asked which they believed to be the most likely explanation. We tried to show the difficulty and excitement inherent in establishing connections between the past and our present, how archaeologists construct an understanding of the past and to see the basis on which they do so. Pupils were also able to select the interpretation that they preferred and to develop their own interpretations so putting into practice the ideas of multiplicity of interpretation.

We also wanted students to be involved in that sense of discovery which is an important factor in archaeology. We tried to maintain the excitement of discovery while demonstrating that archaeology is more than simply finding things or a process of discovering facts waiting to be found in the soil. We wanted to show that interpretation is central to the writing of history and prehistory.

Fig. 6.2. One of the roundhouses under excavation with the door marked by
ranging poles and stakeholes by yellow flags. (Photo. Bill Bevan, copyright PDNPA.)

Fig. 6.3. Whiteways Primary School, Sheffield discussing the meaning
of rock art with Hoe the farmer. (Photo. Bill Bevan, copyright PDNPA.)

Each school party had a tour of archaeological features on the moor and of the trenches so that they could see at close-hand how archaeologists excavate and record an area, see the latest finds, ask the archaeologists questions and offer interpretations of what they could see. The tour was interspersed with a series of encounters with Prehistoric People, in the form of the theatre group.

The Days formed part of a class-based module in environmental studies for 7 to 12 year olds on prehistoric life, environmental change and archaeological investigation which was developed in partnership with the Derbyshire Educational Authority's Chesterfield Urban Studies Centre (Dymond 1998). As most archaeologists working in education are aware, the national curriculum omits anything prior to the Romans from history. So how are we meant to know what the Romans did for us if we're not told what life was like before? Environmental studies proved a successful route to take prehistory into the classroom. Each participating school was provided with a teaching pack of information, materials and activity ideas for teachers. Introductory sessions for both teachers and pupils were undertaken by Park Rangers and project archaeologists, led by the project-based educational archaeologist who also visited the schools. We tried to gain a balance in the schools who visited the Edge, including rural schools within the National Park, urban schools in nearby cities and special needs schools. We consciously invited some schools with a large ethnic mix to counter the argument that people of non-white British backgrounds are not interested in the archaeology/past/heritage of Britain. One Sheffield school comprised people with backgrounds in Yorkshire, the Yemen, Somalia, Pakistan and India. Neither ourselves nor the teachers could see any difference in participation or understanding by children of different ethnicities with the whole school being extremely interested. I am convinced this is because of our 'people-centred approach', and think that if we had taken a more traditional 'heritage of Britain' approach then many of the children would have been left disinterested because it can often present the past in a more nationalistic, even patriotic, way - lineages of kings, battles won or lost, great national achievements. These can be more difficult to identify with when your ancestors do not come from this nation.

Act 3 - Enactment
All three characters argue while gathered around the stones, centre stage, facing audience

There they are again, this time gathered around a large boulder deep in conversation. As the children approach they can hear them arguing, seemingly they are getting very excited about the stone itself. One (who calls herself Snare) claims it tells her where the deer can be found, another (known as Hoe) that she knows when to plant his crops by the stone, and the third (did he say his name was Brink?) that it aids him to navigate across this land

without upsetting others who live here all year. This, thinks one of the children, is absurd...obviously it looks like the wheels of a car so proceeds to tell this to the shabbily dressed adults. Then before you know it, the school party are telling the Neolithic people that its a waffle, a game, a bicycle...until a plane flies over and one of the children has to explain what a plane is and that it is not a 'funny bird'. They begin to exchange flint tools for sunglasses, pens though one class tries to swap one of their mates for all the land of these Neolithic people. Except that the teacher stops that.

Before the field season began the group worked with the site directors and the educational archaeologist to develop their roles and gain a grounding in archaeological theory and method to avoid common preconceptions or stereotyping of past societies. They adopted the roles of farmer, hunter-gather and thinker to animate different themes and interpretations of life in Prehistory. As the school groups toured prehistoric features surviving on the moorland Mike Dymond (the on-site educational archaeologist) encouraged them to make their own interpretations of what they could see (fig. 6.4). Between these stops, the children would come across the theatre group acting out a tableau on a theme related to the feature they had just visited or were about to visit (fig. 6.5). These, in language suitable for their age, included seasonal movement across the landscape, the social significance of boundaries, dissemination of ideas, the meaning of the rock art and different perceptions of landscape – including their contestation. They also encouraged the children to think about their lives and society today in comparison to prehistory, and to discuss whether there is one right way of living or many different ways which are equally valid. Each encounter was followed by a question and answer session where pupils were encouraged to explain what they had just seen or taken part in.

One such scene was an argument between the hunter and farmer characters over a fence (fig. 6.6). The hunter approached the farmer angrily, demanding the fence be removed because it prevented her from following traditional hunting routes and she believed that the land should be open to follow 'game'. The farmer argued that she needed the fences to keep her animals from getting lost and to define her land from her neighbours. The hunter conveyed ideas that she perceived the land in relation to where animals moved and congregated, to her movement across the landscape, and that the animals could not be owned by anyone. The scene ended with the hunter kicking over the fence. The educational archaeologist then got the children to answer questions about what they had seen. This dramatically animated how the linear piles of stone were boundaries which had been part of a social landscape in prehistory different meanings to different people.

The day ended with a procession into the Neolithic enclosure. The school parties were divided into three

Fig. 6.4. Mike Dymond holds a question and answer session about a clearance cairn. (Photo. Bill Bevan, copyright PDNPA.)

Fig. 6.5. State of Flux discuss the benefits of new-fangled bronze. (Photo. Bill Bevan, copyright PDNPA.)

Fig. 6.6. Hoe the farmer and Snare the hunter argue over one of Hoe's new fences.
(Photo. Bill Bevan, copyright PDNPA.)

groups to be rotated between different activities; drawing rock art, archaeological planning using a planning frame and learning a song (fig. 6.7). Each of the three Neolithic characters led the singing with a different group and taught a verse related to their character with a chorus common to all. After the three groups had participated in each activity they gathered outside of the enclosure and lined up in their groups behind their Neolithic character. They then simultaneously set away to process towards the enclosure while singing their song. Each group entered the enclosure via one of the original entrances and once inside they came together again to form a circle in a small clearing amongst the boulder field. Here each group took a turn to sing their verse to the others then finished by singing the chorus together. This was again followed by a question and answer session with the educational archaeologist which covered the themes of communal gatherings and ceremonies, and why they would take place within enclosures. With the visit complete, the pupils left the excavations being very animated, often glancing back to look at the Neolithic actors before they were lost to sight.

Act 4 – Unusual Suspects
Audience participation led by the hunter
Lucy, aged 7³/₄, did not like Snare the Hunter, who talked about killing and skinning deer with those sharp stones and spears. She tried to reason with Snare, explained

why killing animals was wrong and when the Hunter said you can not live off plants alone, she was able to remember most of the reasons why you can. She even tried siding with Hoe, until she found out that the farmer kept cattle and sheep to eat.

The key to all of this was not to turn the children into a passive audience and present them with a single answer, nor to state that an interpretation was inherently wrong. Instead we encouraged the children to actively give their own interpretations to explore the difficulty and excitement inherent in establishing connections between the past and our present. At certain places pupils were asked to give their own interpretations and at others they were presented with different interpretations, each using the same evidence which lay in front of the pupils, and they were asked which they believed to be the most likely explanation. This exercise allowed pupils to see how archaeologists construct an understanding of the past and to see the basis on which they do so. It also empowered them to select the interpretation that they preferred and to develop their own interpretations so putting into practice the ideas of multiplicity of interpretation.

This is more than just about giving pupils lots of information with which to tell stories. Individually the children bring different perceptions, experiences and understandings of the world to these activities which inform their interpretations in the question and answer

Fig. 6.7. A school group learn the song of one of the Neolithic characters, effectively summarising Mark Edmonds' Ancestral Geographies of the Neolithic *into 3 verses and a chorus. (Photo. Bill Bevan, copyright PDNPA.)*

sessions or their interactions with the Neolithic characters. Social roles and individual identity are very fluid and dynamic during childhood. The Discovery Days provided a very stimulating, and unusual, arena for these to be played out amongst the pupils. Hence Lucy explicitly brought an important element of her identity to the day by discussing vegetarianism, which was not just directed at Snare but also to her classmates. Similarly this informed the pupils' interpretations of the rock art and the explanations they gave to the theatre group about modern objects.

Act 5 – Adult Oriented Rock
titter ye not
Aaaah, look young ones here we have strangers come to visit, they look like elders of their community – good day to you.

The theatre group also interacted with adult visitors, either casually as these visitors came across the group working with the school parties or more formally as part of open days. The moorland is open access land and attracts many ramblers who came across the excavations by chance as well as people who were specifically visiting the project. The response of adults was generally very positive, though some tended to be more inhibited when interacting with the actors.

During the open days the theatre group would host their own activities, short scenes based on those they developed for the schools Discovery Days. They also intermingled with visitors generally as the visitors crossed between trenches or watched demonstrations such as flint knapping or pot-firing. This overcame the reticence that many adults otherwise had when engaging with the theatre group. It helped to break down barriers between visitors and 'demonstrators', and helped to reduce the passive object:subject relationship of these demonstrations. The slightly irreverential side and added fluidity made the demonstrations less formal. Often in demonstration situations both parties are waiting for the other to initiate conversation. With the theatre group a third element was introduced, with which visitors and demonstrators could interact and identify. The theatre group enabled people to feel they could ask questions of the demonstrators, and in some cases encouraged the demonstrators to be more vocal about what they were producing without waiting to be asked by a visitor.

Epilogue
Curtains close, lights dim and the audience departs
Hoe: That was a tiring one today.
Brink: Yeah, but largely because of how good a bunch they were.

Snare: They're usually more tiring the more interested they are.
Hoe: Or argumentative. They loved the fight scene, did you see those boys really getting into taking sides?
Snare: But I banged my foot on that flaming fence of yours. I thought you weren't going to stick it so hard into the ground today.
Brink: Ah, we all must suffer for our art.
Hoe and Snare: Oh SHUT UP!

Much of what the theatre group did on Gardom's Edge was interactive improvised promenade theatre rather than living history days. This approach to educational or public archaeology is very dynamic. It goes beyond having a costumed figure to explain the past to school parties about the past by encouraging students to interact with them. This does require the on-site interpreter to dispense with the need to be an authoritarian figure distributing solemn facts and truths: rather, they need to be a facilitator who guides the subjects and themes to be explored without aiming to get the students to accept a right answer. This turns students from passive and potentially bored observers, who may in the end only regurgitate what they have been spoon-fed, into excited participants with their own evidence-grounded opinions and interpretations.

The imaginations of the school parties are more stimulated when they participate in interpreting the past. The school parties are therefore much more actively involved than in those situations where children visit a site to passively receive information solely from lectures or tour guides. Many issues, such as individual perceptions and interpretations of features, and relationships between individual and community, cross-over because there is lots to identify with in the people-centred approach of social theory when stripped of its jargon. Children from different backgrounds, and with varying abilities engaged with the Gardom's Edge prehistoric landscape. Those otherwise potentially mundane piles of stones, at least to the eyes of your average school child, were animated into life.

Acknowledgements

Thanks first and foremost to the members of the State Of Flux Theatre Group – Amanda (Hoe), Mickey (Snare 1), Saffron (Brink 1/Snare 2) and Jonty (Brink 2) – who developed the programme in conjunction with Mike Dymond and the site directors with great enthusiasm and understanding, and worked tirelessly with the school parties during the Discovery Days. Mike Dymond, Gavin Bell, Keith Clarkson, Jane Featherstone of the Chesterfield Urban Studies Unit, Mark Simmons and Caryl Hart were instrumental in developing and conducting the schools project. The Peak District National Park Authority and the Department of Archaeology & Prehistory, University of Sheffield backed the project. The Estates, Information and Rangers Services of the Park provided logistics and support throughout. John Barnatt and Angela Piccini made valuable comments on this paper.

References

Ainsworth, S. & Barnatt, J., 1998. A scarp edge enclosure at Gardom's Edge, Baslow, Derbyshire. *Derbyshire Archaeological Journal*, 118, 5-23.

Barnatt, J., 1987. Bronze Age settlement on the gritstone east moors of the Peak district, Derbyshire. *Proceedings of the Prehistoric Society*, **53**, 393-418.

Barnatt, J., Bevan, B. and Edmonds, M., 2001. A Time and a Place for Enclosure. In Darvill T. & Thomas, J. (eds.). *Neolithic Enclosures in Northwest Europe*. Oxford: Oxbow/Neolithic Studies Group. 111-131.

Barnatt, J, Bevan, B. & Edmonds, M. (in press). Gardom's Edge: a landscape through time. *Antiquity*.

Bender, B. (ed.), 1993. *Landscape: politics and perspectives*. Oxford: Berg.

Beswick, P. & Merrills, D., 1983. L. H. Butcher's survey of early settlements and fields in the southern Pennines. *Transactions of the Hunter Archaeological Society*, **12**, 16-50.

Bevan, B., Barnatt, J., Dymond, M., Edmonds, M. & McElearney, G. (in press). Public Prehistories: engaging archaeology on Gardom's Edge, Derbyshire. In Henson, D., Stone, P., & Corbishley, M. (eds.), *Education and the Historic Environment*. London: Routledge.

Dymond, M., 1998. Not Just a Day Out! Archaeology and Education on the Gardom's Edge Project. *Assemblage*, http://www.shef.ac.uk/~assem/4/

Edmonds, M. & McElearney, G., 1998. Web Sites and Public Access at Gardom's Edge. *Assemblage*, http://www.shef.ac.uk/~assem/4/

Edmonds, M. & McElearney, G., 1999 Inhabitation and Access: landscape and the internet on Gardom's Edge. *Internet Archaeology*, http://intarch.ac.uk/journal/issue6/edmonds_toc.html

Gosden, C., 1994. *Social Being and Time*. Oxford: Blackwell.

Tilley, C., 1994. *A Phenomenology of Landscape: paths, places and monuments*. Oxford: Berg.

7

Changing interpretations.
Public access and interpretation on a developer-funded excavation at Braehead, Glasgow.

Ronan Toolis and Clare Ellis

Introduction

In the summer of 2001, AOC Archaeology Group carried out the total excavation of a rare survival of an Iron Age settlement within the City of Glasgow at Braehead. An interpretation package designed to make the process and results of the excavation accessible to the public was implemented in tandem with the excavation. Although the site was not one of the most visually appealing or intelligible of archaeological monuments, a considerable investment of imagination and effort in presenting the site to a wide range of audiences paid off with large numbers of repeat visits and overwhelmingly positive feedback from visitors.

The site was a plough-truncated, ditched and palisaded enclosure, some 4800 m^2 in extent, located on the floodplain of the river Clyde. It comprised three concentric oval ditches with the entrance to the interior located on the eastern side (fig. 7.1). Numerous bedding trenches for a series of palisades lay within the interior and over the backfilled inner ditch. Palisades had also been used to narrow and redefine the entrance. Excavation revealed six probable roundhouses, although two of the structures may not have functioned as dwellings. The interior contained evidence of other severely plough-truncated structures. The artefact assemblage was small, but characteristic of prehistoric, west coast Scottish sites. It included coarse local pottery, an interesting assemblage of coal bracelet rough-outs, rubber-stones and hammer-stones and a few lithics.

The archaeological site was located on the edge of the Braehead Shopping Centre, in an area targeted for expansion of the retail facilities of the Centre. West of Scotland Archaeology Service were the archaeological advisers to the planning authority. The full archaeological excavation of the enclosure was a commercial venture, subject to planning permission. The planning permission required an element of public participation, which AOC Archaeology's client, Capital Shopping Centres, was enthusiastic to embrace and support, given the careful design of the public participation package to promote a positive public image.

Public interpretation was a key feature of the Braehead excavation from the outset. The purpose of our interpretation package as a whole was to provoke in the visitor a desire to search for a better understanding of the Braehead Enclosure. To achieve this we created an exhibition, a web site, a schools resource pack and a competition. Guided tours provided free and accessible interpretation for anyone wishing to visit the site. The working week was modified so that the excavation was open throughout the weekend to maximise opportunities for people to visit the site while it was being excavated. However, schools and local archaeological societies could book guided visits to the site during the week. Public participation in the excavation was also actively encouraged (fig. 7.2).

The on-site exhibition

The initial access point of our interpretation package was an on-site exhibition, open to the public every weekend during the 10-week duration of the excavation. The exhibition itself was composed of six exhibition panels, comprising three designed specifically for the Braehead excavation and three that addressed general topics relating to the archaeological background of the Braehead Enclosure.

At Braehead, the panels were displayed within a large portacabin located at the edge of the site. The panels introduced the public to what we perceived as the story of the site through interpretative, not decorative, images, photographs and maps, which we hoped would *provoke* interest in, enable visitors to *relate* to and *reveal* the essential thrust of our archaeological excavation.

Since less than 1% of visitors might actually read all the exhibit copy (Veverka, 1994, 135), we did not design the panels in a way that demanded that everyone read all the text before understanding the subject. Instead we separated the text into two parts, 'headlines', or primary information, followed by 'explanations', or secondary information. The primary information was composed of a series of points, which formed the bones of the subject. These headlines were carefully planned so that readers might grasp several key points about the subject of each

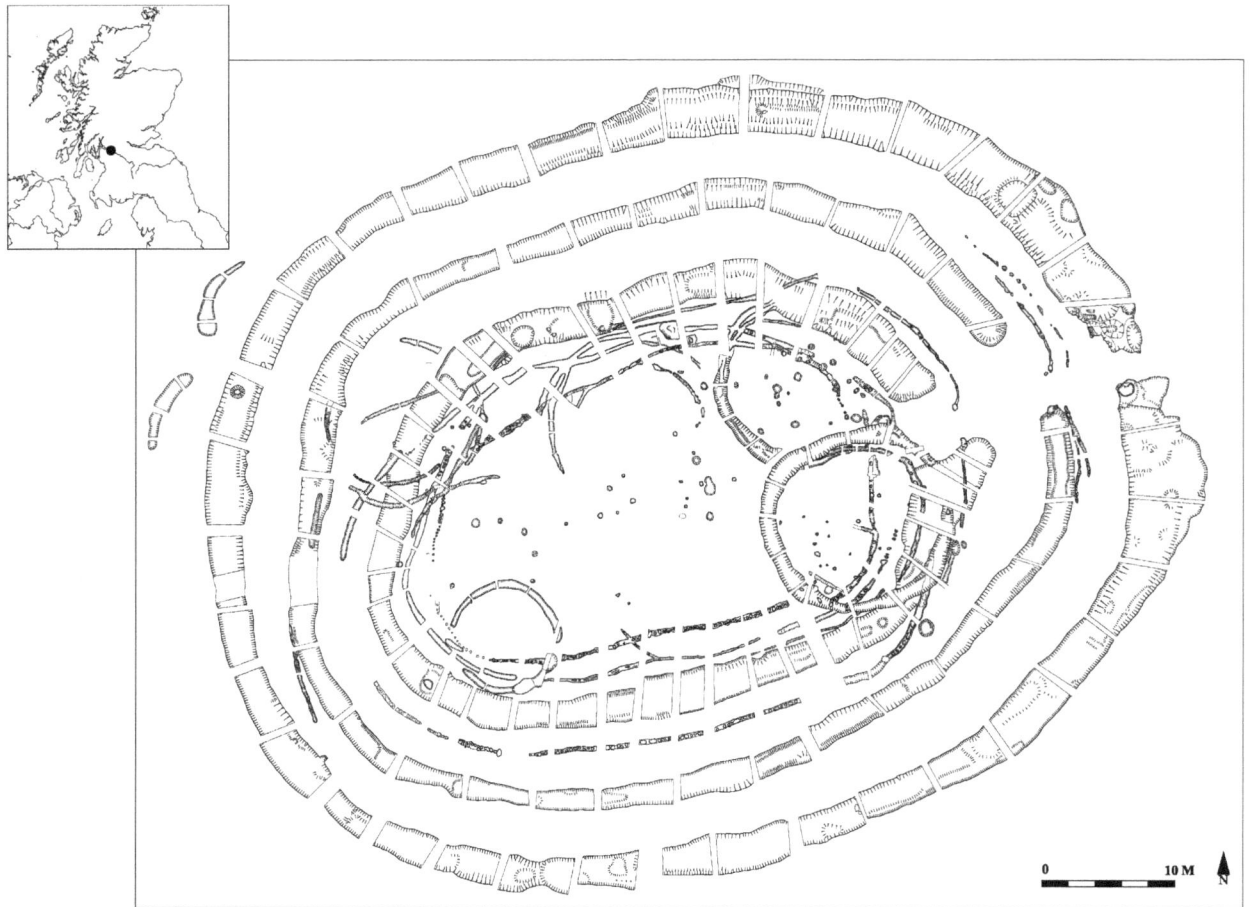

Fig. 7.1. Excavation Plan of the Braehead Enclosure

Fig. 7.2. Aerial Photograph of the Braehead Enclosure under excavation. This photograph was taken from a model aeroplane operated by volunteer Mr Bill Kerr, seen standing to the right of the viewing platform.

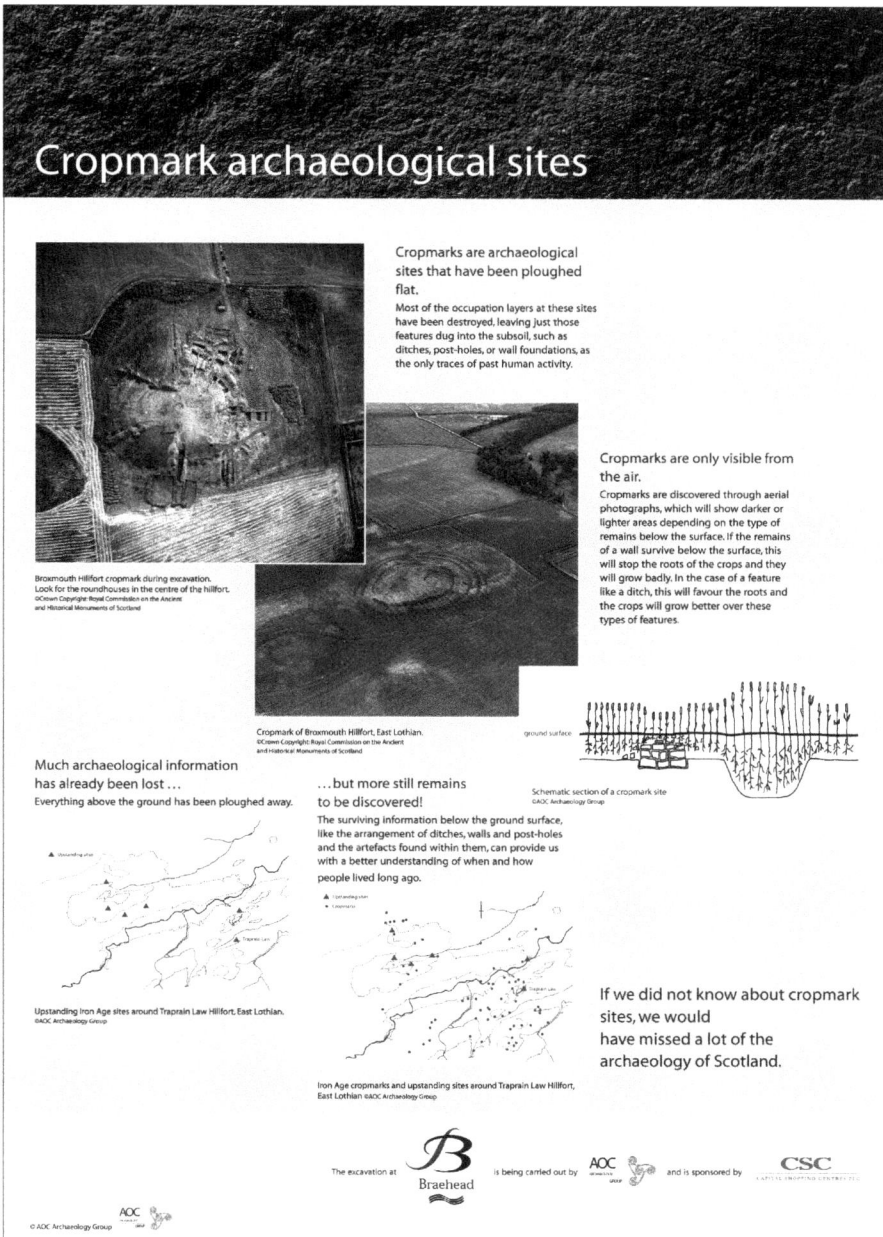

Fig. 7.3. Braehead Exhibition Panel.

those who did want to find out more about specific points could do so.

When designing the panels, we agreed a clear learning objective for each one. Each objective comprised a limited amount of information that visitors could take away from the exhibition. The principal objective of the panel illustrated in fig. 7.4, for instance, was to help visitors understand what was going on at the excavation during the subsequent guided tour. By demystifying the archaeological process of excavating and making it 'open, accessible and reinterpretable rather than closed and known' (Parker Pearson, 1993, 230), we hoped to make the whole experience more interesting for visitors.

By illustrating the importance of recording contexts one learning objective of the panel, illustrated in fig. 7.4, was to explain how archaeologists might build up an understanding of an archaeological site through excavating it. By illustrating what visitors may see archaeologists *doing* on site we wanted to enable them to understand the *point* of doing those things. Equally valuable was the emotional objective of the panel, to provoke a level of anticipation before leaving the exhibition area for the site tour, which might then provoke more curiosity amongst visitors when actually viewing the excavation.

panel simply by skimming the panel. These key points might be termed the essence of each subject, as exemplified by the headlines for the 'Cropmark archaeological sites' panel (fig. 7.3).

However, we hoped that the headlines would provoke visitors into reading the passages of secondary information, placed beneath each headline and composed of more thorough explanations for the headline statements. Although we didn't expect many people to read all of these, it was important to include a more detailed level of information than the headlines so that

The panels, by themselves, might have enlightened visitors to a limited extent as to why and how we were excavating at Braehead but they were not planned as a discrete stand-alone exhibition. Rather, the exhibition panels were designed to introduce visitors to some of the fundamental aspects of archaeological procedures and the background to this particular excavation and provoke questions in their minds, questions that they could ask the archaeological guides during the subsequent tour of the excavation.

A camera link from the site to a television within the exhibition also allowed visitors to see the excavation under progress before commencing the guided tour. It

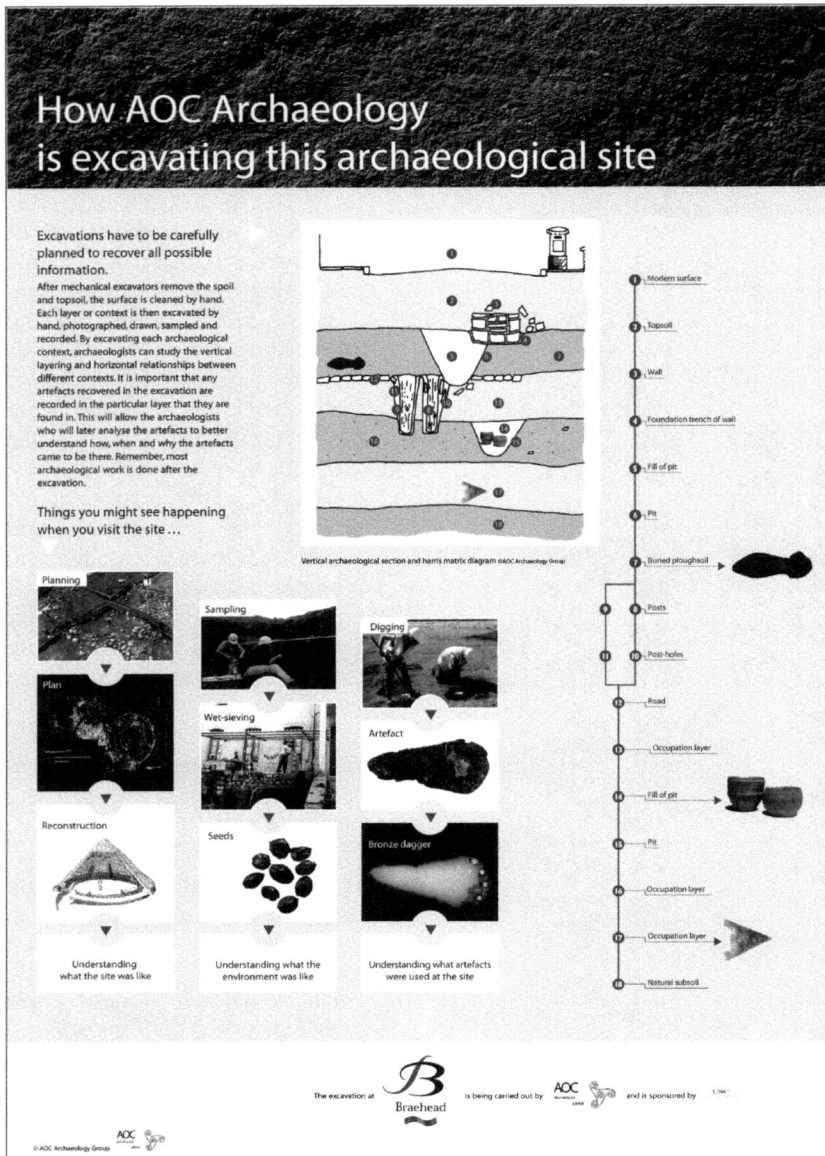

How AOC Archaeology is excavating this archaeological site

Fig. 7.4. Braehead Exhibition panel.

was hoped that this would provoke anticipation and emphasise the fact that the excavation was the process by which our understanding of the site was changing. As new finds and information affecting our interpretation of the site were revealed during the excavation the archaeological guides updated a 'news board' within the exhibition and the web site. This provided the interactive element of the exhibition and allowed the visitor to trace the progress from initial assumptions about the site to new interpretations as the excavation proceeded. For instance, they were able to see the evidence as it emerged that demonstrated that two of the three proposed reconstruction illustrations of the enclosure displayed at the exhibition were wrong.

The news board also addressed the problem of presenting interpretation of a site before its excavation is complete.

Relatively fundamental information, such as dating evidence for instance, had not yet been recovered let alone analysed. We decided to use this to our advantage in trying to make our exhibition slightly more interactive. Passive, 'flatwork' exhibition panels are recognised as perhaps not the most intrinsically interesting or effective means of interpreting a site to the public (Ververka, 1994, 129; Lee Davis, 1997, 94). By encouraging visitors, particularly visiting school groups, to guess the date of the site and enter our competition for prizes donated by various heritage groups, such as the National Trust for Scotland, the National Museums of Scotland and Historic Scotland, we hoped to provoke them into actively interpreting the information from the site themselves. For if people remember 90% of what they *do* as opposed to only 30% of what they read and 50% of what they see (Ververka, 1994, 25), an exhibition that *engages* will make a more effective impact on visitors' perception of a site.

Perhaps the key concept underpinning the Braehead interpretation package was the way in which our understanding of this archaeological site might change and evolve *during* the excavation. This was not only important for demonstrating to the public and our clients what excavations actually achieve but necessary for avoiding the recognised pitfall of 'over' interpreting, of leaving nothing to the imagination (Goulding, 1999, 65). It has sometimes been a criticism of the presentation and teaching of the past that it does not show 'that history and the way we interpret it is not carved in granite...and that the study of history is always unfinished' (Lowenthal, 1998, 117). The potential to change our interpretation of the past was an integral part of the structure of the interpretation package we produced for Braehead and particularly so for the schools resource pack. The point of interpretation is to encourage people to think for themselves (Parker Pearson, 1993, 227). The significant number of visitors who regularly revisited the excavation is an indication of the success of the theme of a constantly changing understanding of the site.

Guided tours

A vital element of our interpretation package was that professional archaeologists were permanently on hand, when the site was open to the public, to respond to questions raised by the exhibition and who took visitors on guided tours of the excavation. This was considered vital because our experience is that an enthusiastic and knowledgeable guide is probably the most effective and flexible medium for conveying interest and excitement, and a sense of meaning to the public. Effective guides were especially required at Braehead, where the plough truncation had rendered the site almost invisible to the uninitiated lay person. In the interests of health and safety, the guided tours were not actually taken into the site, however, but to a raised viewing platform at the edge of the excavation (see fig. 7.2). As the site was flat, it was essential that visitors could view the site from a height to enable them to see the activity and what was being revealed of the monument. From this vantage point the guides could point to specific areas of the site and explain what was being carried out there by the archaeological team. The activities on view from the vantage point included both excavation and post-excavation tasks, as we had established a marquee at the edge of the site where the sieving and sorting of palaeoenvironmental samples could be carried out. This allowed the guides to introduce their audience to the concept of post-excavation analyses.

Public participation

Public participation formed an important part of the interpretation package. From the outset of the excavation,

a large rota of volunteers from the Renfrewshire Local History Forum and Glasgow Archaeological Societies joined the team and under supervision undertook excavation alongside the professional archaeologists. The volunteers were joined by others who had learned of the excavation through the Braehead Enclosure web site and word of mouth. While only a self-selected portion of the visiting public participated in this manner, it nevertheless engaged them in an active role in uncovering and interpreting their own heritage.

Publicity

In total over 1,000 people visited the exhibition and excavation, many of these repeat visits. The vast majority of visitors (96%) came from the local area (Glasgow, Renfrewshire and elsewhere on the West Coast of Scotland). The feedback from individuals, on the presentation and content of the exhibition and guided tour, was overwhelmingly positive. The origin of most visitors reflected the concentration of publicity in local media. The publicity package comprised press releases, leaflets and posters provided by AOC Archaeology but co-ordinated and distributed by our client, Braehead Shopping Centre. While the posters and leaflets (fig. 7.5) were distributed solely throughout the local area, press coverage of the excavation did occasionally reach national media too.

Fig. 7.5. Braehead Excavation Publicity Leaflet.

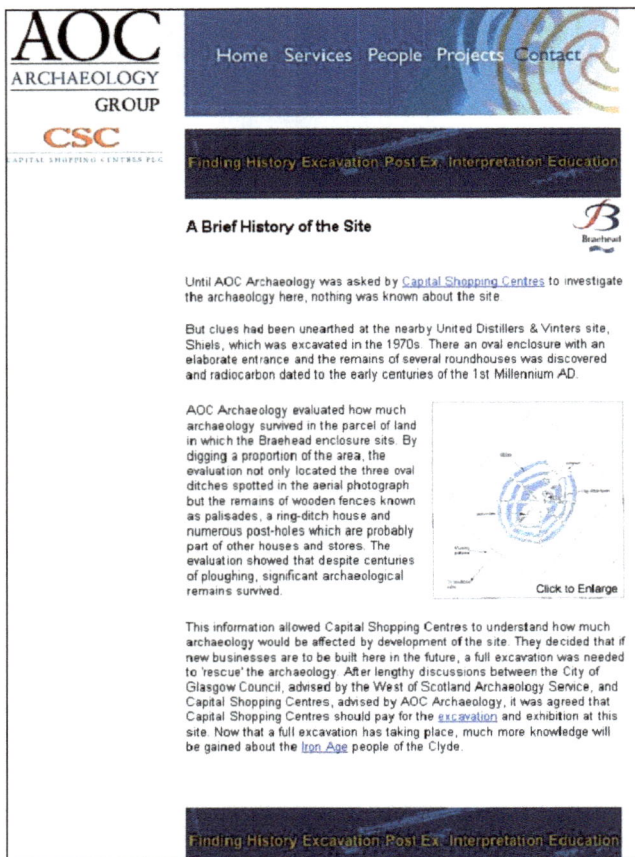

Fig. 7.6. Braehead Excavation Web Site.

The web site

Over six times the number of people who physically visited the site visited the web site over the duration of the excavation. Even after the excavation had been completed the web site continued to receive over 1,000 hits a month. This has provided the impetus to regularly maintain and update the web site with information from the post-excavation process like the overall site plan and a summary of the results to date, together with a guide to the techniques used.

Designed in co-ordination with our on-site exhibition and linked to the web sites of AOC Archaeology and our client, Braehead Shopping Centre, the Braehead Enclosure web site (fig. 7.6) promoted the exhibition and excavation to a potentially much wider section of the public than perhaps would have been reached by the more conventional means of posters and leaflets. It also allowed more people to 'visit' the excavation. The web site also formed a flexible and cost effective medium of interpretation because it could be and was regularly updated with new finds and information. In this way visitors to the site could 'return' to the site time and again to view the progress of the excavation and learn about what was being discovered during the post-excavation analysis of finds from the site.

The School Resource Pack

Within days of the launch of the Braehead web site, various schools booked several hundred children to visit the excavation after downloading the schools resource pack. This had been designed specifically for the Braehead excavation, in consultation with the Council for Scottish Archaeology. The Braehead School Resource Pack was available for any school or Young Archaeologist Club to download from our web site free of charge. The structure of the resource pack (fig. 7.7) followed 5-14 curriculum guidelines (Scottish Office Education Dept, 1993, 34-35; Scottish Executive, 2000, 11) and used previous archaeology and education projects as exemplars (e.g. Dreghorn, 1996, 15). The Braehead School Resource Pack comprised several activities that provided opportunities for pupils:

- to look for and *record* evidence of a site
- to *interpret* the evidence based on observations
- to *present* and *evaluate* interpretation

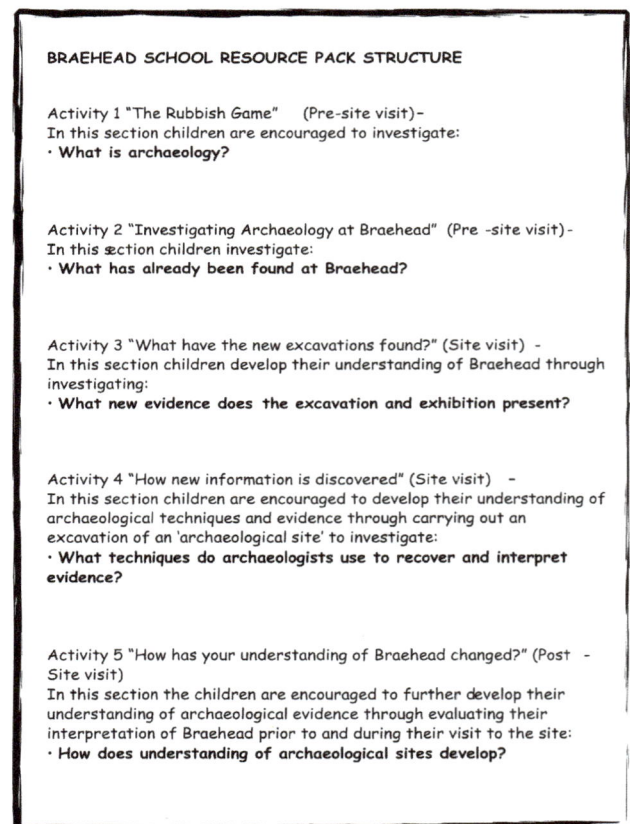

Fig. 7.7. The Braehead School Resource Pack Structure.

These activities enabled schoolchildren to build *knowledge & understanding* and *develop informed attitudes* through visiting both the exhibition and the excavation. The emphasis of the resource pack was in guiding, provoking and enabling school children to research the site and re-interpret the site using their own observations. In addition to the information handouts available from the Braehead School Resource Pack, the visit to the exhibition and the guided tour of the excavation, the school children also carried out a mock excavation of their own (Activity 4, fig. 7.7). This was done in an 'archaeologically sterile' area of the site that had been carefully constructed into archaeological zones. Various artefacts had been planted within this area and a photographic catalogue of these artefacts, from AOC Archaeology's own teaching collection, enabled the children to record and interpret what they had found. This exercise enabled the children to develop a better understanding of how archaeological evidence is collected and interpreted and was a crucial element of the resource pack because it enabled them to better evaluate both their own and our interpretations of the site.

Conclusions

Apart from the occasional evening lecture given to a local heritage society and perhaps an open day, it is relatively rare that the results of commercial archaeology are disseminated in an effective way to local people in Scotland. There is currently a trend for projects that receive public money to include some form of public access. Often this is in response to a condition from grant sources such as the Heritage Lottery Fund and it has still to trickle down in a meaningful way to developer funded archaeology. However, local planning authorities are beginning to look for more public benefit in return for planning consent for the development of sites where there is perceived to be some form of public loss. At Braehead, public interpretation was an integral part of the negotiated mitigation measures that formed part of the planning conditions for the site laid down by the West of Scotland Archaeology Service, in consultation with Historic Scotland. As an example of a commercial excavation that incorporates accessible interpretation Braehead represents an all too rare opportunity for a wide cross-section of the local community to experience aspects of their local archaeology as it is being 'discovered'. It is, perhaps, an example of the type of opportunity that can be created through a combination of curatorial and developer support.

The blueprint of the interpretation package prepared for Braehead is capable of being developed in the future for other developer-funded excavations and part of AOC Archaeology's corporate policy is to maximise public gain wherever it is appropriate and feasible. Where public access is not possible to a site, due to health and safety concerns for instance, as at another large excavation we carried out at Kintore, Aberdeenshire, we negotiated with our clients a contract to present our excavation results at a specially built facility once the housing development was complete. And following our programme of building recording at Patons Mill, Alloa, we prepared material for a publicly accessible resource pack for the local museum.

It seems only right, when there is so much interest in archaeology amongst the public, that a commercial archaeology unit makes more effort to make archaeology accessible to the public. Encouraging public interest in local archaeology can only strengthen the protection of archaeology by local authority archaeologists. But this practice is difficult to maintain, under the pressure of cut-price commercial archaeology, without the support of local authority archaeologists and organisations like the IFA, Historic Scotland, English Heritage and CADW. It is, therefore, perhaps worth stressing that the public participation package for Braehead only cost 8% of the project value. As has been pointed out before (Parker Pearson, 1993, 225), perhaps it is time that public interpretation is included more often in the archaeological briefs provided by curatorial archaeologists for developer-funded archaeology projects.

However, this comes with a price tag for the developer and one that fully merits the inclusion of 'public archaeology' costs in the planning gain package for the site. Planning gain is precisely the context into which we should slot programmed public presentation of archaeological information for local and wider social education. As a social act, it merits social support. Councils jealously hoard the funds, services and infrastructural developments usually considered legitimate spoils of planning gain. In comparison with these costs, the cost of public archaeology is trifling. Can we hope that local authority archaeologists, supported by bodies like Historic Scotland, English Heritage, CADW and the IFA, apply pressure in the future in this direction?

References

Dreghorn, P., 1996. Education in the Middle of Nowhere. In Curtis E. & N. (eds.), *Touching the Past Archaeology 5-14*. Edinburgh: Scottish Children's Press. 5-16.

Goulding, C., 1999. Interpretation and Presentation. In Leask, A. & Yeoman, I. (eds), *Heritage Visitor Attractions*. London: Cassell. 54-67.

Lee Davis, K., 1997. Sites Without Sights: Interpreting Closed Excavations. In Jameson, J.H. (ed), *Presenting Archaeology to the Public*. Walnut Creek, California: AltaMira Press. 84-98.

Lowenthal, D., 1998. *The Heritage Crusade and the Spoils of History*. Cambridge: Cambridge University Press.

Parker Pearson, M., 1993. Visitors Welcome. In Hunter, J. & Ralston, I. (eds), *Archaeological Resource Management in the UK*. Stroud: Alan Sutton Publishing Ltd. 225-231.

Scottish Executive, 2000. *Environmental Studies: Society, Science and Technology 5-14 National Guidelines*. Dundee: Learning and Teaching Scotland 2000.

Scottish Office Education Dept., 1993. *Environmental Studies 5-14.* Edinburgh: Scottish Office Education Dept.

Veverka, J., 1994. *Interpretive Master Planning.* Tustin, California: Acorn Naturalists.

8

'Valley of the First Iron Masters'.
A case study in inclusion and interpretation.

Peter Halkon

Introduction

Recent pronouncements concerning widening participation in the historic environment (English Heritage, 2000), the current debate about Article 3 of the Valetta Convention (e.g. Selkirk 2001) and the role of volunteers in archaeology, provide an appropriate background for this article. Without the inclusion of several hundred enthusiastic volunteers the project outlined here would not have been possible. Since 1980, we have examined a landscape block in lowland East Yorkshire, extending northwards from the River Humber to the Yorkshire Wolds. Due to the discovery of one of the largest prehistoric iron industries in Britain associated with the River Foulness, we have called this the 'Valley of the First Iron Masters'. The origins of our investigation and my own interest in archaeology however, go back somewhat further, to my own upbringing at Hasholme Hall, Holme on Spalding Moor, where my father farmed. It was here, encouraged by my parents and friendly neighbours, that I picked up Roman pottery sherds and helped in the excavation of a pottery kiln by the East Riding Archaeological Society (henceforth ERAS) as a schoolboy (Hicks and Wilson 1975). It was near this same spot that Martin Millett and myself were to recognise and excavate the Hasholme Iron Age log boat (Millett and McGrail, 1987). I hope I can be forgiven this autobiographical vignette as it highlights the importance of early encouragement and inclusion. A number of archaeologists of my acquaintance were similarly inspired - a few minutes spent identifying a small piece of pottery for a child or other member of the public may sow beneficial seeds and create a lifelong interest.

On my return to this region after gaining a degree in Ancient and Medieval History and Archaeology, and securing a teaching post at a school in Hull, I rejoined ERAS, where Peter Armstrong, an archaeologist of the former Humberside County Council encouraged members to aid in SMR enhancement. I chose to explore my former home area and fieldwork, carried out with ERAS members, was focussed initially along the River Foulness, especially at Bursea and Hasholme. We were lucky in securing the services of Jim Pocock of Bradford University who carried out geophysical survey at several locations. Prehistoric and Roman activity was found to be more intensive here than expected (Halkon 1983). An opportunity to take the project further was provided in

1983 when I was introduced to Martin Millett, a newly appointed Archaeology lecturer at Durham University, eager to research Roman impact on a relatively little known archaeological area and provide field opportunities for students. Thus began our ongoing collaboration. It is not the intention here to provide a full account of the archaeological results of this work, which appears elsewhere, but to highlight the contribution that volunteers can make to such an enterprise and outline our attempts to interpret our findings to a wider audience. As a background to this, however, it is necessary to provide a brief outline of the project.

Outline of the project

Phase one

An 8x8km block was selected around Holme-on-Spalding Moor with a view to fieldwalking a representative sample of each square kilometre based on around 55 farms. This was undertaken by ERAS volunteers, evening class groups and children from local schools. Sites were then selected for research/training excavation. Volunteers of all ages and backgrounds were, and still are, welcomed. Some have substantial theoretical knowledge and wish to improve practical skills. Others, through participation in field work, have become so motivated that they have gone on to take extra-mural and indeed full-time archaeology courses.

First phase discoveries included over 130 scatters and concentrations of Roman material presumed to be foci of settlement and industry, 30 pottery kiln sites and an extensive Iron Age iron industry. At Moore's Farm, Welhambridge, we excavated one of the largest prehistoric iron slag-heaps in Britain, dating from c 300BC (Halkon 1997; Halkon and Millett 1999). Our most spectacular discovery was the 12 metre long Hasholme log boat, with a felling date of c.300 BC, which had sunk in a creek of a former tidal inlet (Millett and McGrail 1987). All this was tied in with a programme of aerial survey, study of soil maps and palaeo-environmental investigation, which provided a landscape context for archaeological discoveries. Ours was first project in the region to do this in such detail. The work around Holme-on-Spalding Moor was runner-up in the Pitt-Rivers Award of the 1988 British

Archaeological Awards for the best work done by a voluntary group or individual.

Phase two

Activities of metal detectorists had been noted for some time on the line of the main Roman road between York (Eboracum) and Brough on Humber (Petuaria) at Shiptonthorpe, where it crosses one of the watercourses associated with the River Foulness. Reporting of a bronze bowl to the writer led to the detailed investigation of Roman roadside settlement. A full report on this phase is in final stages of preparation (Millett forthcoming). Fieldwalking, again largely carried out by ERAS volunteers, was combined with soil chemistry and geophysical surveys (Taylor 1995) the latter revealing the clear plan of the road flanked by a series of plots used for housing, stock and a cemetery. During the following programme of research excavation (1985-91), a section was cut across the Roman road and a complete plot next to it was excavated. This was found to contain a sequence of timber buildings and a waterhole, the latter containing evidence for structured deposition including well-preserved shoes, animal bones and pieces of wooden writing tablet.

Phase Three

In this ongoing phase we are investigating 3x3 km around Hayton, further west along the Roman road and close to becks, which form part of the Foulness valley drainage system. A Roman fort was photographed here by St Joseph in 1974, which was subsequently excavated (Johnson 1978). Sporadic investigation was done in the early 1980s by the writer who did some fieldwalking around the fort. Metal detector users also frequently visited Hayton (McLinden 1990) and Bryan Sitch of Hull Museum followed up some of their discoveries. Our involvement resumed in 1993, when a local farmer showed me hypocaust tiles which had been brought to the surface by deep ploughing in preparation for planting potatoes. Subsequent gridded fieldwalking by a local evening class group located a Roman building which was shown by geophysical survey to overlie a settlement consisting of a 'ladder' of ditches on a gravel ridge parallel to Hayton Beck. The series of training/research excavations (1995-2001) was undertaken by students from Durham, Southampton, Leeds and Hull universities, overseas students and large numbers of volunteers from ERAS and the local community (fig. 8.1). Sixth Formers, several of whom are now undertaking post-graduate Degrees in archaeology, participated as part of a bursary

Fig. 8.1. Excavations at Hayton 2000. Community archaeology in action.

scheme. In 1999 we were greatly helped by BP, who as their Teeside to Saltend Ethylene pipeline cut through our site, funded that season's excavation as a community archaeology programme. During these excavations, which were integrated with programs of field walking and geophysical survey, we revealed a settlement sequence including Iron Age roundhouses and Roman timber buildings, which were in turn replaced by a range of stone buildings. Discoveries included burials of humans and animals, a well lined with 28 oak timbers, whose backfill included painted wall plaster and a unique piece of decorated Roman furniture (Halkon *et al* 2000; Halkon, Millett and Taylor 1997).

Further fieldwalking and geophysical survey was targeted on an extensive Roman roadside settlement and watching briefs were carried out here during the construction of turkey sheds and the digging of various service trenches to them.

Inclusion

From the above it can be seen that volunteers of all ages and varied experience have been integral to the project. At Hayton, as well as pot-washing and finds sorting, small numbers of closely supervised children have excavated features, drawn sections and recorded levels with an EDM (fig. 8.2). At Holme-on-Spalding Moor, children from the County Primary school there have undertaken fieldwalking and subsequent analysis of finds, which was incorporated into a local study as part of the KS2 National Curriculum (figs. 8.3, 8.4). Full and part-time university students have written projects and dissertations based on excavation and field walking or fulfilled their course requirement for excavation experience. One member of a Certificate in Archaeology course at Hull wrote a GIS based computer program to plot field walking data from gridded surveys. MA in Archaeological Survey students undertook geophysical and geochemical prospection. The many students from urban backgrounds who have participated in our project will have also taken with them greater awareness of rural life. Participation has by no means been restricted to students, as members of the local community have joined in the excavation. Such volunteers often bring with them useful skills and experience from which we can learn.

The inclusion of so many disparate groups and individuals has not been without its logistical costs, particularly in time. The biggest number working on site at once has been around fifty, but we have been incredibly lucky in the quality of our site supervisors, the majority of whom have been research students or staff members from participating universities. As well as coping with the day to day work on site, they have patiently explained methodology or aspects of the archaeology on site. In the 1999 season at Hayton, due to the impending construction of the pipeline, they also had

to cope with the demands of developer funded archaeology.

Fig. 8.2. Volunteer children recording post holes they have excavated with an EDM.

Largely due to demographic and regional factors, few members of ethnic communities have taken part, though they would of course be most welcome to participate. We have had some disabled diggers, one of whom, a Thalidomide victim, trowelled brilliantly with her feet, though lack of funding has precluded us from coping with wider access. Some volunteers with less serious disabilities can bring with them greater problems. One such case was a pupil who had social and behavioural difficulties who had always wanted to take part in a dig. Many of the supervisors on our excavation found her difficult to deal with and in the end she worked with me. I have heard subsequently that her time on the dig had a beneficial effect back at school.

Interpretation

Interpretation is defined here in both the conventional archaeological sense and its American meaning, as presenting our results to the wider public. Whenever

Fig. 8.3. Despite the light snow, which melted quickly, children from Holme-on Spalding Moor Primary School were able to find much Roman material in this fieldwalking survey near their school in January 1994.

possible, we have welcomed visitors to our excavations and explained what was going on. Visitors have included casual passers-by and organised groups. On several occasions the former have been so enthused that they have ended up working on site with us.

Perhaps the most successful and well attended of the planned events were the annual Family Archaeology Days at Hayton, organised with the help of the Yorkshire Wolds Heritage Trust and ERAS. St Martin's Church was specially opened, and as well as enjoying its fine Romanesque features, visitors were refreshed by tea and scones provided by members of the local community. The project directors led tours round the excavation and we were also able to set up an exhibition of finds and displays about our work at Hayton and the project as a whole in the village hall, which doubled as our site HQ. During the 2000 season, a simple, cheap and effective way of aiding understanding on site, was the marking out with canes and safety tape of the 18m diameter round house, excavated the previous year, its exact position being located with the EDM. Though of course lacking the impact of reconstructed round houses such as those at Castell Henllys (see Bennett, this volume), visitors were

none the less able to experience a sense of space and appreciate the effect of such a structure on the landscape setting. Other activities were principally aimed at younger visitors, including washing and sorting pottery, tile and animal bones. Peter Edwards, Head of Art and Design at Pocklington School who lives close to the site and who has contributed in many ways to the success of our Hayton excavations, produced a fine interpretative reconstruction drawing which we supplied to visitors. Since 1995 he has also kept a video diary. It is most interesting to see how our recorded interpretations changed as the site unfolded! This idea was taken further with the production of a video clip by the AV Department at Hull University to go out on the History Department's web-site. Under the direction of Martin Millett, some Southampton University Archaeology students also prepared and posted web-sites as part of assessed coursework.

During the construction of the Ethylene pipeline, BP were particularly anxious to involve local schools to which representatives from AC Archaeology, the main contractors, made visits. Children from Barmby Moor Primary school were also able to come to the excavation, and after a tour were given slightly simplified site plans and asked to produce their own reconstruction drawings. Many of these were very impressive and we awarded the prize of a book to the best. During the Hayton excavations, extra funding from the Faculty of Arts, University of Hull and BP enabled us to produce interim reports in the form of illustrated booklets.

Widespread interpretation and dissemination of the project as a whole was greatly aided by generous sponsorship from BAe Systems (formerly British Aerospace). We were delighted that they won the Wedgwood Sponsorship Award of the 2000 British Archaeological Awards, 'for the best private sector sponsorship of archaeology by an individual, company, organisation or charity in the United Kingdom'. To quote the citation made by the judging panel:

'They have made possible a number of popular and academic publications, provided help with audio-visual systems, provided a designer to work on leaflets and displays and provided high quality display stands. The Panel was especially impressed by the way that the sponsorship related to education and community involvement with their environment. In many instances this meant bringing archaeology into the classrooms of local schools. Some of the publications certainly deserve wide circulation, while the importance of the Foulness Valley in the early development of the iron industry in Britain is something that, as a result, will no doubt creep into textbooks and works on the subject over the next few years.'

(British Archaeological Awards 2000)

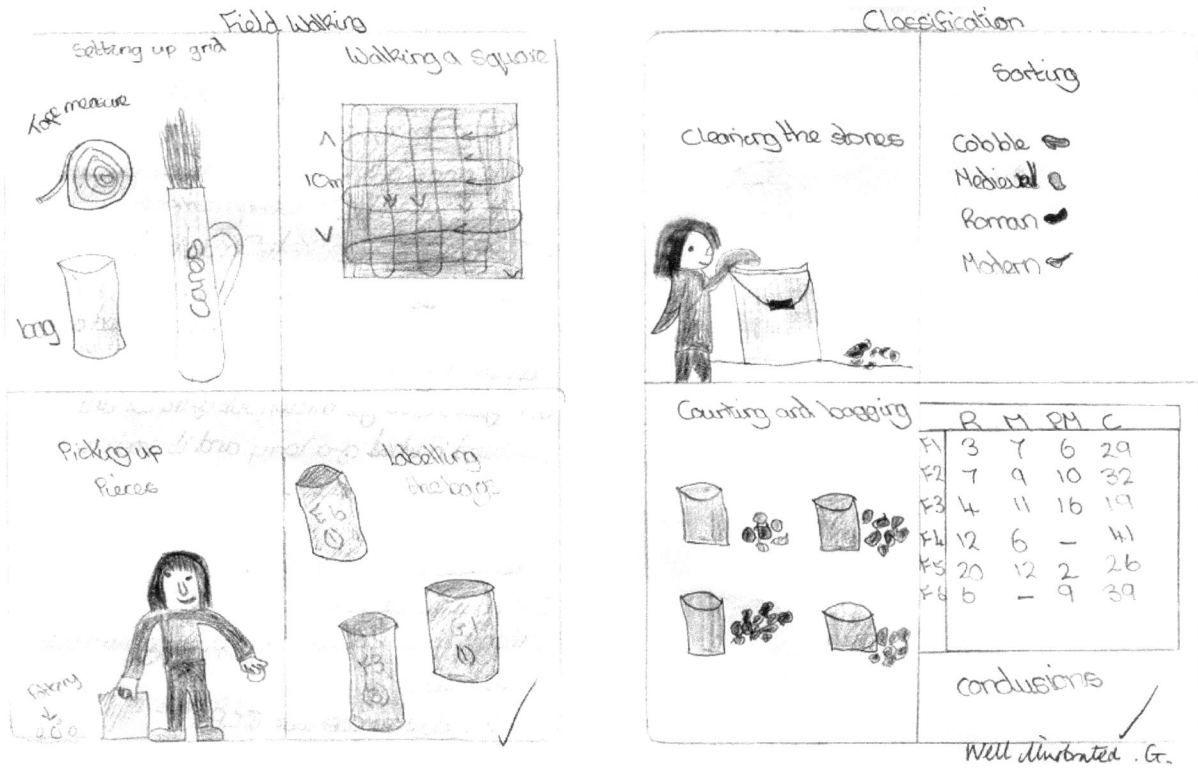

Fig. 8.4a & b. Follow-up work on fieldwalking by Catherine Brown, Holme County Primary School

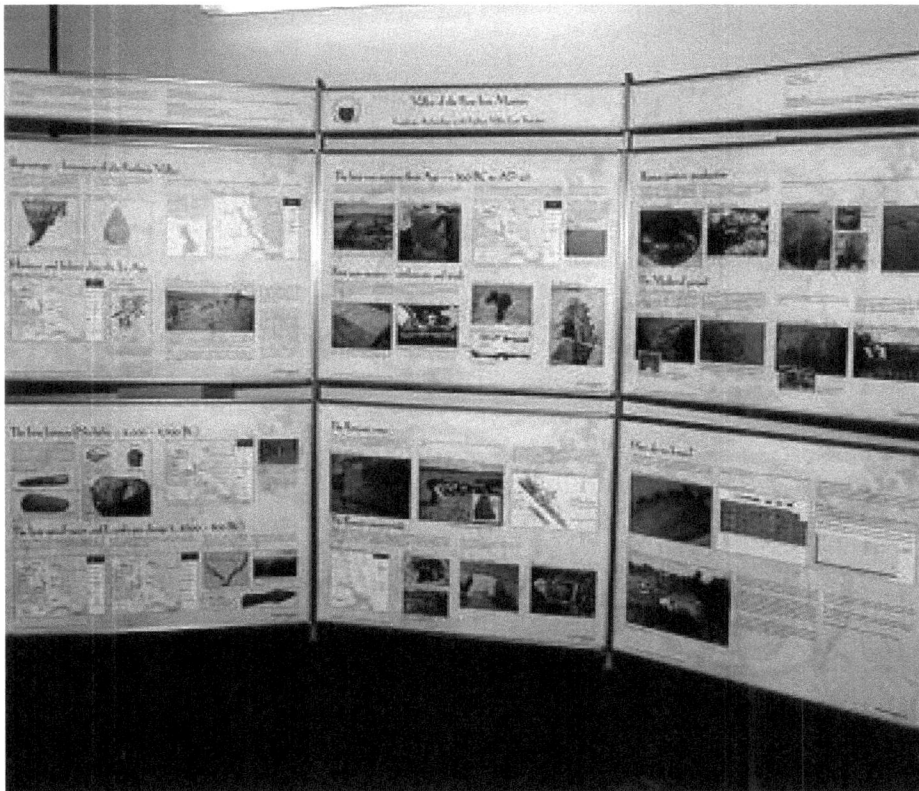

Fig. 8.5. Valley of the First Iron Masters display.
Sponsorship of this won BAe Systems the Wedgwood Sponsorship Award of the
British Archaeological Awards 2000.

The display boards (fig. 8.5) have been well used, exhibited in libraries, schools, conferences and village halls all over the region. The accompanying 'popular' colour booklet, which normally we could not have afforded, has been very well received and has been read by many more than would usually read archaeological reports. What was perhaps most remarkable was BAe's sponsorship of the full academic report of the first phase of the project, which has also been favourably reviewed. In this report, which incorporated the work of many specialists, we tried to go beyond the usual account of the 'digs' and provide an integrated view of this ancient landscape. We are seeking similar sponsorship for extending the display boards and producing colour booklets to go with phases two and three.

Conclusion

Much of what we have done in terms of inclusion and interpretation is not particularly new, however, we are taking steps towards increasing accessibility still further, by the production of a 'virtual landscape' of the Foulness Valley, to be carried out jointly by the University of Hull and the East Riding Archaeological Society, which will be available through the web, generously sponsored by the Heritage Lottery Fund in March 2003. Most of our efforts to broadcast our results have, however, been inexpensive, such as the talks held in the Village Hall at Hayton which have always been very well attended. Such forms of communication are still very important and the pride of place and interest in the local environment shown by local community members at these events is particularly striking. At the launch event for the 'Valley of the First Iron Masters' booklets/display boards and 'Rural settlement and industry' (Halkon and Millett 1999) the large village hall at Holme-on-Spalding Moor was full beyond capacity. This was partly due to a feature covering our work on *Look North,* the BBC's regional TV news programme earlier that evening.

The welcome we have received from many farmers and landowners has been striking. During the Holme-on-Spalding Moor survey we investigated land on 55 farms and were only refused access to one area owned by a large company. The stated reason for denying permission was a bad experience with archaeologists on their land elsewhere in the county! The attitude of the others was fortunately very different, as they provided practical help in the form of equipment, pointing out discoveries they had made themselves and even assisting with field walking. Many felt a strong sense of identity with the landscape, the most eloquent expressing the feeling that they were merely the current custodians, empathising with their predecessors, who, without the aid of the tractor and combine, had striven to make a living from the soil. One of my most moving experiences of adult education was watching a group of farmers who had come along to one of my day schools, pondering the practical capabilities of a Neolithic polished stone adze. Perhaps this inherent interest in the historic as well as the natural environment should be given greater emphasis during the current debate about reform of CAP and its replacement by agri-environmental forms of subsidy, all the more pertinent in the aftermath of the recent foot and mouth outbreak. It is possible to reintroduce species of plant and animal and go some way towards habitat restoration, but once an archaeological feature has been ploughed out it cannot be replaced in the same way. Farmers need to be given greater financial incentive to preserve such landscape elements than current schemes such as Countryside Stewardship provide. I hope that in some way our field work and its interpretation has reinforced or awakened an interest in their own archaeology amongst those who are its natural guardians, and that in acting as such they will receive benefits rather than further burdens.

A clear example of the benefits of educating local populace to cherish their own archaeological heritage happened at the time of writing this account. A farmer, bordering a housing development in one of villages within our study area, was most concerned when he noticed the builders removing archaeological features as well as topsoil. The police were informed that human remains had been disturbed and the follow up investigation revealed more graves, Iron Age and Roman features. Despite PPG 16 regulations specified by the county archaeologist, demanding full archaeological assessment, the developers continued earthmoving, with what turned out to be only outline planning permission. Villagers were so concerned about the damage being done to the archaeological deposits that they insisted on action being taken. A senior planning officer and associated curatorial archaeologist eventually put a stop to further work until appropriate steps were taken. Without the public-spirited action of the local populace, the damage could have been even greater.

Public education in its broadest sense has always been fundamental to our project and as the above example shows can create a strong bond between a community and its archaeology. The long-term nature of our work has provided us with advantages not possessed by many 'contract' archaeologists. The projected costs for most development generated archaeological interventions do not include the provision of site display boards or popular syntheses, explaining what the archaeologists are doing or what they have found (but see Ellis and Toolis, this volume, for a commendable exception). Tight schedules and safety issues often preclude site tours, though I am very grateful that a number of 'contract' archaeologists in this region have been very generous in allowing groups of my students to visit and even participate in their excavations. It is not specified how much of the estimated £20m to £30m expended annually on archaeological sites by developers (English Heritage 2000, 36), is spent on such educational provision, but if archaeology is to be justified, it is surely essential. The end products of most interventions are slim reports, which satisfy the demands of the planning process but seldom move beyond the SMR office. Whilst many watching briefs may not be of great interest, there is a need to draw together the results of larger archaeological activities in order to create narratives of the past for public consumption.

We hope that through our attempts to interpret our results and encourage participation, we have gone beyond doing archaeology for sake of archaeologists

References

English Heritage, 2000. *Power of Place. The future of the historic environment*. London: English Heritage.

Halkon, P., 1983. Investigations into the Romano-British Landscape around Holme-on-Spalding Moor, East Yorkshire, in B. Whitwell (ed.) *East Riding Archaeologist* **7**. 15-24.

Halkon, P., 1997. Fieldwork on Early Iron working sites in East Yorkshire *Historical Metallurgy* 3, no 1: 12-16.

Halkon, P. and Millett, M., 1999. *Rural Settlement and industry: Studies in the Iron Age and Roman Archaeology of lowland East Yorkshire*, Yorkshire Archaeological Report **4**. Leeds: Yorkshire Archaeological Society Roman Antiquities Section and East Riding Archaeological Society

Halkon, P. Millett, M. and Taylor, J., 1997. Fieldwork and excavation at Hayton, East Yorkshire, 1996. *Universities of Durham and Newcastle upon Tyne Archaeological Reports* **20**: 39-41

Halkon, P., Millett M., Easthaugh E., Taylor J. and Freeman, P., 2000. *The Landscape Archaeology of Hayton.* Hull: University of Hull

Hicks, J. D. and Wilson, J., 1975. The Romano-British Kilns at Hasholme. *East Riding Archaeologist* **2**, 49-70

Johnson, S., 1975. Excavations at Hayton Roman Fort. *Britannia* **9**, 57-114.

McLinden, J.A., 1990. Roman coins from Hayton East Yorkshire. *Yorkshire Archaeological Journal*

Millett, M. and. McGrail, S., 1987. The Archaeology of the Hasholme logboat. *Archaeological Journal,* **144**, 69-155.

Millett, M.J. (forthcoming). *Shiptonthorpe, East Yorkshire: Archaeological studies of a Romano-British roadside settlement.* Yorkshire Archaeological Society Roman Antiquities Section monograph.

Selkirk, A., 2001. *Current Archaeology,* **174**, 281.

Taylor, J., 1995. Surveying small towns: the Romano-British roadside settlement at Shiptonthorpe, East Yorkshire, in A. E. Brown (ed.) *Roman small towns in eastern England and beyond*: 39-52. Oxford: Oxbow books.

9

Roundhouses in the landscape.
Interpreting the Iron Age at Castell Henllys.

Phil Bennett

This paper presents a consideration of the relationship between coppice building materials and the later prehistoric landscape based on the reconstruction of an Iron Age roundhouse at Castell Henllys, Pembrokeshire.

Castell Henllys is an Iron Age inland promontory fort owned and managed by the Pembrokeshire Coast National Park Authority. The site delivers a range of the National Park Authority's key corporate objectives including those aimed at providing for the conservation, understanding and enjoyment of its natural and cultural heritage. The fort is a scheduled ancient monument and is one of many later prehistoric promontory forts within the National Park.

Castell Henllys is a unique visitor destination in the UK. It is the only Iron Age Fort to have roundhouses and other buildings reconstructed on their original, archaeologically excavated foundations. The award winning success of Castell Henllys, both as an educational resource and as a visitor attraction, is founded on the ability to bridge the gap between archaeological research and visitor understanding.

Castell Henllys occupies a spur of land overlooking the Nant Duad in a valley formed at the end of the last ice age from glacial melt water. The site was fortified around the beginning of the Iron Age, most probably by the local aristocracy of the time, partly as a display of power and status and also to provide defence for that elite against the threat of attack. Towards the end of the Iron Age and the advent of the Roman period in the first century AD, the focus of settlement at Castell Henllys shifted. This was manifested in the establishment of a defended farm between the inner and outer great ramparts and in the abandonment, probably for economic as well as social reasons, of the fort itself. By the fourth century AD, and possibly associated with the establishment of a new, Irish influenced local elite, the position of power shifted from Castell Henllys and the site was abandoned (Mytum 1999). Throughout the Iron Age the surrounding landscape was formed, managed and dominated by successive generations of leaders at Castell Henllys.

The interpretation of Castell Henllys Iron Age Fort is inextricably linked to the development of its landscape. One could not exist without the other. The formation of the Castell Henllys landscape has been determined through its management by the residents of the fort and

their successors. Successive landscapes of managed woodland, cultivated fields and open grazing present a palimpsest of the past which has been imaginatively interpreted through the dramatic reconstruction of the fort and its domestic buildings. We can interpret elements of the landscape surrounding the fort from the materials required to build roundhouses and other structures. Many of those materials, such as oak posts and hazel wattle are dependent for their growth on careful management.

The archaeological record holds the key for interpreting not only people but also the landscape in which they lived and the habitats for the floral and faunal communities that were supported by it. The process of reconstructing the fort has required a programme of practical management for its surrounding environment providing for the regeneration of hazel and oak coppice, the conservation of wetland and traditional grassland maintenance. This management has helped provide for the conservation of bats, dormice, ravens and dippers, otters and orchids, lichen communities and other flora and fauna already present at Castell Henllys, sometimes in large numbers. In short, the story of Castell Henllys can just as easily be related through the eyes of a dormouse as it can by a chieftain. The stories will differ but they will be of equal importance and, combined they highlight the diversity of wildlife and sustainable woodland and landscape management present in the Iron Age and Roman period and being reconstructed and recreated at Castell Henllys today.

The long-term programme of archaeological research and the subsequent attempted reconstruction of Iron Age buildings on their original, excavated foundations make this an important site. As an interpretative resource for visitors, school children and students, Castell Henllys is unique (fig. 9.1). The reconstructed area of the fort lies next to areas under archaeological excavation while nearby fields are used to demonstrate prehistoric farming practices with Iron Age breeds of livestock. Since its purchase by the National Park in 1991, Castell Henllys has become an important visitor attraction in north Pembrokeshire, receiving around 30,000 visitors per year and providing a significant input into the local economy.

Fig. 9.1. Engaging with the past.

The site is a model for innovative interpretation and a prime example of best practice in sustainable tourism. The reconstructed roundhouses form the focus for the interpretation of the site.

As a result of an engineer's structural survey commissioned by the National Park Authority, the need to periodically replace or rebuild the structures at Castell Henllys was identified in order to avoid a perceived sense of decline especially by visitors returning to the site. In 1998, in partnership with the European Regional Development Fund, the National Park Authority decided to attempt to reconstruct the largest known Iron Age roundhouse to have existed at Castell Henllys. The house platform chosen for the project had yielded comparatively little information during excavation by the University of York (Mytum 1989). Its probable diameter was gauged from a partially surviving wall foundation gully and the lack of internal postholes suggested that the roundhouse had a free-spanning roof. This paucity of information allowed a free approach to the project allowing the opportunity to experiment with construction type and methodology, whilst enabling reconstruction on the original site of a roundhouse with the same dimensions and maintaining a sense of shared space for visitors. By originating and recording every detail of material procurement and construction methodology (Bennett forthcoming), a focused attempt to consider the longevity of roundhouses and the resource implications of the construction of roundhouses on the local landscape in the Iron Age has been possible.

Castell Henllys dominates its local landscape not by being sited on the highest available point, but rather by appearing to be the raised centre of a natural amphitheatre to those parts of the surrounding landscape higher than it (fig. 9.2). The chosen house platform for this project is not only the largest at Castell Henllys; its position is the most dominant. With this in mind, as well as the demands of modern building regulations, our intention was to build a high status roundhouse with the best materials and craftsmanship available. The new roundhouse required the appropriate planning consents and visits from the Building Officer and Fire Officer at the various stages of its construction. The material requirements were massive. The new structure followed the foundation trench of its Iron Age antecedent and is 13m in diameter with a roof apex of 8m. The wall is 1.2m in height and of wattle, woven around posts approximately 1m apart. The roof was constructed with oak rafters with a surface slope of c. 45 degrees to facilitate the run-off of rain and snow. The roof is thatched with water reed tied to hazel and ash purlins.

The strength and stability of the building is provided by three ring-beams (fig 9.3). The first, a wall plate of mortise and tenon jointed split oak lengths was constructed at the top of the wall to bear the outward pressure caused by the weight of the roof and to provide a base to which the rafters could be joined. The second, and main ring-beam is positioned just over halfway up the roof. A central post was erected and secured with ropes at the beginning of the project to help in the positioning of rafters and the ring beams. The main ring-beam was constructed in the shape of a wheel with

Fig. 9.2. Aerial view of the fort.

Fig. 9.3. The roof under construction.

spokes radiating out from the central post to the principal rafters; the wheel's rim effectively joins all the rafters together and provided a surface to which secondary rafters were joined. The main ring-beam braces the roof and transfers the pressures on the roof due to weather from one particular point to the whole of the structure, increasing its strength considerably. A smaller, upper ring-beam was constructed just below the apex of the roof to facilitate the positioning of the tops of the principal rafters. When the ring-beams had been constructed and the roof rafters jointed and set in place, the central post was cut off just below the level of the main ring-beam leaving a free-spanning roof.

The water reed thatch was laid onto purlins of ash and hazel fixed to the rafters with hemp twine and wooden pins. Each of the purlins were joined together around the rafters, forming separate hoops 1metre apart covering the area of the conical roof. The reed was attached to the purlins under strips of split hazel, which were then tied down with hemp twine. When approximately half the roof had been thatched, the wall was daubed both inside and outside the roundhouse. The daub mixture was made from six parts clay to one part cow dung together with partially rotted straw and water reed. The daub was pushed hard into the wattle then smoothed off. Around 15 tons of daub was used for the wall, which had to be patched up as the drying daub cracked. The finished building is impressive, particularly from the inside. The house is spacious, cool in summer yet remarkably warm in the winter when the door is closed. It is clearly visible and dominant in the surrounding landscape. Buildings of this size, complexity and sophistication should not be described as huts.

Untreated timber rots very quickly in the acid soils of West Wales. The internal oak supporting posts in another of the Castell Henllys roundhouses rotted out and had to be replaced after only ten years (Bennett 2001). The roof superstructure and thatch of a well-built roundhouse will always outlive the wall stakes and posts where they are set in the ground and yet there appears to be little evidence at Castell Henllys to suggest that major maintenance and repair was undertaken to replace them. It would be easy to interpret this lack of evidence to suggest that roundhouses had a short lifespan.

The positioning of a wall plate at the top of the wall might explain the lack of need for substantial wall supports below ground thus eliminating the need for their repair or replacement. Peter Reynolds has suggested that the weight of the building might provide stability even when wall stakes have rotted below ground (Reynolds 1993). The engineer's report commissioned by the NPA maintains that outward pressure provided by the conical roof would eventually cause the walls to splay (Whitby and Bird 1997). If, however, the structural integrity of the roundhouse roof can be maintained by the main ring beam then the wall plate should effectively stop any splaying of the rafters and wall posts joined to it caused by vertical and horizontal pressure from the weight of the roof. This could imply that the structural function of the wall is simply to support the tension ring at a height above ground convenient for those living in the roundhouse. The longevity of the roundhouse can thus be determined by the lifespan of the roof rafters, tension ring and the section of the wall above ground, rather than those surviving parts of the wall posts below ground level. If the roof has been carefully thatched by a craftsman and is subsequently maintained to a high standard the reed should survive for more than fifty years. If the roof rafters and wall plate timbers are large and protected from rain by good thatch above and smoked from the hearth below, they will actually get stronger with age. There is good reason to suggest that large roundhouses could have survived for generations.

By closely studying the material requirements for the construction of roundhouses we may be able to reconstruct aspects of the local landscape around areas of population in the Iron Age and consider the value of such resources. The timbers used in the construction of the latest roundhouse at Castell Henllys are all coppice products: that is they were all derived from trees, such as oak, hazel and ash, which have been regularly felled on a planned rotation to encourage the rigorous and straight re-growth of shoots. The time-span of a coppice rotation depends on the tree species and its intended use.

One hundred bundles of hazel rods were used in the construction of the roundhouse, mostly for the wattle wall and the roof purlins. The bundles of hazel consisted of around twenty-five hazel rods each up to three metres long. Depending on the quality of the coppice, two hazel bushes might be required to provide one bundle of hazel. Such hazel requires a coppice rotation of up to eight years. One bundle of hazel was needed for each metre of wattle wall; therefore around eighty hazel bushes were needed to produce enough hazel for the roundhouse wall alone. Those eighty hazel stools (stumps) would have been at risk from browsing deer, cattle, sheep, pigs and wild boar for at least four years out of the eight required within a given period before rotation.

The roof required twenty-four straight oak rafters up to 9m in length and twenty-two 2m-split lengths cut for wall posts and more for the ring beams. Coppiced oak may take up to twenty-five years to grow to the length required for the rafters. In all around thirty-four oak trees were needed for the building in addition to the hazel. The thatching of the roof used two thousand bundles of water reed which, ironically, were imported from Turkey. Many of the reed beds in Britain are now managed for nature conservation rather than for commercial purposes and supply can be problematic. Water reed also suffers from the high nitrate levels in many of our watercourses making the reed structure friable and reducing its lifespan as a thatching material. Combed wheatstraw can be used for thatching but is not so long lasting as water reed.

The relationship between resources and roundhouse construction cannot be ignored. It is unlikely that the materials for such buildings would have been widely available in the landscape without extensive and long-term woodland management. Woodland work without modern tools is very labour intensive and one wonders whether such work would have been possible without the control and organisation of work forces by local elites. The large scale coppice requirements for roundhouses, palisades, fences and other structures places a value on those resources easily forgotten when considering the Iron Age. To what extent, for instance, would charcoal have had a role as the primary fuel for heating and cooking? Again, without modern tools, the cutting of firewood into manageable lengths is hugely labour intensive while charcoal can be produced from long lengths of timber in large quantities in the woodland and is a more efficient and easier to transport fuel. As firewood, coppiced timber is an expensive use of a valuable resource; it is most likely that a combination of charcoal and the small diameter trimmings from the management of coppiced woodlands would have been used for fuel. If our attempts at reconstruction indeed echo those of the Iron Age, it would be astonishing to think that the effort involved in cultivating and gathering coppice products would have been undervalued by a lack of subsequent woodland management. Similarly it is unlikely that large roundhouses might have been constructed for relatively short-term use.

The demand for coppice products in the Iron Age would have been influenced by the frequency, size and density of contemporaneous surrounding settlement. The longevity of roundhouses would, in part, have also determined the management of resources. The sustainability of managed woodland resources in the Iron Age would have been directly related to the value placed on these limited resources by local leaders. Whether or not Iron Age elites bothered about the human time consumption (conspicuous or not) related to woodland work, has to be considered against material requirements and the conservation and management of the resource. If we accept that the construction of Iron Age (and earlier) roundhouses was reliant primarily on coppice products, then the landscape implications would have been considerable. In this light, there seems little doubt that coppice products were greatly valued by people in prehistory.

The use of different levels of interpretation at Castell Henllys is an effective way of communicating the past to visitors, students and schoolchildren and it can also provoke research into related subjects. The retrieval and interpretation of archaeological information provides the basis for the experimental reconstruction of Iron Age roundhouses on their original sites. The study of the materials used in the buildings illuminates those areas of the prehistoric landscape previously hidden to us through being located outside the area of archaeological investigation. This reversal, whereby the desire to provide interpretation provides a basis for research, encourages the presentation of innovative hypotheses that can motivate new archaeological research to test them.

References

Bennett, P., 2001. Approaching the Past. *The Archaeologist* (IFA Journal) 42.

Bennett, P., (forthcoming), *Building the Past - experimental design and reconstruction at Castell Henllys Pembrokeshire.*

Mytum, H., 1999. Castell Henllys. *Current Archaeology* 161.

Mytum, H., 1989. Excavation at Castell Henllys, 1981-89: The Iron Age Fort. *Archaeology in Wales* 29

Reynolds, P., 1993. *Experimental Reconstruction.* Edinburgh University Monograph No 1. Edinburgh: Edinburgh University Press.

Whitby and Bird, 1997. *Castell Henllys Iron Age Fort Structural Appraisal.* Unpublished report for the Pembrokeshire Coast National Park Authority.

10

High Street, Londinium.
Reconstructing Roman London.

Hedley Swain

Introduction

Between 1994 and 1996 the Museum of London Archaeology Service undertook a major excavation in advance of the redevelopment of 1 Poultry in the heart of the City of London. The excavations uncovered the largest and best preserved section of early Roman London yet found (Rowsome 2000). Once the excavations were completed the long and slow process of recording, conserving and analysing the thousands of finds and records began.

In 1999, with the site archive and assessment complete and detailed analysis on the 1 Poultry material underway the Museum decided to use the excavations as the basis of one of its major special exhibitions. The aim was to show the public how archaeology could be used to reconstruct the past and also to try and give an indication as to what it would really have been like to live in 1st century Roman London. Here the Museum was also conscious that it would be trying to correct a popular conception of the Roman world. A novel, though not unique approach was taken to the exhibition. Its main feature would be a 1:1 scale reconstruction of part of the Roman town as excavated at Poultry (Hall and Swain 2000).

The Exhibition

As designed the exhibition was divided into three distinct spaces: an introductory area; the reconstructed buildings; and finally a display of the finds from the excavation. The main part of the exhibition was the area of reconstructed buildings. The idea here was to take the ground plan of part of Roman London, as revealed at 1 Poultry, lay it out to exact scale in the exhibition space and then, using the archaeological evidence reconstruct this part of the 1st century town. We wanted to give visitors an 'experience' of Roman London so the reconstruction not only had to look authentic but also feel and smell authentic. There would be no real objects in this space and no captions or explanatory text. Instead visitors were handed a large leaflet, which acted as a guided map to the space and provided explanations of areas they were walking through. Unlike other exhibitions, such as Jorvik the York Viking Centre, visitors were allowed to walk through the reconstructed spaces at their leisure, touching

everything. This obviously called for a reconstruction that would 'feel real' at a very detailed level, and would also be extremely hardy – the exhibition lasted six months.

Creating the buildings brought together three groups: the Museum of London field archaeologists and archaeological finds and environmental specialists who had excavated and analysed the results from the excavation; the Museum team of curators, interpreters and designers, and finally the external creators of the reconstruction, Sands Films. Sands had worked with the Museum on several previous smaller scale projects and had an established reputation for creating extremely lifelike sets for films. Additional props for the interiors were provided by a series of craftspeople experienced in making Roman style pottery, glass and leather.

The process involved extracting from the archaeologists all possible evidence about the three buildings and their immediate surroundings. This involved not just the size, shape and construction of the buildings but the objects that were found in them and might point to their function. This was then used by the Museum curators to create a 'contents list' for the recreation: where doors and windows would be, what would be in each room, what the floor surfaces would look like etc. Sands then started work off-site to create the buildings into which the contents would be placed (the Museum's tight special exhibition timetable meant that there were only three weeks to install the exhibition, so as much as possible was pre-fabricated off site) (fig.10.1). With different elements there was an initial period of experimentation over exactly what doors and other features would look like, and how they could best be constructed. Although no attempt was made at total authenticity in the reconstruction it was our policy to use original materials and techniques wherever possible in order to create the most realistic experience. So newly felled oak prepared with adzes was used for the roofs, windows and doors. Forged iron was used for the door hinges. But mud brick and daub were not used for the walls and most nails were modern with resin copies of Roman nail heads hiding them.

An area in which Sands proved masterly was in creating a feeling of mucky reality. Floors were carpet tiles prepared in a resin mud solution that almost everyone commented on when they first entered the area: very few museum

Fig. 10.1. Constructing the Roman buildings off-site. Freshly cut oak was used and a combination of traditional and modern tools. (Photo. Museum of London.)

Fig. 10.2. One of the interiors from the High Street Londinium reconstruction. (Photo. Museum of London.)

visitors expect to find themselves walking on mud. Mosses, weeds and general dirt were also added wherever appropriate (fig. 10.2).

One problem area was lighting. The buildings masked most of the Museum's own gallery lighting. The Roman buildings almost certainly would have been dark spaces, the occupiers trading light for warmth. However what we couldn't re-create were the lamps, candles and open fires that they would have had to compensate for this. We used as many windows and doorways as we could to shine lights into the buildings but in the end the Museum's electricians had to use all their ingenuity to create background ambient light effects. The result was still some murky spaces, which greatly added to the atmosphere but did in places make the leaflets hard to read.

One reason for the lighting problem was an early recognition that it was easier to create a sense of reality by producing internal spaces with daylight shining in,

than external spaces, so the Roman building plans were used to fill as much of the exhibition space as possible with building interiors. In fact, however, so strong were the recreations, and so used are the public to dealing with 'un-real realities' that none of them seemed put off by the small areas of the exhibition which revealed the walls and ceiling of the gallery (fig. 10.3).

We could only take the archaeology so far. We were totally confident about the building floor plans and floor surface. We could be equally confident about the general construction of the buildings based on evidence from other sites. The use of the buildings could be worked out from finds evidence in two cases; the third was a best guess. Obviously the exact layout of props within the buildings was more conjectural but the archaeologists and curators felt confident that no liberties had been taken with the archaeology, and therefore the trust of the public. The buildings were a bakery and 'café', a carpenter's workshop and house, and finally a foreign pottery and spice shop.

Fig. 10.3. The exterior of the building shown being built in fig.1, in the exhibition. (Photo. Museum of London.)

The entrance area of the exhibition included a five-minute video, which explained the nature of the Poultry development and excavation, and how the reconstruction was realised. The purpose of this was to put what visitors would see in the reconstruction into the context of the archaeological process, to explain to them that the reconstruction was based on actual archaeological evidence from an actual site within the City. The video was created by Paul Larsman, a professional television director, based on a synopsis of the points the Museum wanted to put across. To emphasise this sense of place and context large graphics showed the location of the site in relation to both Roman and modern London. Finally an architect's model of the new Poultry development was displayed.

The final area of the exhibition was a display of the actual finds from 1 Poultry including many items that the visitors would have seen as replicas in the reconstructed area. The Poultry site was very productive and included many wooden items that seldom survive. However it was still incredibly gratifying how much time visitors spent poring over these objects having had them put into context in the reconstruction.

We were extremely happy with the reconstruction but it was obviously empty of people. How to create the atmosphere and feel for a lived in space? We felt strongly that mannequins would intrude into the sense of reality. It was also impossible to people the space with real people full-time, even if this were desirable. Three partial solutions were found. Trained actors dressed as Roman-

Britons inhabited certain rooms on certain days – aimed primarily at school groups (fig. 10.4). This simply expanded on the arrangements the Museum of London already had in place for the permanent Roman gallery and its room settings. Craft demonstrators (pottery, wood, bone and leather workers) were also used on certain days in one of the rooms. A soundtrack was also used to give background atmosphere. However the most ambitious attempt at introducing life into the exhibition involved a film. One of the three buildings, a pottery shop, included the shop-front facing onto the via Decumana – the high street of the exhibition's name. Onto the view out of this front was projected a continuously running 10 minute loop of film. This was of about 70 individuals from Roman reconstruction groups walking past a Roman street set. Despite the obvious artifice of this process it proved hugely popular with visitors and helped make the link between the interiors, the people of Roman London and the town itself in which the buildings were set (fig. 10.5).

Once created (as with all museum exhibitions work finished a few minutes before the press view) we had to face the problem of how to advertise and market an exhibition for which there would be no images until the day it opened and which would be relying heavily for its visitor appeal on senses other than vision. This problem led to quite heated debate within the project team with very different concepts discussed. In the end a campaign of radio adverts and posters, which focused on the reality as opposed to the myth of Roman life, were used that had no direct relationship to the exhibition. But the exhibition

Fig. 10.4. Encountering a Roman: the general public come across an actor in one of the reconstructions. (Photo. Museum of London.)

Fig. 10.5. Filming members of reconstruction societies in front of a Roman street set for the film used in the exhibition. (Photo. Museum of London.)

more-or-less sold itself. It received very favorable early press coverage, excellent early visitor figures, mainly families during the 2000 school summer holidays, and word clearly got round that it was worth a visit. The Museum also developed a large programme of well-publicised public events relating to the exhibition.

Wider discussion

Was High Street Londinium the right exhibition for the Museum? High Street Londinium was certainly a great success by many criteria. It received very favorable media coverage, excellent visitor figures, and supported very good commercial sales. Visitor comments were also extremely favorable. The one continuing complaint from visitors was that it was only a temporary exhibition, and should have been made permanent!

It was also a success at other levels. It showed clearly that the Museum was at an advantage in having a large body of archaeologists as part of its staff. It also demonstrated the Museum's ability to stage very different exhibitions, particularly in the context of the exhibitions that were staged before (Vivienne Westwood) and after it (Creative Quarters – London's art world). However is this the wrong sort of exhibition for museums to be putting on? In an article in *The Independent* Mark Ryan described it as 'tacky literalism at its worst'. His complaint was that this was a museum giving the visitor too much, taking away their need to imagine the Roman world for themselves. Was High Street Londinium leaning too far towards being a theme park? Were there too few real objects? Was it a museum exhibition at all in the true sense? All archaeological interpretations are just that, interpretations. There was much in the exhibition that we could not guarantee was accurate.

The Museum was aware of these possible accusations but would argue that they come from the wrong perspective. The prime aims were to give visitors a new, different and enjoyable experience that they would remember; secondly to convey to them the nature of the archaeological process and how a office development can lead eventually to a revised understanding of the past; and thirdly to convey what it would have been like to live in 1st century Roman London, and how different this would have been to most people's impression of the Roman world. We would argue that the methods we used achieved these aims more successfully than a more traditional exhibition type. We would also argue that although we have a responsibility to relate the evidence we have as it is, we should not be frightened of using the expertise we have to make interpretations of the past.

Visitors clearly did enjoy the exhibition and did not think they were being patronised, or being deprived of using their imagination. As archaeologists we often underestimate how intelligent and discerning the public can be, but also how much help is needed in understanding the deep past – especially as popular culture has tended to simplify that past from 'Carry On Cleo' to 'Gladiator'.

Archaeologists should not be frightened of entertaining. There is no law that states we must not display objects until at least 10 years after their discovery and only then in a glass case divorced of context and with an impenetrable caption. Reconstructions should always be a part of how we communicate the past. They fail when they are not based on interpreted data, when they are divorced from the archaeological process, or when they are just plain bad and embarrassing.

More straightforward observations can be made. Visitors are used to coming to museums to see real objects in glass cases, which they cannot touch. It was actually quite difficult to persuade many visitors to take full advantage of the reconstructions and to touch sets and objects. Others had difficulty with the difference between real and replica objects.

High Street Londinium will live on. A full Quick Time Virtual Reality video was made of the whole exhibition. Although this will obviously not allow the same sensory experience as the main exhibition through links it will show the close relationship between the reconstructions and the real finds. Work on developing this as a gallery and web service are underway.

Summary

For archaeology to appeal to a wide audience it needs to be linked to discovery and process and to be relevant. Its display should also be imaginative and fun. Reconstructions like those used for High Street Londinium have an important part to play in the communication of archaeology and history, if they are firmly set in the context of scholarly investigation.

Acknowledgements

Banca di Roma sponsored High Street Londinium. Key members of the Museum's project team for the exhibition were Jenny Hall, Moira Gemmill and Lucie Amos. Francis Grew worked with Adaptive technologies to complete the Quick Time film of the exhibition.

Portions of this paper have been previously published in Issue 16 (2001) of *Museum Practice*.

References

Hall, J. and Swain, H., 2000. *High Street Londinium.* London: Museum of London.

Rowsome, P., 2000. *Heart of the City, Roman Medieval and Modern London Revealed By Archaeology at 1 Poultry.* London: English Heritage and MoLAS.

11

Access to the evidence.
Interpretation of an excavation at a Scottish castle.

Adrian Cox

Introduction

This paper focuses on the interpretation of an archaeological excavation at Caerlaverock Old Castle to visitors, and presents an evaluation of visitors' reactions to the archaeological work and its presentation. An opportunity has been taken to assess and discuss what we have learned from the experience, about visitors' perceptions of archaeology and about how the subject can be presented to the general public in a stimulating and effective way.

With spectacular views over the Solway Firth and the distant Lakeland fells, Caerlaverock Castle, situated around nine miles to the south-east of Dumfries (fig. 11.1), is among the most impressive medieval castles in Britain. During the summers of 1998 and 1999, Historic Scotland sponsored the excavation of the site of an earlier fortress (Caerlaverock 'Old Castle'), situated 200 metres to the south of the present castle in an area of wooded marshland (NGR NY 027 654; fig. 11.2). The principal aim of the excavation, directed on behalf of SUAT Ltd by Martin Brann, was to inform a scheme for the laying out and interpretation of this important site to visitors. The programme of educational work undertaken in relation to this project was designed and carried out by the author, very capably assisted by a small team of volunteers.

Setting the scene

Caerlaverock Castle stands near the edge of the coastal salt marshes known locally as the *merse*. This shoreline is the habitat of a very important and fragile wildlife ecosystem, and is now a National Nature Reserve extending to almost 8000 hectares. Its proximity to England brought Caerlaverock Castle into frequent conflict throughout its existence, and it has a fascinating and turbulent history, interwoven with the story of the Maxwell family (Grove 1994, 16).

The lands of Caerlaverock were granted to John de Maccuswell in c1220, and the construction of the earlier fortress (Caerlaverock 'Old Castle') is thought to date to this period. Both documentary and dendrochronological evidence indicate that the old castle was occupied for only a short time (around 50 years), before being replaced

by the present castle to its north. Adjacent to the old castle is a harbour basin, formerly accessible from the Solway Firth.

It has long been Historic Scotland's intention to enhance the presentation of Caerlaverock Old Castle to the public, and among the main objectives in commissioning the excavation was to reveal sufficient of the castle's ground plan and structural details to enable its laying out and interpretation. It was hoped that the excavation would reveal a snapshot of 13th-century life at the castle, and shed more light on its dating, its sequence of development and the reasons for its abandonment. The harbour basin and other earthworks in the immediate vicinity were the subjects of a less detailed, but parallel, investigation.

The Old Castle site is truly a time capsule. Its remains were clearly visible in the late 18th century, as reported by Grose (1789). In the 1860s, an excavation on the castle mound exposed lengths of the sandstone wall foundations, leaving the site scarred by deep radial trenches, apparently not backfilled. Surveyors from the Royal Commission noted after visiting the site in 1914 (RCAHMS 1920, 11) that even within living memory the site served as a convenient quarry for the neighbourhood. By the time of their visit, the site was overgrown with trees and they were only able to estimate the general arrangement and dimensions of the castle.

The recent excavation was carried out over thirteen weeks from June to September 1998 and an additional four weeks in June and July 1999. A full account will be published in due course. The excavated evidence does not appear to contradict the established view that the old castle was occupied for around 50 years during the 13th century, and demonstrates a phased expansion of the castle during this short period. Post-abandonment activity on the castle mound included iron smithing and the construction of a keyhole-shaped oven (Brann 1998, 25; 1999, 23).

Outreach at the Caerlaverock excavation

Professional archaeological units such as SUAT Ltd are increasingly dependent upon developer funding, and against this background it sometimes proves difficult to

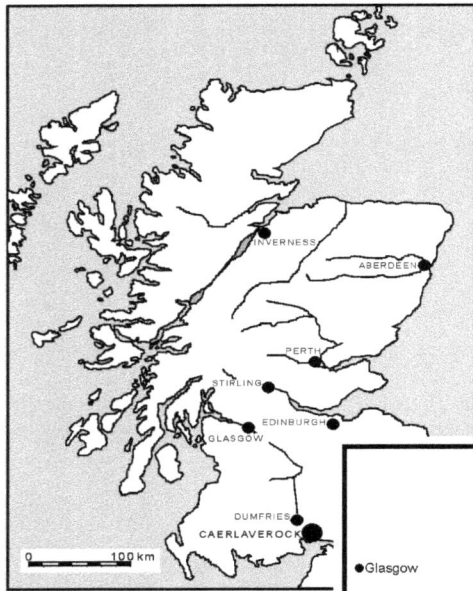

CAERLAVEROCK

Location Map

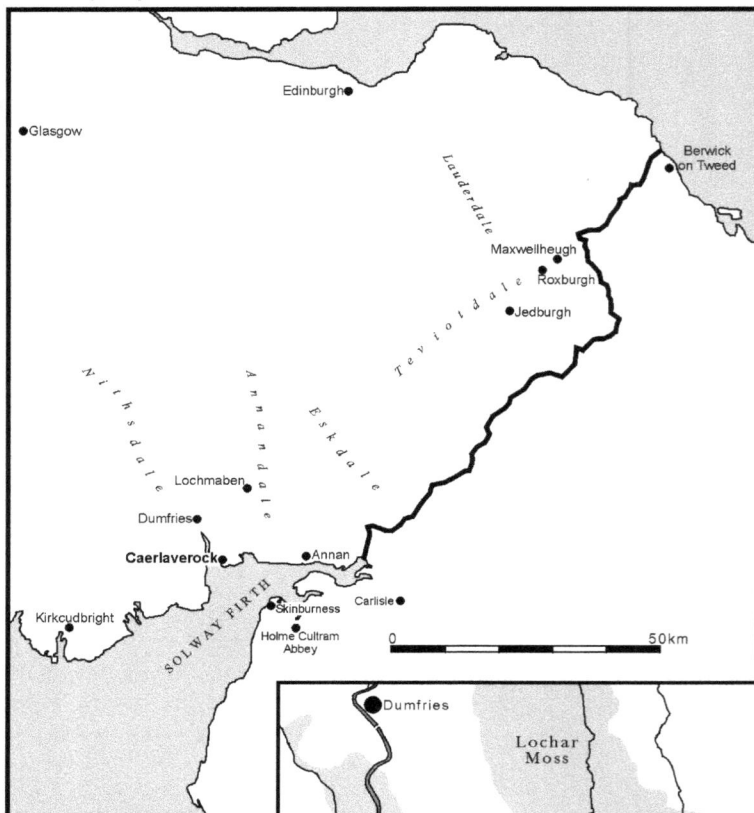

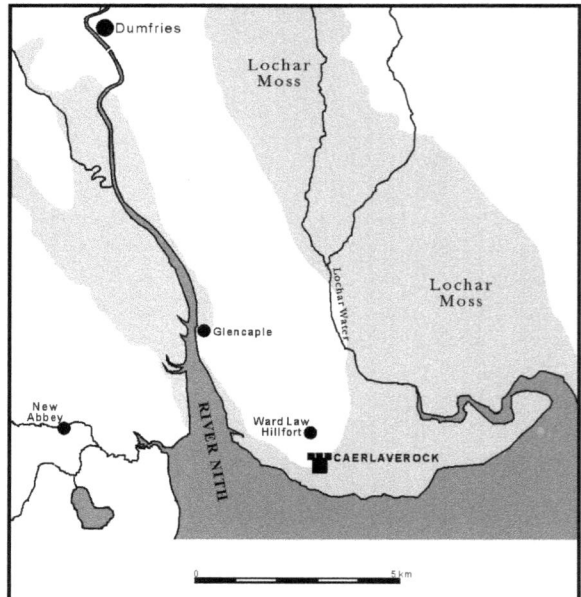

Fig. 11.1. Location map.

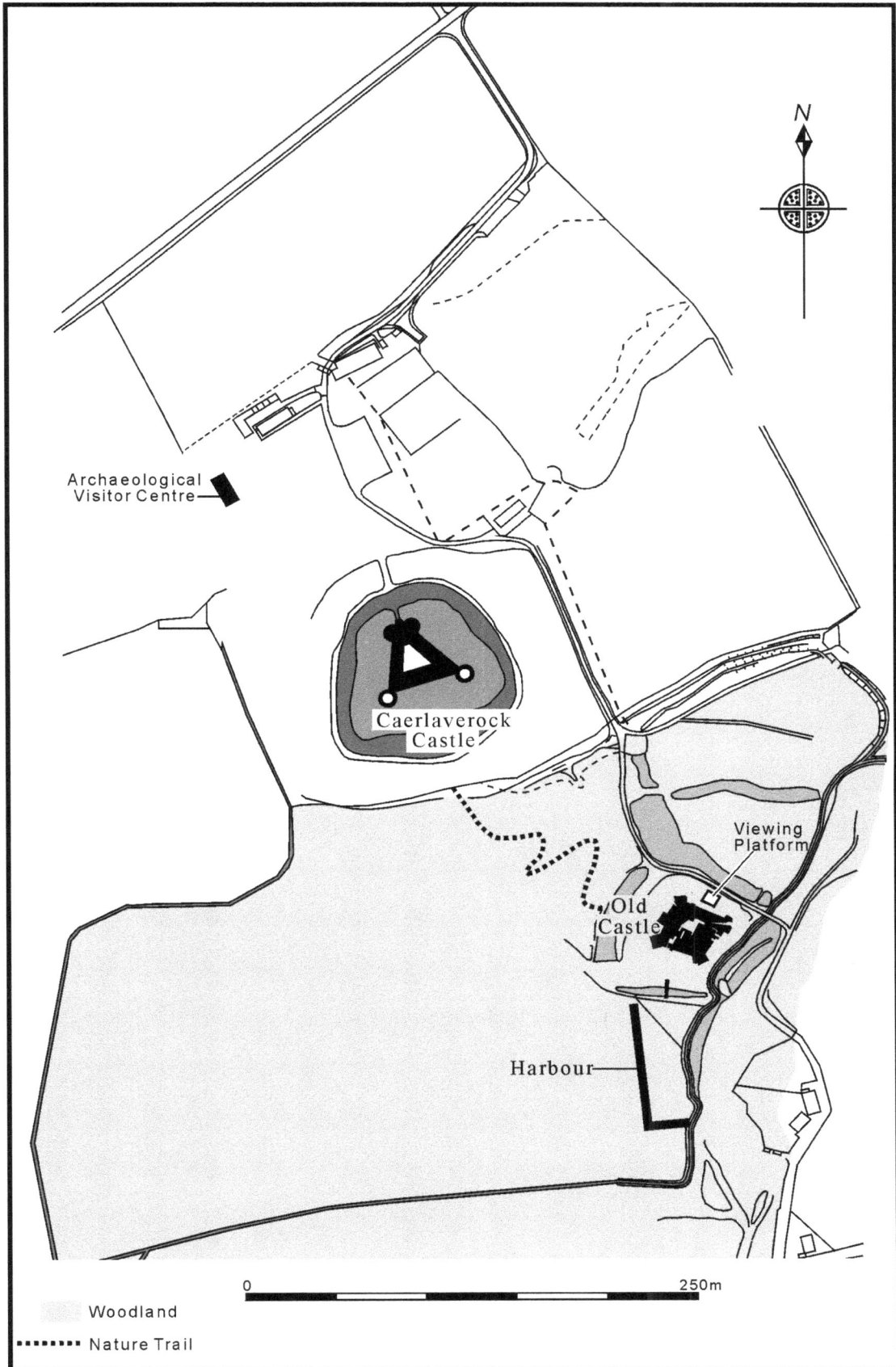

Fig. 11.2. Location of castles and of visitor facilities.

support educational work. Nevertheless, partly by staff contributing some of their own time, we are able to maintain a small-scale outreach programme at SUAT (Cox 1996). I feel that archaeologists benefit greatly from the exercise of interpreting and explaining the results of their work to non-specialist audiences. This challenge helps us to understand our own results, and encourages healthy scrutiny of our methods. The excavation at Caerlaverock provided an extremely welcome opportunity to demonstrate the value of including a major educational element in a large excavation project. It provided an opportunity to communicate our enthusiasm for archaeology to visitors of all ages, both from the local community in Dumfries and Galloway and from all over the world. Altogether, the archaeology was presented to over 10,000 visitors.

In order to maximise public interest and involvement in the project, excavation took place during the summer months, the busiest period for visitors to the castle, and a rotation system ensured that archaeologists were always working on the site, seven days a week. A visitor centre was set up in a portacabin at the northern end of the site for the duration of the project, containing an exhibition describing the excavation's objectives and the results as work progressed. This included a display of finds, and alongside the static display was a range of materials used in interactive educational work (eg artefact-handling, primitive spinning and drawing) with younger visitors. The interactive materials varied as the excavation progressed, but all were

intended to provide insights into the everyday lives of the inhabitants of a medieval castle. The visitor centre provided a focus for those interested in the archaeological work, and was a logical starting point for organised guided tours of the site.

The character and route of the guided tours was carefully considered in advance of the excavation. A flexible approach to the route ensured that all visitors, including people with disabilities and those with very young children, were able to experience and enjoy the tours. The safety aspects were, of course, also carefully evaluated. En route to the old castle site, an opportunity was taken to describe the later castle and set both castles within their historical and geographical context. At the site of the Old Castle itself, Historic Scotland erected a viewing platform which stood above part of the moat on the castle's eastern side (fig. 11.3). From here, visitors were able to view the excavation at very close quarters.

Local schools were actively encouraged to take advantage of the opportunity to visit a 'live' archaeological excavation. Schools were contacted at the outset of the project and invited to visit, and a group of local schoolteachers was given a detailed guided tour of both castles in order to emphasise the value of class visits to curricular studies.

We endeavoured to provide opportunities for the direct involvement of the public in the project, as volunteers

Fig. 11.3. The viewing platform from the Old Castle mound.

assisting on the site itself, in day-to-day finds processing activities and in the provision of guided tours. As the excavation progressed and visitor numbers increased, volunteer assistance became invaluable, and thanks to the hard work and dedication of a small group of volunteers we were able to reach many more visitors than would otherwise have been the case.

Guided tours provided for school groups were designed to encourage interaction and feedback from the pupils. As well as providing the essential information about the archaeology and the site, we encouraged the children to actively participate and to look for evidence themselves, giving them opportunities to ask questions and to contribute their ideas. Experience has shown that children value this opportunity to contribute rather than simply being lectured to. We need also to be mindful that, in bringing the past to life, sometimes a multiplicity of interpretations is possible, and youngsters need to be given some freedom to construct their own understandings of the past.

Organised groups from local historical societies and other organisations also took advantage of the guided tours and participated in activity sessions. Special open days were held for Friends of Historic Scotland and to mark Scottish Archaeology Month. Branches of the Young Archaeologists' Club were invited to visit, and the branch closest to Caerlaverock, from Stranraer, enjoyed a very successful day at the site. Members of the Perth branch (in which SUAT has an involvement) and of other branches across the UK, visited with their families.

In order to provide wider accessibility to the unfolding results of the excavation, a dedicated web site was created. Updates were added every few days. The hope was not only to give wider access to the results but also to provide a valuable educational resource. The internet can be a valuable medium for getting the message across, but of course its success depends on people's access to and familiarity with it.

A quiz sheet for young visitors, devised in partnership with Historic Scotland's Education Unit, posed a range of questions, such as 'Why do archaeologists have to be very careful and take lots of measurements and recordings as they work?' and 'Why do you think a second castle was built near the first castle but not on the same spot?'. Many children completed these sheets, illuminating them with their own interpretations.

It is not known what percentage of visitors had been attracted to Caerlaverock Castle because of the archaeology in progress there, but this certainly appeared to boost visitor numbers in what otherwise (in 1998) was a disappointing year for Scottish tourist attractions due to unfavourable currency exchange rates and very wet summer weather. The actual doing of the archaeology proved to be of as much interest as the results, and many local people returned often to watch the archaeologists working and learn of any fresh discoveries. Visitors'

support and appreciation of the work was very heartening. The archaeology was like an unfolding mystery; a detective plot. It was exciting. Archaeology is exciting, after all, and, as archaeologists, we need to nurture and encourage this excitement and enthusiasm.

Visitors' preconceptions

Visitors to an archaeological excavation each bring their individual experience and perception. Each can leave with valid and successful insights. Archaeologists need to share their insights as effectively as possible. It is clear that people have different perspectives, and our visitor-oriented approach to this project allowed them to learn from and enjoy the experience of their visit, and to express themselves.

To most people, archaeology means excavation. However, a longstanding image of archaeologists, especially among children, as elderly male professors, always excavating (Dyer 1983, 54) is steadily changing to reflect a situation closer to reality, partly thanks to increased media coverage of archaeology and to the impact of popular television series.

One common preconception about archaeological work, judging from visitors' comments, is that it is undertaken by students. We were frequently asked, during guided tours, if the on-site team (nearly all professional archaeologists) were students. A few visitors were genuinely surprised that people actually make a living from archaeology. This is a view that the profession as a whole would be wise to take notice of. As it is, the professional status of archaeologists is belied by the salaries they are paid, their working conditions and employment security. However, people are willing to accept that archaeologists do difficult, demanding and valuable work, and expect that they should be highly trained and highly skilled.

Young visitors, quite naturally, also arrived with preconceptions about castles. There are, of course, strong associations between castles and warfare, and those who visit castles such as Caerlaverock expect to learn about sieges, weaponry, dungeons, prisoners and executions. These topics were less relevant, though, to our investigation of the old castle site. The focus here was principally on the site's development, on trying to understand the sequence of structural episodes and understand its function within its landscape. The excavation revealed many aspects of daily life within the castle, particularly through the artefacts recovered. This rather different emphasis, upon investigating the castle itself and the lives of those who inhabited it, rather than upon warfare and sieges, provided, I feel, a refreshingly different perspective on medieval life, especially for youngsters.

The concept of castles being associated with warfare and sieges is strongly reinforced at Caerlaverock. It is, after all, an ideal place to learn about siege warfare, being the setting for a famous siege in 1300, now the focus for a new display area at the site. In 1300, Edward I led an invasion of Galloway, one of the strongest centres of Scottish resistance, and Caerlaverock Castle, in such a prominent and strategic position, was a prime target. Although a marginal incident among the turbulent events of the time, the siege of Caerlaverock was immortalised thanks to a detailed account of it written by a member of the besieging forces (Grove 1994, 20). This account, Le Siège de Karlaverock, written in the French language of the English court (Wright 1864), is one of the most fascinating and important contemporary accounts of siege warfare recorded for any medieval castle in Britain, hence the strong focus on this aspect of the castle's history in its presentation to visitors.

There is a perception, too, that castles stood in isolation, their thick walls forming a barrier to the world outside. In fact, as at Caerlaverock, settlements grew up around them, and they were often focal points of settled communities. Of course, the influence of a castle extended well beyond its curtain walls.

Responses to the archaeology

The archaeological work at this site had to be undertaken in such as way as to minimise disturbance of the fragile wildlife habitat. The careful removal and protection of the topsoil, which contained many thousands of bluebell bulbs, was among the aspects warmly appreciated by visitors. They also understood why it was important not to disturb too great an area of this important habitat. Only very minor intrusive work had been carried out in the harbour basin, for example.

On the platform overlooking the excavation, the guides explained the principles of archaeological excavation. We pointed out that it was an expensive operation, sometimes undertaken as a last resort, and was, in this case, seen as the only way to reveal more information about this particular site. The concept of rescue excavation (with which we at SUAT are very familiar) was often also explained. A clear and understandable explanation of archaeological methodology was an aspect of the tours that seemed to appeal to visitors. I feel it is important to explain how we discover information about a site, and how we reach the conclusions we reach. At SUAT, we have been able to get the concept of archaeological stratigraphy across to youngsters by means of illustrated classroom talks, with carefully-chosen images, and by use of small-scale simulated excavations (Cox 1996, 35).

Many visitors commented that the archaeologists' work was 'meticulous' and 'painstaking', requiring a great deal of patience. Many, in a quiet moment, would confide to

us that they had always wanted to work in archaeology, or at least to give it a try. Experience shows that the role of archaeologists actually enjoys a very positive view from the general public.

Scientific dating techniques, for example dendro-chronology and archaeomagnetic dating, both used at this site to important effect, proved to be of interest, as did the concept of waterlogging and organic preservation, also particularly relevant here. On the subject of water, the weather in the summer of 1998 was a popular talking point in itself. Many guided tours were conducted in the rain, but nevertheless, visitors listened and participated in the guided tours with great interest.

It was important for us to give visitors genuine opportunities to comment on and ask about anything they wanted to. They were given these opportunities, and we were rewarded with many insightful and intelligent observations in return.

Responses to the outreach methods

As mentioned above, the on-site visitor centre formed a natural starting point for learning about the archaeology. The layout of the exhibition was initially regarded as being at an evaluation stage, and, by monitoring visitors' responses to it, we were able to make some small modifications to make it even more accessible. Simple, informative labelling, understandable by children, was used for the artefacts display, and this was viewable from child height. Many people used the visitors' book to make favourable comments.

The guided tours were universally well received. People appreciated the particularly close access to the excavation and the wide-ranging content of the tours. They enjoyed the opportunities to ask questions, to explore our ideas about the archaeology for themselves and to express their views. The website also received a very positive response. It attracted over 3,500 hits during the project, and people were able to catch up with progress having been enthused by a visit. Schoolteachers used the website to keep their classes informed about the progress of the excavation.

Visitors were given an opportunity to see day-to-day finds work (cleaning, labelling and recording of finds) being carried out. Many joined us, and helped for a while in cleaning the finds. Among the materials on display was metalworking debris, associated with an iron smithing workshop on the site. People more often think of the products of an industrial process or craft activity than of its waste products, but of course archaeologists regularly deal with the latter. We found that visitors to the project were fascinated by all kinds of material evidence that can tell us something about past lives.

In providing artefact-handling experiences, we gave people opportunities for individual exploration of the archaeological evidence. In SUAT's school-based artefact-handling activities with youngsters the emphasis is on active learning and asking questions (Cox 1996, 34-5). Children value this opportunity to handle and explore real archaeological material. It holds their attention far better than a picture in a book or a static display of objects behind glass in a museum. Replica artefacts were used, along with the finds from the excavation and from SUAT's own small handling collection, to investigate with children how objects were made and used in the medieval period, and what archaeologists could learn from the artefacts recovered during the excavation (fig. 11.4).

Processing of environmental samples, using a flotation tank, also took place in public view, and there were brief demonstrations by Historic Scotland's Caerlaverock-based squad of stonemasons of the specialised stone working techniques used to repair historic monuments. In giving visitors such close access to the on-site work and to the evidence recovered, offering them opportunities to be at the heart of the learning process and to express themselves, we attempted to provide an experience with real depth.

Interpreting the ambiguous

The success of a work of art, for example a Van Gogh painting, depends on the particular way in which a viewer experiences it, and the range of different and powerful responses can be great. A painting can be experienced both as something outside the individual, but also within that person. Visitors to an archaeological site also personalise their experiences, and take away different insights. Perhaps one abiding memory of the Caerlaverock Old Castle excavation will be the sound of birdsong mixed with the sounds of scraping of trowels over stony clay. A range of different sensory responses was stimulated in this particularly peaceful setting.

In describing the form of the old castle in guided tours, use was made of a simple plan of the features thus far revealed, and certain architectural details provided important clues, easily visible from the viewing platform. These included chamfered stonework, rebates identifying doorways, and the base of a flight of steps leading to the missing first floor level. Visitors were invited to imagine a rather different environment for the old castle, closer to the shore since the coastline has receded southwards in the intervening centuries. The adjacent harbour basin, now dry for most of the year, would have played an

Fig. 11.4. A school group investigating medieval artefacts.

Fig. 11.5. One route to the Old Castle, with Carr woodland at either side.

important role in the siting of this castle. Since no reconstruction drawings or artists' impressions were available at this stage, visitors were invited to use their imaginations to bring the scene to life and to 'people' it. We were able to present the evidence, and present hypotheses, but also encouraged questioning. Ideas about the past are not fixed, but open to questioning and individual interpretation. I wanted to help people to engage with the archaeology, to be stimulated and enthused by it, and to feel it offered them something valuable and distinctive.

Many visitors asked about the origins of the building stone used at Caerlaverock, and this frequently prompted interesting discussions of the available evidence. Having discussed its possible origins, another frequent query was 'Where has all the stone gone?'. Here, some of the clues were strongly linked with the concept of recycling. Much of the better quality stone may have been transported the short distance to the later castle and incorporated in the buildings there. The old castle has no doubt also served as a convenient quarry for the local neighbourhood since its abandonment (RCAHMS 1920, 11).

The apparent absence of a well on the site also fascinated people. The excavation had not revealed a well, although this did not necessarily mean that one did not remain undiscovered. It was also worth considering why there might not have been a well inside this castle. Possibly, with the abundance of fresh water streams available around the site, there was no need for a well, and the construction of one may have posed great difficulties given the high water table and the nature of the geology.

Here is an example of there being no immediate and definitive answer, but it was interesting to discuss the possibilities, and visitors were thus empowered to participate in the interpretation of the archaeological evidence being uncovered. Their opinions are always valid. There are often no absolute right or wrong answers in archaeology. People can contribute their own ideas about the past.

The geographic and natural setting of the castles was also discussed. A nature trail links the two castles, winding through an area of Carr woodland, dominated by Alder (*Alnus glutinosa*) (fig. 11.5). Many visitors enjoyed learning a little about the diversity of local fauna and flora here, and there was a genuine two-way exchange of information, as local people had much to tell us about the local wildlife. In the past, people enjoyed a much closer relationship with their natural environment, making use of the resources locally available. In Scotland, there was a myriad of superstitions concerning different kinds of trees and other plants (Lamont-Brown 1996, 17). Alder itself, for example, was, in folklore, valued as a cure for fever, toothache and warts. It was also used to keep pests away from crops, and was highly valued in gunpowder manufacture as it makes excellent charcoal.

There was much interest in the reasons for the abandonment of the old castle. Among the visible hazards were the situation of the castle on marshy ground possibly affected by flooding from the sea and the instability of the structure due to inadequate preparation of its foundations on the clay. Less tangible, but perhaps equally valid, would have been the Maxwells' need for a large, strong, defensible residence; also a more comfortable one. Once again, discussing the possibilities with visitors was rewarding.

Discussion

Among the findings of visitor surveys carried out at the British Museum in the late 1970s (Alt 1980) was that most family visits were planned at quite short notice and were casually made for the purposes of leisure, recreation and general interest, rather than specialised interest. This is probably also true of visits to a place like Caerlaverock Castle. Most visitors arrive without detailed knowledge of its history or about archaeological processes. Although a small minority were reluctant to join one of the guided tours, the excavation must have been difficult to fully understand without one. Unguided visitors could read the brief explanatory information at the site itself and could see short stretches of wall foundations, but whatever their preconceptions about this early fortress were, they probably would not have been much changed unless we had a chance to talk with them. Guided tours are particularly valuable for youngsters, since their early impressions of archaeology may colour their perception of the subject for many years.

The experience of working alongside local volunteers was also a very positive one. The volunteers were highly motivated and brought valuable experience to the project, as well as deriving fulfilment from the work. Their contribution enhanced the work being done by the professional team, and thanks to their efforts we were able to communicate with many more visitors than would otherwise have been possible. It is also recognised that volunteers are the lifeblood of museums across Britain (Hall 1995, 25).

Visitors' responses to archaeology and archaeologists are discussed above, but what about archaeologists' responses to visitors to their excavations? The picture is not universally positive. I think the profession needs to be more responsive, more geared up to involve people. The investigations we carry out can have great significance to local communities and archaeologists should be respectful of the needs of these communities. Fortunately, there are many fine examples across Scotland of enlightened archaeologists appreciating the value of involving the public in their work.

I gave a lot of thought to ensuring that the needs of all visitors to the Caerlaverock excavation could be met. I think we achieved our aim of making sure that everyone had equal access to the information and experiences available. Disabled visitors with limited mobility who might otherwise have fallen behind during a guided tour were given individual tours at a gentler pace. There was also full access to the exhibition area and to the object-handling activities. The information in the exhibition was produced in large print so as to be accessible to people with impaired vision. I gave a personal guided tour to a blind gentleman who commented that he had very much enjoyed the sound of the excavation - the characteristic scraping of trowels on stone, the quiet conversation between on-site staff, all mingling with the birdsong in the woodland. The object-handling experience also appeared to be very valuable. Disability has come to be understood, in recent years, as a condition imposed by an able-bodied society rather than the inevitable consequence of impairment. Barriers of attitude can be as impassable as physical or sensory barriers.

We were able to engender an honest and respectful relationship between tour guides and visitors. There needs to be a certain chemistry between them. Much of the feedback was personalised and reflective; and it was all very valuable. Many visitors were in family groups, and evidence suggests that adult recreational choices are far more closely linked to recreational experiences begun as a child in a family than in school (Kelly 1977). This makes it vitally important to reach out to families and present archaeology positively and effectively to them.

Conclusions

The experiences of this project have provided many valuable insights. Guided tours proved to be the most effective way of helping visitors to engage with, and learn about, the archaeology while they were actually there looking at it. Well-designed information boards (and those at Caerlaverock are exceptional) can provide the key points, but the opportunity to listen to a more detailed perspective, to participate and to ask questions, is very valuable.

The best kinds of visitor experiences are those where the visitor feels interested, engaged, and comfortable. People should not feel intimidated, alienated or overwhelmed. Giving people opportunities to get involved and to make a contribution is also important. Experience of this and other educational projects has shown me that there is huge potential for the general public to be interested in archaeology. People are generally very supportive and are hungry to learn more about the subject. Children, whilst also being very perceptive and sometimes asking very searching questions, are generally prepared to support and understand the attempts of archaeologists to preserve and interpret the past. From this we can derive great encouragement.

Archaeology has something unique to offer the public. The Caerlaverock project provided unique experiences, quite different from an ordinary visit to a castle. Involving people also offers significant benefits to archaeologists. Here, we benefited greatly from visitors' local knowledge, thoughtful insights and useful feedback. The archaeological research developed in tandem with the interpretation.

At Caerlaverock, there is a unique relationship between wildlife, archaeology, the sea, the land, those who live here and those who visit the place. Our efforts to increase people's awareness of the contribution archaeology can make to this relationship and to their community will hopefully be valued by those who shared the experience with us.

Acknowledgments

I would like to thank Doreen Grove, Marion Fry, Chris Tabraham, Mike Rains, Peter Ransom, Richard Welander and Peter Yeoman, for their encouragement and support during the project. Warm thanks are also extended to the District Custodian Alec Little and his excellent staff at Caerlaverock Castle, for their interest in and assistance with the smooth running of the educational work. Thanks, also, to all those who visited the project and offered such valuable encouragement and kindness, including Bill and Sheila Cormack, Alfie Truckell, the late Jack Scott, Alistair and Lizzie Penman, Ray Chadburn, Isabelle Lousberg, Samantha Curry, John, Jean and Martyn Stewart, colleagues at SUAT Ltd and all at the Wildfowl & Wetlands Trust, Caerlaverock, to mention but a few. Figs. 11.1 and 11.2 are by Dave Munro. The project was funded by Historic Scotland.

Special thanks are due to the volunteers who worked with me on the outreach project, John Williams, David Jardine, Sheila Tindal, Stewart Duncan, Jane Gallagher and Sue Cromarty. A finer and more dedicated team would be difficult to find. I would also like to express my thanks to all who visited this project, and to the local community who made us feel very welcome.

References

Alt, M. B., 1980. Four years of visitor surveys at the British Museum (Natural History) 1976-79. *Museums Journal*, January 1980.

Brann, M. L., 1998. Caerlaverock Old Castle. *Discovery & Excavation in Scotland* (1998), 25.

Brann, M. L., 1999. Caerlaverock Old Castle. *Discovery & Excavations in Scotland* (1999), 23.

Cox, A., 1996. Interpreting the evidence: Education from an archaeological unit's perspective. In Curtis, E and Curtis, N (eds) *Touching the past: Archaeology* 5-14. Edinburgh: Scottish Children's Press. 34-37.

Dyer, J., 1983. *Teaching Archaeology in Schools*. Aylesbury: Shire.

Grose, F., 1789. *The Antiquities of Scotland*. London: Printed for S.Hooper.

Grove, D., 1994. *Caerlaverock Castle* (Historic Scotland souvenir guide). Edinburgh: Historic Scotland.

Hall, E., 1995. All for love. *Museums Journal*, October 1995.

Kelly, J. R., 1977. Leisure socialisation: replication and extension. *Journal of Leisure Research, 9*.

Lamont-Brown, R., 1996. *Scottish Folklore*. Edinburgh: Birlinn.

RCAHMS, 1920. Old Caerlaverock Castle. In *An Inventory of the Monuments in the County of Dumfries*. Edinburgh: RCAHMS. 10-11.

Wright, T., 1864. *The Roll of Arms of the Princes, Barons and Knights who attended King Edward I to the siege of Caerlaverock in 1300*. London: J.C.Hotten.

12

'But Didn't the Horses Drown?'
Interpreting historic narrowboats in the Working Boats Project.

Jo Bell

The working boats of Britain's canals, and the culture associated with them thrived until the 1950s. The boating community and its material culture mixed the industrial and domestic intimately. The Working Boats Project re-uses twentieth century boats to interpret these lives for a wide local audience.

Introduction

We all know the difficulties of conveying to the visitor that a muddy hole in the ground is worth the admission charge, let alone that it was home to a vibrant and complex community in Roman or Medieval times. Interpretation in this sense does not mean our understanding of a site or artefact as archaeologists. Rather, it is the process by which we share that understanding with the public, communicating by whatever means necessary to give them access to their own history. One might think that an industrial archaeologist working with twentieth century remains has an easy life when it comes to interpretation. After all, ours is an embarrassment of riches – well-preserved technology, standing buildings, drawings, photographs and in my case the ultimate luxury of living sources. Despite this – and sometimes because of it – even the very recent past can be subject to ambiguities which hinder presentation. This has been illustrated in several ways during recent work with British Waterways' Working Boats Project.

The Working Boats Project

The Working Boats Project is a British Waterways initiative, funded by substantial grants from the Heritage Lottery Fund and other partners. Based in the Midlands, we aim to conserve, restore and re-use ten of the narrow 'working boats' which carried heavy cargoes on local canals until the 1960s (fig. 12.1). The oldest of the ten boats dates from 1912: the youngest, 1958. Most are restored to the style and form they had in the mid 1950s. They stand (or float) at almost the farthest edge of historic archaeology. Indeed, some readers will feel that 1958 barely qualifies as archaeology. Nonetheless, these boats require as rigorous an approach to recording, conservation and interpretation as any other large artefact (fig. 12.2). They are surveyed before conservation work

begins, and the work is done by master boatbuilders liaising closely with British Waterways staff.

Five boats are already back on the water, and it is on these that we have used the interpretative methods outlined below. The issues of archaeological compromise raised when we try to reach high standards of conservation, accessibility, sustainability *and* safety cannot be addressed here. Many of the decisions on individual boats were made before the present archaeological approach was adopted. Decisions on interpretation, however, are ongoing.

It will be helpful to explain a little about the culture of working boats, the work that we do with our fleet and the audience we need to reach.

The subject matter

The phrase 'working boats' describes any of the craft which worked on Britain's canals and inland waterways from the eighteenth century to the mid-twentieth. The archaeology of canals has been relatively well studied, but the boats which moved on them have been neglected by our profession. In the 1760s, the Duke of Bridgewater's pioneering Manchester canals used simple wooden boats called 'starvationers' because of their protruding ribs (Ware 1980, 8). Thereafter, working boats developed a rich regional typology and technology. Most were cargo boats and some were specially adapted to carry chemical or liquid loads. In pre-railway days, some carried passengers or mail on non-stop flyboat runs. There were specialised boats for canal maintenance, and pleasure or trip boats. Wooden boats were replaced with iron and later steel hulls. All classes of boat were driven by man, horse or sail power until the later nineteenth century, when steam engines came into use. Diesel engines followed in the last century.

Fig. 12.1 Loaded coal boats in transit near Birmingham, 1949. © Colin Scrivener.

Fig. 12.2 EDM survey of tunnel tug Birmingham, by University of Leicester Archaeological Services.

As custodians of the inland waterways, British Waterways do not usually take an explicitly curatorial role. However, the organisation acknowledges its responsibilities in heritage management. It has many listed and scheduled structures in its ownership, and a number of historic narrowboats in its operational fleet. The Working Boats Project is a recognition of their significance, and shows a willingness to support practical conservation. The project fleet of ten is a representative mixture of maintenance boats, tugs and the distinctive narrow boat pairs which characterised Midland boating from the 1930s until the 1960s. It should be noted that the phrases 'narrow boat' and 'barge' are not synonymous. Narrow boats have a width or beam of around 2.2m. Barges are around twice as wide, and the two should not be confused.

Narrow boat pairs were a common and distinctive sight on the canals within living memory, and it is to them that this paper refers. A pair consisted of a motor boat with (usually) a diesel engine, drawing behind it a 'butty' or engineless boat, similar in dimensions and carrying a similar load of up to 25 tons. Each boat had a small furnished cabin, c.3m x 2.2m. In these two cabins lived the working family, sometimes with many children. Long-haul journeys (eg. Birmingham – London, four days) and poor wages had made family life on land impossible, so that by the mid nineteenth century the boats were both a home and a workplace. The importance of 'the role of the individual in the creation of material culture' (Palmer and Neaverson 1998, 7) is very clear in this joint domestic/industrial setting. There were strong cultural traditions, including crafts such as fender making (these being the rope 'bumpers' which protect the boat from scrapes), and folk art such as rose-and-castle painting (fig. 12.3). This painting had well-defined regional styles, originating from individual boatyards (Chaplin 1989, 72). Working boat artefacts are distinctive and highly decorated, such as the water cans in which fresh water was kept or the polished brass items which were often collected and displayed in the cabin.

Central to this culture were the skills required to load, steer, work and display the boats. Many skills survive only in oral tradition, as the boaters were largely illiterate and their community insular. One of our aims in the Working Boats Project is to record these techniques and spread knowledge of them, so that restored boats can be worked in the proper way. Boating people inevitably had (and survivors still have) a very linear sense of geography, with good knowledge of a lock system 60 miles away but very little knowledge of villages or towns a mile from the canal. Their sense of community likewise was of a long thin neighbourhood, stretching for many miles and with individuals constantly moving off or reappearing. The history we are interpreting therefore incorporates the material culture, art, technology and social history of working boats.

The audience

To explain whom we are interpreting for, a word should be said about the day-to-day work of the project. The boats travel the waterways of the Midlands, from Staffordshire and the West Midlands through to south Warwickshire. They no longer carry heavy loads, but do carry a mock cargo. They appear at public events such as boat gatherings, where thousands of people see them. Many hundreds step aboard to see inside the cabins. Some of these people know nothing about canals: many are pleasure boaters with no knowledge of working boats: others grew up on working boats. The boats are also used for formal, curriculum-based schools work. Children visit a pair of boats in their local area as part of a themed study – transport, local history or design and technology, for instance. 'Education' also encompasses our volunteer group, Friends of the Working Boats. Volunteers are learning to work the boats, preserving skills and shedding light on the fabric of the craft. Like much industrial archaeology, working boats have hooks, holes and attachments which can only be explained when one actually uses the craft. Community work with the boats will include work with youth groups, the visually impaired, the elderly, people with learning disabilities and arts groups. The audience for the project clearly includes a very wide range of ages and levels of

experience. It also includes staff from British Waterways itself, who are learning that the working boats provide a unique focus for educational, community and press relations work.

Fig. 12.3 An example of rose and castle painting.

Interpretation

In this project, conservation and interpretation decisions are interdependent. Each has implications for the other.

Our first important decision, affecting all subsequent decisions on interpretation, was to keep the boats on the water. Several important inland boats are preserved out of the water (for instance *Friendship* at the Ellesmere Port Boat Museum), or in the water at inland waterway museums (Ellesmere Port, Gloucester and Stoke Bruerne). There are good curatorial reasons for this and we sometimes wistfully recall the words, 'the care of boats can be more difficult than that of any other larger object….Keeping the boat in the water creates additional difficulties' (Ball 1997, 44). We feel though that our own fleet must be capable of moving around the canal system. Only then can we achieve the joint aims of preserving waterway skills and taking the history of working boats to a wide audience. We regard them as floating listed buildings – with all of the problems of a listed building and the additional challenge of keeping it afloat. By keeping boats on the water and using them in their original landscape context, we ambitiously hope to avoid the accusations of fossilising them and making them nostalgic visitor attractions.

Our second decision was what period to interpret. The history of the boats offered several possibilities. The seven cargo boats in our fleet were in use from the 1930s to the 1980s in various forms. A boat might be built in 1935 with a wooden bottom, have a new steel bottom fitted in the 1950s, a different cabin in the 1960s and finish its working life in the 1980s as an open boat used for dredging. At each stage, its fabric was adapted. Each period has its own legitimacy, and each would allow us to tell a different story through interpretation. Sources of information include the fabric of the boats themselves and documentary sources such as company records and boatbuilders' plans. Photographs of working boats from the late nineteenth century onwards (fig. 12.4) show important details of working techniques, ropework and clothing.

We chose to restore most of the boats to their 1950s form, which allows us to explore many important issues. The 1950s were a time of great change in the boating community. Challenged by road freight and cultural pressures, commercial carrying was virtually extinguished. Working boat life was increasingly difficult. Boaters' children could not attend school if constantly on the move; pay and working conditions were poor compared to other trades; canal infrastructure and waterway commerce were alike neglected by government. The social stigma of belonging to the boating class was strong, and they were often dismissed as 'water gypsies' by non-boaters. The wartime predominance of women on the canals – known as the 'Idle Women' because of their Inland Waterway insignia – and the post-war nationalisation of the waterways can be discussed. There are also practical advantages to choosing the 1950s for interpretation. The technology and construction of that time is still generally available, so that where replacement of a component is unavoidable we can replace like with like. This period of decline is also within living memory, allowing us to learn from former boat people on technical and social issues.

In two cases, interpretation has involved more swingeing changes to the fabric or presentation of historic boats. These decisions were made before the project took its present stance on conservation, but were taken for good interpretative reasons. Firstly, it must be conceded that very substantial changes were made to the narrow boats *Sagitta* and *Carina*. They no longer have the traditional profile of working boats. They do, however, offer a unique interpretative space with extremely good access for the public (fig. 12.5). The holds of these boats are now well-equipped classrooms, and one has a mechanised chairlift so that wheelchair users can come

Fig. 12.4 Working boats moored at Regents Dock, London in the 1940s © The Waterways Trust Archive.

Fig. 12.5 Explaining a narrowboat cabin.

aboard. They each retain the traditional boater's cabin but Sagitta's cabin has been completely reversed. The usual form of the cabin, opening on to a small stern deck or counter, limits access to three or four visitors at a time. The reversal means that up to thirty people can sit in the relatively spacious hold of the boat, looking into the cabin as an interpreter explains it. The second significant compromise or adaptation is to a 1951 piling boat and rig, which will not be put back on the water. Instead they will be installed in a landscaped area outside a British Waterways office in the Black Country, as part of an interpretative display. The boat will be an essential part of a display explaining canal maintenance and ecology. This is a compromise made partly out of practicality and partly to allow closer study of the boat than would otherwise be possible.

Having made the decisions outlined above, other decisions become easier. The fixtures and furnishings of the boats must not be anachronistic, and any 'living history' or costume used in association with them must also be correct for the 1950s. The very nature of boats imposes certain pressing restrictions. Anything used in interpretation must be mobile, aesthetically appropriate and capable of being stowed in the hold. There is therefore no static or fixed interpretation, in the sense of

boards or installations to help the visitor decipher the 'site'. Indeed, the craft often move from one historic location to another, and interpretation needs to be flexible. Explanation of the boats will differ between a former canal maintenance workshop and a former private sawmill, and different issues can be touched on at each mooring.

Interpretation also has to be appropriate to the culture of the working boats. We keep leaflets and written interpretation to a minimum, as the written word was not commonly used amongst boaters. The physical environment of the boats, and 'props' associated with them, have proven by far our most effective weapons. The main interpretative tools are:

- The boat cabins, furnished as in the 1950s. Fold-away beds and tables, cutlery and crockery, crocheted 'lace' and blankets, ribboned plates, brass knobs, period photographs, a solid fuel iron stove and rag rugs are all displayed and explained. Roses and castles painting is done by well-known craftspeople in appropriate regional style. In the case of Sagitta and Carina, access is maximised by the complete reversal of one cabin and the addition of a wheelchair lift.

- Living history presentations by professional interpreters. From spring 2002 living history and storytelling will be important components of the educational programme. This links the working boats very closely to national curriculum work in local schools. Typical activities include a pretended engine breakdown, where the boat is forced to stop. The 1950s couple on board come ashore to do their washing, trade with children and talk to visitors about their living conditions.

- Presentation of the boat exterior in the correct livery, with correct paintwork including the bright geometric patterns, furnishings such as the traditional water can and mop, fancy ropework and sign-written wording.

- Period costume for visitors, especially children, to 'get into role'. A neckerchief and waistcoat, flat cap or scarf increase the feeling of involvement and make the visit more enjoyable. They also allow us to explain the costume. An apron, for instance, protected work clothes from dirt and coal dust: a bonnet kept the sun and wind off the head for women who spent the day steering a boat.

- Mock cargo, displayed in the hold with access by wooden steps. Visitors can step into the hold of the boat and look into sacks or wooden crates. The sample cargoes are typical of those carried by working boats – tea, coffee, crockery, coal, grain (fig. 12.6).

- Interactive models and games. These include large upstanding games such as a jigsaw of the boaters' cabin, and models demonstrating the difference between road and water carriage. Artefact boxes, for use in schools or by the visually impaired, include items such as coal (not familiar to many children), a painted water can, flat iron, potty and small fender.

- Painted A-boards, in the sign-writing style of the boats. These give a biography for each craft and an outline of the Working Boats Project.

- Our volunteers in the Friends of the Working Boats group. Volunteers act as skilled intermediaries, explaining the history of individual boats and the culture associated with them. Many volunteers are themselves former boaters. Often volunteers work in period costume, doing third-party interpretation to explain boating techniques. Short films can also be produced to record and pass on technical skills such as methods of ropework and loading.

Fig. 12.6 Explaining cargoes to a visitor.

- Oral history and recordings of former boat workers. These can be played back in the cabin so that the boats are explained by the people who actually lived on them, rather than being interpreted solely by well-meaning professionals.

- Demonstrations of boating crafts such as fender-making, rag-rugging and sign-writing. These complement the display of the boat itself and provide a starting point for conversation about it.

Multi-level access to information is vital. Complete newcomers should feel that they have learnt without being intimidated, but people who already have a good understanding must still be able to learn. For children and many adults, the most effective tool is the furnished cabin. The cramped space, the warmth of the stove, even the smells of cooking, coal dust and Brasso are all aids to understanding living conditions on a narrow boat. Such stimuli have a genuine force and immediacy which cannot be rivalled by any photograph or museum replica cabin. There is a snobbish temptation to dismiss these as gimmicks, but they help us to see an artefact – in this case the boat – as it was perceived in its working life. This is high-quality learning with many physical stimuli to questioning. Why does the table fold up like that, where do the children sleep? and so on.

Ambiguities and issues

The boats' mobility gives them the ability to reach tourist hotspots such as Stratford, and to reach new audiences there. They also are able to visit poor areas, or run-down urban settings where access to museums or similar facilities may seem limited or irrelevant. These are amongst our most important target areas. The disadvantaged parts of the West Midlands are areas where working boat culture thrived, for instance in parts of Birmingham and the Black Country. Here, working boats were the vital transport link that brought the Industrial Revolution inland. We strive to make our visits locally relevant, using local references to communicate the boats' former work. High concentrations of disadvantaged and ethnic communities are settled here, and the issues encountered by the project may be of interest.

Although the Working Boats Project fleet is extremely recent in archaeological terms, the history of the boats remains unknown to many local people in all the areas where we work. For some adults and almost all children, the way of life on these boats in the 1950s is as alien as life in an Iron Age hillfort, and requires as thorough an explanation. The cabins were tiny spaces with no electricity or running water, no school for the children and a constantly shifting view outside the window. Visitors are encouraged to explore the appealing and unappealing aspects of such a life. The issues raised when professional archaeologists interpret so distinctive a working-class culture should not be overlooked. We aim to minimise, though we cannot remove, the impression of 'outsiders looking back' (Lewery 1996, 9).

One would hope that such recent history would present no ambiguities of interpretation. In fact it can seem that the information available, particularly from the oral evidence of veteran boat people, contradicts itself. There is more than one way to skin a cat, and very many ways to rope a pair of boats together or work them through a set of locks. The working boat community was illiterate to an unusual degree and up to a very late date, so there has never been a body of written instruction. To supplement the physical evidence of our own boats and others, we have oral tradition and a limited amount of photography or film footage. From the late 1950s there were several books and biographies concerning working boat life, but even at that date some were coloured by nostalgia and poetic license. In fact we seldom have direct contradictions, and usually these can be explained by extremely localised traditions. It is important however, to convey to the public that there may be alternative methods or materials to those we are using. We are also learning ourselves. Occasionally we find ourselves in the embarrassing position of being corrected by a visitor with thirty years' experience of the life we are describing – not a problem faced by the prehistorian!

The benefits of such direct and physical interpretative archaeology are clear. The work done with schools in the Walsall area, particularly, has demonstrated the value of the project for children who do not have English as a first language. Some have come to Britain very recently. For these children and for many others, the canal is an entirely unfamiliar environment. The working boats offer an insight into the canal and help us to explain why it is there. They are a useful tool to explain the changing local landscape and natural environment, the history of the immediate area and the function of nearby buildings and places. The boat cabin, its furnishings and the language used to describe them are unfamiliar to *all* the children. They are put on an equal footing even if only by bewildering them in equal measure. The boats provoke thought about different ways of living, as well as conversation and interaction.

The restoration of boats to their 1950s form could perhaps make it difficult to explain the important earlier stages of canal boat history. The reasons for building canals in the first place, and the many decades of horse boating, might seem to be excluded by our 1950s setting. We have overcome the latter, at least, by devising a scenario for children in which our main character Harry talks about his family. Though he works on a boat with a diesel engine, his father was familiar with horse boating, and 'Harry' is able to explain the principles.

The project's contact with children is more structured and themed than that with adults, and exposes the gaps in our own explanations. As children are wont to do, they show us where we are taking too much for granted. Nowhere is this clearer than in our attempts to explain horse-boating. From the eighteenth century, narrow boats were drawn by horses walking on the towpath. This method continued into living memory and the physical evidence remains clear in many places. Deep grooves in brickwork or cast iron furnishings show where the wet ropes rubbed repeatedly, and certain hooks or fixtures can be seen which were put in place to help the horse take up the strain. To children who take the combustion engine for granted this is a very hard concept to grasp. When asked what animal could be used to pull the boat along, there is usually a cry of 'fish'. On one recent occasion, several voices suggested 'squirrels'. When the idea of the horse is introduced, it becomes clear that some children cannot imagine how or why it would pull a 25-ton boat. Doubtless this is a failing on our part, but occasionally a trembling voice asks, 'but didn't the horses drown?'

Conclusions

Interpretation is a responsibility for all of us, whether we work on open excavations, building survey or the reconstruction of steam engines. We have the privilege to work at the coal face of history. It is incumbent upon us to share our findings with as wide an audience as possible, in whatever format they may find accessible and informative. We are striving to make archaeology a part of people's lives, and vice versa. However, we cannot claim to know everything about the artefacts or sites we work with. There will be ambiguities in our interpretation and we should admit this. If this is true of the Working Boats Project, where the material is never more than a century old, it must certainly be true for colleagues working on more remote periods. Ambiguity is the price we pay for honesty in interpretation. No, we don't know what that did – can you tell us? We think that the boats were loaded like this – do you know better? We aren't sure – but this is our best guess. In this project, at least, good interpretation relies on humility, candour and humour. Humility is needed because our public sometimes knows more than we do, and we must be willing to learn from them. Candour is needed to acknowledge the gaps in our understanding, and explain them in our interpretation. And humour is necessary whenever a visitor asks if the horses drowned.

(**Note:** The views above do not necessarily represent those of British Waterways. Illustrations © British Waterways except where stated otherwise.)

References

Ball, S., 1997. *Larger and Working Objects: a guide to their preservation and care.* London: Museums & Galleries Commission.

Chaplin, T., 1989. *Narrow Boats.* Stowmarket: Whittet Books.

Lewery, A., 1996. *Flowers Afloat.* Newton Abbot: David & Charles.

Palmer & Neaverson, 1998. *Industrial Archaeology: Principles and Practice.* London: Routledge.

Ware, M. E., 1980. *Narrow Boats at Work.* Stafford: Moorland Publishing Co.

13

Endpiece.
Whither interpretation?

Peter Stone

'Every archaeological job in Britain is dependent at the end of the day on public support for archaeology and the historic environment. The effective provision of information to the general public about our archaeological heritage must, therefore, be a major priority, if not the major priority, underlying everything we do as archaeologists.'

(Frodsham, this volume)

But it is not. Nowhere near. Nor has it ever been. Many archaeologists have claimed recently, at an anecdotal level, that the failure to interpret or present (differences that I shall return to below) archaeological fieldwork is the result of the domination of developer funded fieldwork. Such a view must be questioned and, I suggest, rejected. For, as a profession, we have never been very good at interpreting or presenting what we do, either to ourselves - long delay of fieldwork reports, eventually delivered in a daunting and off-putting format that frequently fail to summarise the important findings (the real interpretation? - the value of that piece of work to the general picture) - or to the general public. There have, of course, been some wonderful exceptions – exceptions that are drawn out quickly as defence to such accusations (think of Wheeler, through numerous MSC inspired publications of the 1980s, to the TV heroes of Time Team). No, despite what has been reported upon in this and other similar volumes and conferences the profession puts the provision of information and interpretation to the public low down on its agenda. Are we not told explicitly (Carver: this volume) that Historic Scotland '...defined its policy on interpretation only recently'? Certainly developer funded fieldwork has not helped the situation and, while PPG 15 and 16 are being revised at present, initial discussion with and representation to members of the re-drafting group provide few crumbs of comfort that PPG42 will serve us much better.

No, archaeology is funded, for better or worse, for archaeology's sake (although see Halkon: this volume for a hope that some work goes beyond this). While this is true of developer funded work (the requirement to fund archaeological enquiry would not be within the planning process if archaeologists had not lobbied for it to be there) it is perhaps even truer of (that increasingly scarce animal) research fieldwork. We may argue that archaeology for archaeology (or archaeologists?) sake is

wrong, that archaeology has a role and purpose far wider than the academic discipline, but such arguments essentially fall on deaf ears. As told to me on more than one occasion by senior figures within the profession: 'you cannot interpret anything until you have done the archaeology'. The truth of this assertion is staggeringly obvious but the response has always been 'but why are we doing the archaeology? Surely *doing the archaeology* includes a commitment and responsibility to interpret the archaeology: otherwise, why are we doing it – frequently with public money and/or at the request of the public (i.e. PPGs) - in the first place?' Yes, archaeology is protected, and indirectly funded, through the planning process, but if the dissemination and interpretation of results to a wide audience were fundamental to that process it would be writ in stone within the present PPGs. As we all know, it is not.

As archaeologists we may, and frequently do, discuss the wider presentation and interpretation of archaeological work as testified by numerous conference sessions and specially arranged workshops and seminars. A number (of the larger) Units have been able to appoint community outreach or education staff (frequently assisted by pump-priming from English Heritage, and especially its Education Service) but these are the exception. In *Profiling the Profession* (Aitchison 1999) no interpretation staff were listed and only three education staff. Of these, one was categorised as a 'senior post' (Aitchison 1999, 108) while the others were categorised as 'other posts' (Aitchison 1999, 107). Not an employment record that reflects '... a major priority, underlying everything we do as archaeologists'.

Given this situation, I pessimistically suggest that, the above papers reflect not the normal but the abnormal state of affairs. Readers may recognise similar activities carried out by others – perhaps themselves - but I would be (pleasantly and amazingly) surprised if anyone could read this volume and react by saying 'this is what happens on a daily basis in my working life'. My guess is that most of the work outlined here relates to the '...all too rare opportunity for a wide cross-section of the local community to experience aspects of their local heritage as it is being 'discovered'' (Toolis & Ellis, this volume). This is not only frustrating but annoying: why should staff from SUAT Ltd have to put their own, unpaid time (Cox, this volume) into work that should be fundamental to the work of all archaeologists? Why should Waddington (this volume) have to put the royalties of a book he has written (and countless hours of unpaid time) into pump-priming further interpretation work in Northumberland? Yes, we all work extra hours and pay for things that in any commercial world might be expected to be paid for by the company. But why do we allow this to continue with such a basic aspect of our work? Such questions raise fundamental issues relating to the funding and nature of archaeological work, and while the latter is central to this endpiece the former is beyond the scope of the present publication. This said, a parting observation must be that competitive tendering for a service that most developers fail to see as anything but a nuisance, must be undermining our own position. Could not all those tendering add a standard 10-15% (8% was all that was needed at Braehead: Toolis & Ellis, this volume) to project costs for public interpretation, thereby avoiding undermining each other but achieving a huge step forward for the profession? If contractors were shy of adding this, could Local Authority Archaeologists as clients impose such a blanket requirement? If Local Authority archaeologists are unwilling or unable to impose, or even suggest, such a blanket requirement, could not English Heritage take the lead?

I should like to put these depressing, and no doubt over exaggerated, views to one side and briefly concentrate on a few of the generic interpretation issues raised by the papers in this volume.

A number of authors discuss who should be doing the interpretation. Waddington argues forcibly and convincingly for the archaeologist to be at least heavily involved – not least because this approach 'keeps archaeologists in employment and reduces the need for expensive interpretation consultants'! Perhaps more – certainly equally – importantly Waddington argues that the archaeologist needs to be involved to ensure 'accuracy of information'. This is echoed by a number of contributors (for example Taylor and Wall) who emphasise the need for team work (and see Waddington's list of acknowledgements for the huge number in his 'team'). I have reported elsewhere (Stone 1994) on the re-display of the Alexander Keiller Museum in Avebury (a re-display now built upon by the work of the National Trust – see Taylor this volume) and noted the dynamic tensions inherent in the team which eventually led to the creation of a 'Neolithic figure' of split appearance. We, as the project team, could not agree on what the person would have looked like (nor indeed, for a long time as to

whether or not there should be a figure in the museum at all!). The resulting split-appearance individual did much to throw our uncertainty back onto the visitor (as encouraged by a number of contributors to this volume) and was seen as a highlight of the redisplayed museum. The point here is that the figure would never have seen the light of day had either the archaeologists involved or the interpreters had their own ways. The archaeologists did not initially want a figure (although Ancient Monument Inspector Brian Davison was instrumental in the final compromise) while the interpreters wanted a figure to show 'what it had been like'. The team worked well and came up with a piece of, to my mind, excellent interpretation: the beauty of team work. However, I should like to take this one stage further. I think (well I would as I was part of it...) this team benefited from an unusually open-minded and educationally aware Inspector (his wife was a teacher and he had had to share offices and had worked with members of the Education Service for some time) and also included a qualified and experienced teacher (interpreter?) and archaeologist (me). Our impact on the team made it rather unusual and atypical. Frodsham (this volume) suggests that there would be a considerable market for a consultancy of specialised archaeological interpreters: '...such practitioners could be archaeologists prepared to learn the rudiments of interpretation, or environmental interpreters with a sound basic understanding of the theory and practice of archaeology'. Putting aside Waddington's fears of cost, I fully applaud Frodsham's view but go a step further and refine and extend it by suggesting that such individuals need specialised training following on from their first degree in archaeology. I immediately open myself to attack for self interest or insider-dealing as I help teach on, to my knowledge, the only taught postgraduate degree in the country specialising in heritage education and interpretation! But the course exists because I, from my experience working in field archaeology and for English Heritage, and others saw it as fundamental to the development of widespread expertise in heritage education and interpretation. Changes within Higher Education, far beyond the scope of this endpiece, make it increasingly impossible for undergraduate programmes to deliver such detailed professional understanding or competence. We cannot expect anyone to take seriously the demand for public interpretation to become central to the archaeological profession if there are no professionals with the expertise to deliver public interpretation. Perhaps this is why much of the excellent advice offered in *Visitors Welcome* (English Heritage 1988) has failed to be universally introduced. Vocational, professionally validated, postgraduate qualifications like those offered at Newcastle should become the norm for those intending to follow a career specialising in archaeological interpretation, just as similar qualifications are the norm for other specialist arms of the profession.

Implicit in this need for specialised training and understanding is an acceptance that the range of interpretation techniques and methodologies at our disposal has grown almost exponentially over the last decade or so. It is a tall order asking for individuals to remain at the cutting edge of both archaeological fieldwork and interpretation or indeed, even of all of the different techniques of interpretation. No one-year MA programme can make individuals experts across the range of interpretation methodologies and techniques available. Rather such courses should be providing students with an understanding of the opportunities offered by interpretation to the profession within the context of the profession and, for example, its managerial and ethical constraints. Such individuals may not be able to deliver everything; but they should certainly 'know a man who can'. My second point is that the papers here present a huge array of different methodologies of interpretation and types of media used (see for example Bell and Bevan). Wall particularly discusses computer-based interpretation – and notes the problems of software and hardware capacity having a major impact on the quality of (or simple ability to access) interpretation. The message here is surely simple: we should be ready to use every possible method and style of interpretation available. Different audiences (see below) will relate differently to different media, and archaeological interpreters should be ready and able to employ the full range of methods in their quest for better and more effective interpretation.

The suggestion that we use this full range of interpretation open to us raises the thorny issue of the full scale (re)construction of sites (and see Stone and Planel 1994). Bennett and Waddington (this volume) both discuss the value of full scale (re)construction of sites as general interpretation for the public and as a means of deepening the academic archaeological understanding of the past. Bell (this volume) moves the debate on a stage by discussing at what stage modification to her boats creates something new – or at least not old. These issues are not new (see the ancient Athenian arguments over Theseus's boat) and are beyond the scope of this endpiece. However, we must never forget the power of walking into a roundhouse or henge, and the fact that that the memory of such experiences will almost certainly survive countless written interpretations encountered by members of the public 'proving' the inaccuracy of the (re)construction.

A number of contributors suggest that interpretation should stimulate visitors to create their own understanding of the past (for example, Bevan, Cox, and Wall). This is where I see the difference between 'presentation' and 'interpretation' being crucial. Archaeologists are in the obvious position of being the best people to present information concerning the past. After all, it is they who have studied the past in detail and it is they, usually, who have worked on the particular material being interpreted. Thus the presentation of this material is usually their sole responsibility. My argument here closely follows Waddington's (this volume)

discussion of the nature of interpretation. That this is a Neolithic handaxe is the presentation of information. How this information is then woven into a story, or image, of the past is interpretation and such information is, obviously, open to multiple interpretations.

That visitors should be encouraged to interact with the presentation and draw their own interpretation is a methodology with which I fully agree and is one I have followed in much of my own work (for example, with the Avebury figure mentioned above). However, there is a slim danger of over elaboration on this front. I question Wall's extreme view (this volume) when he actually argues that 'Interpreting the ambiguous also presents us with opportunities to say **your** interpretations are just as valid as **ours**' (his emphasis). I may read too much into this statement and my criticism may be regarded as nit-picking and unfair, but if archaeological interpretation is to 'come of age' then its proponents need to be extremely careful how they evangelise. I do not believe that the interpretation of a lay member of the general public will normally be as good as that of a trained archaeologist. Yes, there may be occasional times when a member of the public may bring specialised knowledge to the interpretation of a particular object or feature, or may come to an interpretation with a fresh mind, but in the construction of a 'wide-angle' of, for example, the Northumberland Neolithic, the expert must surely win every time. This is precisely because they are the experts, having spent many years learning their trade and collating information concerning the area or topic. It is these experts who should be able to be open-minded and skilled enough to offer different interpretations based on their own presentation of the information.

Finally, I think we need to review why we believe we have an obligation to interpret our work. Carver (this volume) identifies three reasons why archaeologists have a responsibility to interpret their work. First, that we have a 'moral and intellectual obligation' to disseminate information to fellow archaeologists. Second, that any commissioned work will require some form of report. Third, that we need to explain our findings to a more general audience. (As an aside, Carver goes on to argue that 'If we are to take our relations with a wider audience more seriously then we must learn to speak with them'. I have no argument with this save that there is not one but many audiences out there with the potential to visit our sites and to be at the receiving end of our interpretation. Each audience has its own needs and peculiarities: no-one said that archaeological interpretation should be easy...). In addition, and almost as a throwaway line, Carver adds that interpretation is part of the mission statement of Historic Scotland – and therefore implicitly adds a fourth reason: we are spending public money on archaeology and the public should get something in return for such funding. In other words, part of our responsibility is rather like a mortgage repayment: the public – or local authorities acting on their behalf - provide archaeologists with either the funding or the planning framework within which to work and should be repaid by archaeologists providing an explanation and interpretation of what has been found. All of these responsibilities are couched in terms of archaeologists repaying – in one guise or another - society. I would add that archaeologists have a responsibility to the heritage itself to interpret their work in order to influence the public to become increasingly aware of the needs of conserving and investigating the historic environment. Similar arguments have been put forward as to why a number of archaeological units have a responsibility to interpret – given their beneficial tax status as educational charities. Surely such arguments, and such responsibilities, relate to all archaeologists.

Other contributors, explicitly and implicitly, agree with these reasons and add others. Wall argues that interpretation should be fundamental to archaeological work for if it is not – 'why is the research being done in the first place'. Taylor perhaps provides some form of answer by stating that if we do not interpret then archaeological research 'could remain the province of experts in dusty tomes on library shelves'. God forbid. Waddington adds that interpretation protects archaeological jobs and Taylor argues that archaeological interpretation should lead to a more informed and conservation-aware public. We should not expect this to be done in a dry academic style, but rather by using the full range of interpretation techniques available to us, by making archaeology fun. We have already seen that a number of contributors have no problem in seeing archaeological interpretation as a form of entertainment: all power to their collective elbows.

However, surely there are more fundamental – deeper? - reasons for archaeological interpretation. 'It should be to stimulate interest in the heritage by encouraging people to think for themselves about what it might have been like to have been alive in the past' (Frodsham, this volume); '…to try and give an indication as to what it would really have been like to live in 1st century Roman London' (Swain, this volume). Put another way, archaeological interpretation is about the people of the past: the 'indian(s) behind the artefact'. But surely even this, in itself, is not enough. Surely such contemplation of the past should lead to a contemplation of the present. What is different now to then? Would we, as parents in the 21st century, feel the same as parents of a two year old who died from meningitis some 4,000 years ago? (see Frodsham, this volume). And might a contemplation of the present not lead us to a contemplation of the future and our role in that future, not only as custodians of the archaeological heritage, but as individuals trying to make sense of an increasingly complex and complicated world?

References

Aitchison, K. 1999. *Profiling the Profession: a survey of archaeological jobs in the UK*. Council for British Archaeology, English Heritage, Institute of Field Archaeologists.

English Heritage. 1988. *Visitors Welcome*. London: English Heritage.

Stone, P.G., 1994. The re-display of the Alexander Keiller Museum, Avebury. In P.G. Stone & B. Molyneaux (eds), *The Presented Past: heritage, museums and education*. London: Routledge. 190-205.

Stone, P.G. & Planel, P. (eds), 1999. *The Constructed Past: experimental archaeology, education and the public*. London: Routledge.